GLOBAL
PERSPECTIVES

A HANDBOOK FOR UNDERSTANDING GLOBAL ISSUES

SECOND EDITION

Ann Kelleher
Laura Klein

Pacific Lutheran University

PEARSON
Prentice
Hall

Upper Saddle River, New Jersey 07458

Library of Congress Cataloging-in-Publication Data

Kelleher, Ann.
    Global Perspectives : a handbook for understanding global issues / Ann Kellerher,
    Laura Klein.—2nd ed.
        p. cm
    Includes bibliographical references and index.
    ISBN 0-13-189260-6 (alk. paper)
    1. International relations—Textbooks. 2. World politics—1945–1989—Textbooks.
    3. World politics—1989—Textbooks. 4. Social history—20th century—
    Textbooks. 5. Social history—21st century—Textbooks. 6. Economic history—20th
    century—Textbooks. 7. Economic history—21st century—Textbooks. I. Klein, Laura F.
    (Laura Frances), 1946– II. Title.
    JZ1242.K45 2005
    909.82′5—dc22

                                                                    2005043157

President, Humanities/Social Sciences: **Managing Editor:** Lisa Iarkowski
    Yolanda de Rooy   **Production Liaison:** Joe Scordato
AVP/Director of Production   **Production Assistant:** Marlene Gassler
    and Manufacturing: Barbara Kittle   **Manufacturing Manager:** Nick Sklitsis
Editor-in-Chief: Charlyce Jones-Owen   **Manufacturing Buyer:** Sherry Lewis
Acquisitions Editor: Glenn Johnston   **Cover Art Director:** Jayne Conte
Editorial Assistant: Suzanne Remore   **Composition/Full-Service Management:**
Marketing Manager: Kara Kindstrom   GGS Book Services, Atlantic Highlands
Marketing Assistant: Jennifer Lang

This book was set in 10/12 Times by GGS Book Services and was printed
by R. R. Donnelley & Sons, Inc. The cover was printed by R. R. Donnelley & Sons, Inc.

Credits and acknowledgments borrowed from other sources and reproduced, with permission,
in this textbook appear on appropriate page within text.

Pearson Education LTD.   Pearson Education Australia PTY, Limited
Pearson Education Singapore, Pte. Ltd   Pearson Education North Asia Ltd
Pearson Education, Canada, Ltd   Pearson Education de Mexico, S.A. de C.V.
Pearson Education—Japan   Pearson Education Malaysia, Pte. Ltd

10 9 8 7 6 5 4

ISBN 0-13-189260-6

CONTENTS

4   Economic Development   61

5   Perspectives on Economic Development   87

6   Human Ecological Sustainability   107

8   Peace and War   151

9   Perspectives on Peace and War   179

PREFACE

Global Perspectives: A Handbook for Understanding Global Issues has been designed to help readers answer important questions about the contemporary world, such as

- Why the thousands of cultural groups in the world have such different customs and beliefs while human beings have so many needs in common
- Why a billion people on the planet are poor and malnourished
- Why it is so difficult to take action to solve the atmospheric problem of global warming
- Why some political conflicts result in war

These questions represent many more questions that can be asked about the problems facing the world at the beginning of the twenty-first century. Issues arise from the trends of cultural diversity, economic interdependence and dependence, deterioration of the natural environment, and political conflict. These general, long-term issues become specific through events in the news.

Making sense of international news is not easy; nevertheless, informed citizens in a participatory democracy must take on the task. This often means they work to become self-educated about global issues, a process made more difficult by the one-sided polemics flowing from the many and conflicting interest groups. For those beginning to learn about international events, the mass media do not always help much. In many cases, television, radio, newspapers, and news magazines have neither the time nor the space to provide needed background information, historical context, or varying perspectives. Thus events are reported as distinct, isolated from one another. They seem to erupt suddenly, presenting major problems. A civil war, an environmental disaster, or an economic crisis, for instance, all produce major controversies over what actions should be taken. How can a person learn enough to be able to analyze available information about the wide range of problems in the world?

Concepts

This book provides a beginning by presenting a process for thinking about the world's long-term trends, and how they are reflected in specific situations. It assumes that explanations for human behavior are possible, that events do not just happen. The following chapters introduce concepts for sorting out what is going on in the world. Learning to think conceptually means using ideas and generalizations that link events to each other and provide explanations for why they occur. For example, this book will define and apply words such as culture, ethnic groups, power, interests, capital, industrialization, development, ecosystem, carrying capacity, and balance of power.

Perspectives

Applying concepts is only the first step. An aware citizenry must know not only the reasons why events happen but also why people disagree so intensely over how to interpret and respond to them. The answer lies in perspectives; that is, the set of interrelated principles, worldviews, and values that people use to determine what actions should be taken. About any given issue there are several perspectives that can reasonably be used to diagnose the problem and decide what to do. If only one perspective had validity, the problem would not become an ongoing issue.

This insight—that different people can honestly, intensely disagree based on valid but opposing principles—explains why issues seem to have a life of their own and go on and on. The problems produced by these issues can seem insoluble. Discussions over an endangered species, or U.S. foreign policy toward China, for instance, can become full-blown disagreements with no resolution. People engaged in an argument apply their own perspectives, sometimes unconsciously. Perspectives imply more than just different points of view, which can be debated pragmatically. Perspectives are value based and embody beliefs about what are the right and wrong actions to take. Learning about alternative perspectives enables a person to understand why fierce debates and conflicts can occur. Therefore, understanding world events means knowing what perspectives are being applied.

Globalization

As a final point, people must realize that, even if they choose not to become engaged in policy debates as conscientious citizens, they still inhabit the planet. The decisions people make in their daily lives become part of worldwide consumption networks. Choices about what to buy and how much water to use, for example, affect people not only locally but in other countries as well. Not paying attention does not mean our actions have no effects. The world is becoming increasingly interconnected through its cultural, linguistic, economic, ecological, technological, and political systems. What we do is part of these systems. Educated people should be aware of the short- and long-term consequences of their lifestyle choices.

The following objectives summarize points made in the preceding paragraphs. Upon completing this book, the reader will be able to

1. Explain the historical development of trends affecting today's world
2. Link current events with general problems and long-term trends
3. Define the basic concepts needed to explain the reasons for trends and specific events
4. Apply several alternative perspectives
5. Evaluate the feasibility and effects of a variety of coping strategies and solutions

The Second Edition

In the second edition we have taken the suggestions of many students and instructors who have worked with the earlier version of *Global Perspectives*, and we have added case studies and emphasized the globalization process that affects all issues. Hence, Chapters 2 through 9 include a specific case to illuminate and show how to apply the concepts in that chapter. We hope that the added examples will lead to more analysis and comparative discussions by the readers. Additionally, the existing cases have been updated in order to reflect the changes of the last few years.

To the Instructor

As an introduction to thinking about the world's interconnected systems and chronic problems, *Global Perspectives* provides useful conceptual tools. Its concepts and perspectives are defined with enough specificity to spark meaningful discussions in class. An appropriate conceptual framework is applied to each of four generic issues facing the world as a whole: cultural diversity, economic interdependence and dependence, deterioration of the natural environment, and political conflict. The two chapters on each issue include some examples to help clarify the points made; however, the book is not designed to cover the myriad, more specific issues teachers and students may decide are important. Some of these may include immigration, developing world debt, U.S.–Japan trade relations, financial problems of the newly industrializing East Asian countries, Albanians in Kosovo, Latinos in the United States, genocide and the War Crimes Tribunal on Rwanda, China's development strategies, U.S. policy toward Iraq—the potential list could extend indefinitely.

As a handbook, *Global Perspectives* offers a structure for analysis, not the knowledge base for a full course. It does not provide the in-depth explanations for a particular category of issues found in textbooks based in a specific discipline. Therefore, additional material needs to be supplied, such as maps, videos, speakers, slides of personal experiences, documents, and anything else useful for focusing on the specific events and issues of interest to both instructor and students. The authors have found novels, autobiographical writing, and videos to be particularly helpful in sparking the interest and involvement of students who are new to thinking about world issues.

Chapter 1, for example, provides a very brief overview of the world before European domination changed trade routes, power structures, and ideas that gave life meaning; in short, whole cultures that had developed over hundreds, even thousands, of years in some cases. The chapter is designed to explain why many of the inheritors of these cultures today have perspectives that differ from those in European and American societies. If instructors using this handbook want to emphasize a historical approach to understanding the contemporary world, Chapter 1 can be supplemented with handouts, articles, or another book.

One point needs to be emphasized. Implied in the handbook's issue-based organization, all four generic trends, as well as the interaction systems they highlight, provide the context for learning about specific issues and events. All four are needed to explain how particular events are interrelated, not only to each other but to worldwide trends and systems.

Acknowledgments

We would like to thank all those people who have helped make this book possible. It is a result of years of teaching and learning from the Global Perspectives course we have team-taught since 1980. Thousands of students have taken the course and have helped us clarify our ideas through their thoughtful questions, challenges, and opinions. Through the years other instructors have also joined the course and made their contributions. We want to thank Drs. Mordachi Rozanski, Robert Erickson, Gina Hames, Gregory Guldin, Elizabeth Brusco, Veeda Gargano-Ray, and December Green, who have all taught sections. All have contributed to the development of the concepts and examples. We need to also express our gratitude for the support of Pacific Lutheran University, which allowed us to design and team-teach the interdisciplinary course.

Many colleagues and friends have reviewed drafts of the book and provided feedback. Drs. Sheri Tonn, David Vinje, Norris Peterson, L. Taulbee, Ms. Ruth Rondema, and Ms. Elizabeth Sullivan have especially given of their time and expertise. We would also like to acknowledge John H. P. Williams, East Carolina University, and Brian G. Wright, Johnson County Community College, for reviewing earlier versions of the manuscript for this book and for their helpful suggestions. The secretaries of the university's Division of Social Sciences have spent many hours working on this manuscript. We thank Peggy Jobe, Sharon Raddatz, and Brenda Murray for their hard work and good humor. We also want to thank our colleagues and friends at Pacific Lutheran University for their support. The faculties of anthropology and political science have been more than patient with us, and good friends and family were vital to our efforts.

CHAPTER 1

Introduction to the Modern World

"The past is prologue."

—SHAKESPEARE

*"Every person takes the limits of her/his vision for the limits
of the world."*

—SCHOPENHAUER

People looking for meaning in world events face a daunting task. In the first place, sorting out the relevant issues, institutions, and interpretations can seem complex, contradictory, and confusing. In the second place, the process must include clarifying one's own perspectives because these act as filters for new information that can lead either to insightful observations or to invidious comparisons. Individuals learning about "foreign" events must recognize that their view of the world is both limited and historically created. People living in different circumstances have different, but no less certain, understandings of the world.

What historical trends have created modern life? How do people perceive the effects of the trends and react to the events and issues they have created? All people have local knowledge of the world and how it functions. Daily life requires such understandings. Yet educated people are called upon to work, make choices, and find meaning in a larger context. In the early twenty-first century, this means a worldwide context.

This chapter introduces thinking about the basics of the modern world. It begins with an exercise in imagination by offering three alternative starting places for understanding the world and its issues; that is, its geographical, political, and cultural divisions. These three alternative images of the planet illustrate the influence of perception as part of the analysis process. The chapter's second and third introductory themes briefly summarize the historical trends that created and changed the modern world: imperialism, with its legacies, and globalization.

PERCEPTIONS OF THE WORLD

Earth provides a home for all humanity who might be expected to understand it in a common way. Differences, however, appear to be more striking than similarities about the nature of the Earth and human life on it. Some regard the world as small, others as vast, and in fact people experience both. In daily living the scale can be minimal, characterized by one-on-one encounters with people of similar backgrounds. Through travel and learning, however, the scale and scope of interaction can increase to planetary proportions. We are the world, but the "we" includes a wide variety of people. The world seems constant, but it is always changing. Given these contradictions, people inevitably explain events and trends very differently. Seeking such explanations becomes more difficult because we are a part of what we want to understand. Even the maps used to image the world are distinct from one another. To some, topographical features are basic to understanding; to others, the world is made up of political units called states; to still others, the world consists of the different peoples inhabiting it. All three characteristics, as well as others, together define the world as we experience it.

The Physical World The map used by those who see the world as the physical planet Earth reflects a topography that has no boundaries or place names. It is a unified reality divided only by natural features. It emphasizes mountains, deserts, rivers, oceans, and lakes. No purposeful human creations are shown on this map. In this context, human differences and constructions seem insignificant and transient. This does not mean, however, that geographical realities are unchanging or protected from human agency. The physical maps drawn of Earth's distant past are different from those of the present. Some of the differences evolved over long periods of time. Volcanoes have grown, erupted, created islands and mountains. Rivers have moved and glaciers advanced and retreated, affecting the land. Even the continents themselves have broken apart or moved together. Other changes, the ones caused by humans, have brought about revolutionary alterations. Deserts have grown, rivers have been dammed, forests cut, lakes and oceans polluted, and large numbers of species killed off in what geologically is a very brief span of time.

The Political World People who regard the world in political terms place an overlay on the physical map. Their map boasts a series of lines that differentiate the states of the world. This representation, which predominates on the walls of many American classrooms, implies that the significant differences among people and places are political. South America is divided into Ecuador, Colombia, and Brazil rather than by the Andes mountains and the Amazon river. Like the topographical map, the political one changes over time but at a far more rapid rate. A political map of the world published in 1990 is terribly out of date. New states have emerged from the division of old ones. The political map of the world 1,000, or even 500, years ago would show vast areas unclaimed by states. Unlike the topographical map, human agency alone determines its features.

The Ethnic World Until recently, cultural maps of the world were found mainly in the offices and classrooms of anthropologists. These maps divide the world into culture areas or portions of the world where the people within the boundaries are more culturally alike than those outside the lines. As collections of related cultures, **culture areas** designate those portions of the world whose people share similar beliefs, customs, languages, and skills. On these maps, South America includes Amazonian Indians, highland Quechua and Aymara (Inca), and urban Mestizos (a mixture of indigenous and Spanish-speaking people), among others. No longer so rare, these maps indicate the growing awareness of the role ethnicity plays in world affairs. These maps, too, reflect changes. The cultural map of 1,000 or 500 years ago would include the Incan peoples and indigenous Amazonians, but Mestizos did not yet exist. Immigrants from Europe and Africa would soon appear and create new cultures in the region. Migrations from region to region have resulted in significant population shifts throughout human history. Humans have moved and adapted to new environments and new cultures. These maps change, like political maps, through human actions.

Each map is a valid image of reality, but none is complete. The world is a complex interaction of physical, political, and cultural elements. When change occurs in one sphere, changes in the others often follow. At any point in history, these elements intersect to form a reality, and people living at that time believe that their world must be both permanent and proper.

EMERGENCE OF THE MODERN WORLD

It follows that the world as we know it is a historical way station on a very long road. Particular events occurred in specific places over hundreds of years, leading to the present situation and influencing the future. Trends and events could have occurred differently, but they did not. It is important to look to the past to understand the origins of the modern world. By doing so, one realizes that the modern state system which seems so obvious and permanent is, in fact, recent and changeable. In the flow of human history, the division of the world's territory into state-controlled areas based on the European model is relatively new. History, however, does not uniformly move in one direction and, over time, states have divided into ethnically defined units just as such units have centralized into states. History suggests that one should expect continued changes in the world system.

The World in 1350 Modern people, particularly those in powerful countries, find it difficult to consider a past when their states did not exist or hovered on the periphery of world events. Trace history back far enough, and all states disappear. In order to understand the modern world, it helps to know what came before, to look briefly at the world before the contemporary system emerged. Even in this concise review, it should become clear that the world system of the past was complex and volatile like the present one and that its history challenges common assumptions about the stability of current social and political systems. Further, because the world as we know it has changed dramatically within the past few hundred years, it is reasonable to expect equally dramatic changes in the future.

This review has its starting point the mid-fourteenth century. At this time, continents that were often pictured as uncivilized by Europeans in later centuries actually had complex civilizations. Every continent had stable, stratified, and economically sophisticated trading societies with elaborate art and architecture. Soon, however, European exploration and colonization would begin creating new power centers which disrupted and then reversed established global trade routes. Even today, people descended from the great civilizations of this earlier time remember their historical antecedents with pride. They were highly developed at that time and considered European society as more primitive.

China could well lead a list of advanced civilizations in 1350. Tracing its origins back a few thousand years, China had developed an elaborate state characterized by a resilient and highly stable social structure, supported by an advanced economy with its vast irrigation systems, and legitimized by profound philosophical and religious systems of thought. The Chinese had produced noteworthy scientific achievements and art forms ennobling human life which have lasted to the current era. Chinese civilization not only survived conquest by the Mongols in the thirteenth century, it absorbed them into its sophisticated system. By 1350 revolts had begun that would lead to the Ming Dynasty in 1368; however, political instability did not disrupt the underlying social system.

Chinese scientists had already developed nautical knowledge and shipbuilding technologies unknown in Europe. The compass and stern rudder, which revolutionized the European economic life and military capabilities, led to the age of sail by enabling Europeans to travel out into the open ocean on the explorations that became imperialism's first stage. In the 1400s another Chinese invention, gunpowder, gave Europeans what would prove to be their decisive military edge in confronting other civilizations. In about two to three hundred more years, the new ocean routes resulting from European explorations would change the world's former trade patterns. For hundreds of years and probably more, luxuries from China had flowed overland through central Asia to the Middle East and then on to Europe. Finding ocean routes to the spices and other riches of Asia enabled Europeans to bypass the societies along the ancient caravan trails. Middle Eastern economies slowly shriveled without their trade lifeblood. In 1350, however, Europe's application of the science and technologies from other civilizations, which would, over the next few hundred years, fundamentally shift global power, were hardly foreseen or even imagined.

In the Middle East, the first great Islamic empires built on Arab conquests and economic development had waxed from the 600s and waned from about the 1100s on, broken into local dynasties that had been overwhelmed by devastating Mongol invasions. Modern Arabs share the legacy of a civilization that in the 800s had arguably the largest cities in the world sustained by intricate irrigation systems and by social services such as pharmacies, universities, piped water, and far-flung trade, complete with a banking system and letters of credit.

By 1350, however, the Ottoman Turks, the people who would again unite much of the Islamic world and even challenge central Europe, were just beginning their expansion. Europeans were discovering from the Moorish civilization in Spain the Islamic learning that had developed over centuries. This discovery was producing the Renaissance, with its profound changes to European civilization. The Arabs had preserved ancient Greek manuscripts with their scientific knowledge and humanistic philosophies and had synthesized, applied, and transported important mathematical advances from India which would underpin future European progress: the concept of zero and the Indian numbering system traveled to Europe after Islamic incubation. Islamic thinkers had advanced medical knowledge and optics; both would be adopted wholesale by European scientists.

Commerce had spurred the growth of Africa's civilizations by 1350. In the north, the city of Timbuktu was a center for trade and learning within the Mali Empire. As a university center it ranked among the finest in the world. Its wealth depended upon the gold and salt it exchanged for goods made from leather, cotton, iron, and copper from trading partners in the region. To the south, the walled city of Great Zimbabwe, in what is currently the country of the same name, was an advanced trade center with goods from the Middle East and Asia passing through its markets.

In what became known as the Americas after colonization, most cultures lived in foraging and simple farming communities; however, some had developed much more complex civilizations. Among the best known, the Mayans lived in what is today Guatemala and Mexico's Yucatan Peninsula. Their elaborate cities with pyramids, temples, and sports fields served as regional centers of religion supported by trade. Astronomy, mathematics, and the invention of a very precise calendar are great Mayan achievements that astonish people in the modern world. Another civilization had evolved in central Mexico, which by 1350 had been taken over by the Aztecs. They had just built their capital at Tenochtitlan, present-day Mexico City, and their trade routes extended far to the north. Mexican artifacts and architectural styles have turned up in the present U.S. southwest. Even farther to the north, the people now known as the Mississippians, because of their geographical location, had a complex class system, long-range trade, and cities characterized by large earthen pyramids.

South Americans had similar cultures to those in the north with one major civilization coalescing in the mid-fourteenth century. The culture of the Incas was just developing, and their empire would grow to control all its neighbors and extend along the Andes mountains from what is today Colombia in the north to parts of modern Chile in the south. Incan building expertise, as evidenced in their vast mountain cities, roads, and irrigation systems, was unsurpassed in the world at the time.

As an age of major transition in Europe, the fourteenth century was a period of almost constant turmoil. French and English monarchs were embroiled in the Hundred Years' War (1337–1453), which was actually a series of intermittent battles, peasant uprisings, and revolts conducted by regional nobles. For most people, the century produced much poverty and suffering. The Black Death (now known as the bubonic plague) reached Europe in 1347, killed millions, and lowered the average life expectancy in England, for example, from thirty-four years to seventeen years at the height of the plague (Tannenbaum 1965, 37–38). Nevertheless it was during this time that Europe absorbed the ideas and technologies drawn from distant lands that were to transform some of its societies and their place among the world's civilizations. By the end of the next century, Europe emerged with the centralized political systems and technological innovations in transportation and weapons of war that enabled it to begin centuries of exploration and dominance.

Early European Expansion: 1400s to Early 1600 Europeans did not know much about the world's other civilizations at the end of the fifteenth century, but they did know about the riches that came from Asia. The spices of "the Indies," used for food preservation and medicines, were traded to Europe at high prices. Europeans wanted to establish a direct route to Asia which would cut costs by eliminating the Ottoman Empire and other middlemen. With improvements in sailing ships and navigation devices, Europeans were ready to move out of Europe to trade on their own terms.

The Portuguese and Spanish were the masters of early exploration. Prince Henry the Navigator (1394–1460) of Portugal, who established a school for navigators, led his country's exploration. In 1445 Portuguese crews discovered that slaves and gold were available in coastal Africa. By 1498 Vasco da Gama had reached India, and Portugal claimed the sea route to Asia. Lisbon replaced Venice as the city for Far Eastern trade, but it soon was challenged by Dutch cities. Spain joined in the competition and, funded by Queen Isabella, Christopher Columbus searched for a western route to what was called "the Indies." He reached the Caribbean in voyages between 1492 and 1502. The Indies seemed at hand in 1513 when Vasco de Balboa first saw the Pacific Ocean. Yet it remained for Ferdinand Magellan to sail from Spain, around South America, and to what became the Philippines in 1519.

For the most part, this early era of exploration was economically motivated, and many trade ports were established. Industrialization, to begin in the 1700s, had not yet provided the incentives that would propel future settlement and conquest in Asia and Africa, but civilizations in the Americas did not receive this reprieve. Spanish conquerors used the Caribbean islands for farming and mining, with indigenous people working as forced laborers. This practice led to their near-total extinction when combined with epidemics spawned by newly introduced European diseases. On the mainland, Spain's goals, often termed "Gold, God, and Glory," also led to disaster. By 1521 Hernando Cortés had conquered the civilizations of Mexico. In the name of religion, all books and artifacts considered pagan were destroyed. Beautiful items made of gold or silver were melted down for their metal value. By 1536 the Incas had suffered a similar fate at the hands of Francisco Pizarro and Diego de Almargo. Spain used its vast imports of precious metals in the mid-1500s to become a dominant power and in the process inflated its currency and deflated economies in eastern Europe and the Ottoman Empire. Spain's depletion of the New World's gold and silver, however, led to a gradual decline which had become evident by the late 1600s.

France and England had less success than the Spanish and Portuguese in the early period of exploration. Their agents searched for a northern route west to Asia, the so-called Northwest Passage. Failing that, the French and English made conflicting claims on North America, which they finally settled by war. The people on this continent had no gold or silver artifacts. Their riches remained to be exploited through settlement by farmers and trappers.

Later European Expansion: 1600s to Early 1900s Europe changed dramatically during the first two centuries of exploration. The rise and decline of European states illustrates the impermanence of power and the inevitably of underlying change. Today's great powers, whose roles seem so firmly fixed in world events, potentially face an evolutionary erosion in the sources of their economic strength and political position. Sixteenth-century Europe experienced the Reformation wars, economic growth, and technological advances which changed the continent. Spain faded into relative obscurity as a European power but kept its extensive American possessions. Similarly, Portugal held on to its Asian colonies and Brazil, but Portugal itself became a small power in Europe. In contrast, northwestern Europe, France but especially England and the Netherlands, began to thrive economically based on their colonial trading relationships and the corresponding growth of their commercial classes.

In the Americas by the eighteenth century, the Caribbean sugar-producing plantation system was in full operation, with African slaves providing the labor. British colonies on the eastern coast of North America were selling furs to Europe and buying finished goods, as was the French settlement of Quebec. Soon tobacco, slaves, and rum would join furs to produce a flourishing source of wealth for Britain from its North American possessions. The French claimed a vast amount of land but did not supply as many settlers as did the British. Particularly in British possessions, epidemics brought by the settlers decimated the populations of native people, and the survivors were pushed off their farmlands.

By the nineteenth century the situation in North America had again undergone dramatic change. A peace in 1763 sealed Britain's defeat of France in North America and left the French with only their islands in the Caribbean. In 1776, however, Britain's thirteen colonies began their successful bid for independence leaving Canada plus some Caribbean islands in the British Empire by 1783. At nearly the same time, the British passed the India Act formally making this rich and ancient land a colony.

The era of imperialism reached its full maturity during the late nineteenth and early twentieth centuries. **Colonialism** refers to the direct administration of a territory and its people. **Imperialism** includes colonialism as well as indirect rule by outsiders over local peoples. During the age of imperialism, parts of the world were considered "protectorates" by European countries. This meant that the imperial powers made important decisions and the local authorities carried them out; for example, such indirect rule characterized British imperialism in Iraq after World War I.

The Industrial Revolution provided the cause and also the means for increased European, later joined by American, expansion. **Industrialization** refers to the shift from handmade products using human and animal muscle plus wind and water as energy sources, to machine production with energy from the burning of fossil fuels, first coal then oil and natural gas. Since machines not only produce much more but also use raw materials more rapidly, industrializing societies needed new markets and sources of raw materials. Other factors also fostered imperialism, including paternalistic missionary zeal and patriotism, the latter because colonial success stimulated patriotic pride. The need to bring Christianity to pagans and civilization to people characterized as "inferior" were often primary rationalizations for colonial enterprises.

The building of the Suez Canal (1854–1869) illustrates, via a specific example, why people in former colonies generally have negative reactions when they recall their history under outside rule. An academic who has studied the canal's history describes the Frenchman who made building the canal his lifework. Ferdinand de Lesseps was "ruthless, shameless, patient, and as brilliant an entrepreneur as lived in a century of Morgans, Guggenheims, Rockefellers, and Rothschilds." The Egyptian government's contract terms "were almost the antithesis of those under which modern concessionaires work." Egypt purchased over half the canal company's stock, but its shares carried few rights, and voting was not one of them. When the canal opened, Egypt received only 15 percent of the profits, in spite of owning more than half the shares. It was contracted to furnish the labor force of about 20,000 to dig the canal and had to pay, feed, and house them (Polk 1981, 85). During the years of construction, the company needed new sources of revenue, and the Egyptian treasury was literally plundered of "untold amounts . . . for indemnities, fraudulent and semi-fraudulent claims, exorbitant prices to purveyors and contractors, and all manner of bribes designed to buy cheap honours or simply respite from harassment" (quoted from David Landes 1958, *Bankers and Pashas*, Cambridge, MA, 316; in Polk, 85). To keep up its end of the bargain, the Egyptian government had to borrow money at usurious rates of interest, such as 26 percent. One loan Egypt contracted in 1865 was for 3 million British pounds; however, the Egyptians actually received only 2.2 million and had to repay 4.1 million plus various fees and penalties (Polk, 86). By the time the Suez Canal opened in 1869, Egypt could receive none of the fees charged for its use because they were committed for loan repayment.

While the European states achieved imperial hegemony over most countries in Asia and forced open trade with Japan and China, the subjugation of Africa tells the story of direct rule. Before the 1880s, Europe's interest in sub-Saharan Africa focused largely on the slave trade. This had allowed the colonies in the Americas to thrive and resulted in prosperity for many Europeans and Americans. The need for and attitude about slavery had changed, however, and by the early to mid-1800s many people considered slavery morally reprehensible. Virtually all contact with tropical Africa was on the coast. Despite 500 years of exploiting African resources, Europeans knew practically nothing of the interior lands or people.

With the British occupation of Egypt in 1882, the European division of Africa and direct rule over its peoples had begun. At the Berlin Conference in 1884–1885, representatives of the interested states convened to divide the continent. The reasons for the conference offered to the public explained its objectives as bringing an end to the slave trade and establishing free navigation and trade in the Congo River basin. European explorers were moving inland, and King Leopold II of the Belgians established the Congo Free State, in the center of the continent, which controlled trade on the Congo River. Delegates at the Berlin Conference affirmed Leopold's claim to the Independent State of the Congo and shortly afterward he began ruling it as a personal possession. It was later deeded to Belgium in 1908, after evidence of horrific labor practices resulting in mass death and suffering became the talk of Europe. At the Berlin Conference, the major European states formalized each other's rule over central and western Africa. Shortly after the conference, east Africa was similarly divided. In the south, the British took control of South Africa in 1902 only after it fought the long and bloody Boer War with the descendents of Dutch settlers in the colony's interior. By the end of the first decade of the twentieth century, France, Great Britain, Italy, Spain, Portugal, Belgium, and Germany ruled virtually all of Africa.

The European states had accomplished the division of Africa in their own interests, with no consideration given to the claims of people already living there. By World War I, few places on Earth remained without the stamp of a European state. Culturally, Christian missions had spread throughout the world and had converted millions to their faith and an admiration of European culture. For a time at least, Europeans had succeeded in gaining control of the world. In the process, they imposed their institutions worldwide, with the state at the center of the international system.

DEFINITION OF THE MODERN STATE

Europeans used their version of the state to achieve worldwide dominance. Its highly centralized organizational structure was capable of concentrating large-scale human and material resources over very long periods of time. Since states have been, and many people think still are, the most powerful decision makers affecting international events, learning about current world issues begins with analyzing the nature of the modern state. Four characteristics define a **state**: territory, government, a loyal population, and the recognition of other states.

Territory This element of a state may seem obvious at first, but the notion of a precise border existing between independent political units is relatively recent. Many empires did not control land so much as populations, often leaving their boundaries inexact because they did not matter very much. As long as subject peoples paid their taxes, fought when conscripted, and did not rebel against the ruling elite, they were allowed to keep their own cultural identity and regulate daily life, such as education, religion, property inheritance, and ownership.

Government All persons living in the territory of a modern state relate to the government directly. Before the modern state, empires and feudal systems considered most of their subject peoples as existing in groups whose leaders spoke for them and saw to it that the rules the government imposed were obeyed. Those in political power were far away, often physically as well as perceptually. The governments of modern states, in contrast, consider their people citizens and indivisible parts of the whole population.

    Government is defined as the one institution in a society that has the legitimate claim to exercising decisive authority over its population. It requires payments and regulates certain categories of behavior. It can even deny liberty and, in extreme cases, life if a person violates specified laws. Governments have a virtual monopoly on force and the right to make and enforce laws that everyone must obey. Thus governments are highly centralized, powerful institutions. The key to their effectiveness lies in the attitude denoted by the word **legitimacy**. A government achieves legitimacy when its people believe that it is justified, that its laws ought to be obeyed, and that its rule conforms to commonly accepted values. Such political values have changed over the centuries. A currently prevailing one accepts government as legitimate if it represents the will of its population, as expressed through elections. A former idea causing consent to governmental authority was the idea of a God-given hereditary monarchy. If major segments of the population begin to consider the government illegitimate, it is forced to rule solely on the basis of its monopoly of force. Inevitably this type of government becomes oppressive and authoritarian. The situation can become dangerous if people avoid compliance or initiate rebellion. In either case, a government relying solely on force has less ability to make enforceable decisions than one that is perceived as legitimate. Legitimacy, therefore, is needed for effective rule.

A Loyal Population Citizens generally identify with the modern state at least to some extent. Their feeling of loyalty, called **patriotism**, is distinguished from **nationalism**, which is an individual's identity with an ethnic (cultural) group based on several shared characteristics, such as language, history, and religion. Empires did not always expect or demand to be the primary focus of identity and loyalty for most of the peoples they ruled. These attitudes were required only of members of the governing elite. The modern state that evolved in Europe, however, fused nationalism and patriotism, at least as ideals. Each state was assumed to have one dominant cultural group, hence the designation nation-state, which was the term used for decades. The "nation" part has been dropped in recent years because every state in the world today includes more than one cultural group.

Distinguishing between ethnic nationalism and state patriotism helps clarify one of the most significant causes of current conflicts. The clash of identity between the two occurs because, generally, one ethnic group controls the government, society's most powerful institution. This creates a situation whereby the dominant group, either consciously or unconsciously, discriminates against other groups. In the 1990s, for example, over forty countries had cultural groups wanting some form of political representation separate from their existing governments, including the Scottish Nationalist Party in the United Kingdom and the French-speaking Quebecois Party in Canada.

Recognition of Other States This trait can become significant particularly when a government changes by revolution. If most countries of the world fail to accept the new government, economic and political difficulties can result. North Korea provides a case in point.

States become weaker if one or more of the four characteristics become problematic. Government leaders, therefore, strive to make policies that attempt to strengthen their control over territory, legitimize their rule, instill patriotism, and gain respect from other states.

TRENDS OF THE POST-WORLD WAR II WORLD

Events in today's world occur in the context of the modern international system. Therefore, adequately explaining the causes of, and responses to, international issues depends on knowing how the current international system functions. The **international system** is defined as the organizations and processes that people use to interact across state borders. The modern state, the most powerful institution in the international system, has a major impact on many others, like the United Nations, by setting their policies. States have changed in their relationships with each other and with international organizations during the decades since World War II (1939–1946). The war altered how the world works. The international organizations and trends constituting the current international system were either established after the war or transformed because of it. Four of the most significant general trends since World War II are U.S. leadership, the Soviet challenge, the end of colonialism, and the world's increasing interconnections.

U.S. Leadership The United States emerged from World War II as a hegemony—a dominant world power. It was the only great power that had not been physically and psychologically devastated by the war. Its economy and confidence were at an all-time high. Internationally, the United States used its preponderance of power to establish the international system's institutions and their rules. These organizations can be divided into two categories: economic institutions, such as the World Bank, and political institutions, the United Nations for example. The general principles underlying these organizations are derived from the U.S. diagnosis of the fundamental causes of World War II. The United States believed its prescriptions would be the best antidotes for a war-prone world.

According to the thinking of U.S. policy makers, as well as many others around the world, the most devastating war in human history had two primary underlying causes, one economic and the other political. The Great Depression of the 1930s devastated the world's economies. Each state's setting higher tariffs to protect its own economy only made the downturn worse for all states and ensured the Depression's spread worldwide. In fact, the highest tariff in U.S. history was passed in 1932. Every state reacted with some degree of political change, but the one in Germany proved to have devastating consequences. The Depression had hit only Germany harder than the United States, and in 1933 Adolf Hitler's Nazi Party, a particularly degenerate and racist version of fascism, came to power in Germany. Its hypernationalism extolled the state as the ultimate good, demanded absolute obedience to the government and its dictator, and predicted that the "master race" of Germans would control the world by eliminating "inferior" peoples. According to the fascists, war benefits society because it destroys the weak. Virtually every analysis of the causes of World War II cites Nazi policy at the top of the list.

The United States and its allies were convinced that following the war, the international system had to be structured so as to foster worldwide economic prosperity, and to identify, plus weaken, potentially aggressor states. Three institutions were established in the 1940s to organize the international economy. Called **international governmental organizations (IGOs)** because states make up the membership, together they were designed to stabilize the international economy and ensure economic growth. The International Bank for Reconstruction and Development, called the **World Bank**, offered economic aid in the form of loans to countries whose projects were approved. This IGO was originally planned to assist in European recovery, but recipient countries changed over the years as former colonies began to become independent in the 1950s and 1960s. Loans for economic development rather than rebuilding became the World Bank's task, a much more massive undertaking. Whereas Europe already had the prerequisites for healthy industrial economies, the newly independent states did not.

The **International Monetary Fund (IMF)** provides its members with loans to restore international confidence in a country's currency if its value plummets. Like the World Bank, the IMF first helped Europe but, over time, its loans shifted primarily to newly independent, less industrialized countries. Both the World Bank and the IMF have weighted voting, which means that those countries paying the majority of the institutions' annual assessments have the majority of the votes. Thus the contributors, not the borrowers, control policy making, and the terms of the loans tend to reflect those of commercial international banks.

The General Agreement on Tariffs and Trade (GATT), the forerunner of today's **World Trade Organization (WTO)**, was assigned the task of lowering tariffs and other barriers to trade. The mechanism devised to achieve increased trade through lower tariffs was called **most-favored-nation status**. In practice, this consisted of an agreement between two states lowering their tariffs with each other to match the lowest that each charged any other trading partner on a specific category of product, such as clothing or automobiles. Over time, as more and more states granted most-favored-nation status to each other, tariffs around the world were reduced substantially. The WTO replaced the GATT in 1995. The new organization has a wider agenda and greater powers of enforcement.

As the worldwide political IGO, the **United Nations** began in 1945 with the adoption of its charter. Its main task then as now was tackling threats to security. The two main United Nations bodies—the General Assembly and the Security Council—have different roles. The **General Assembly** provides a forum in which every member state is equal, with one vote each and no weighted voting. The **Security Council** has the key role in responding to threats to the peace. Some of the Security Council members have more power than others. Of the fifteen states in the Security Council, five have permanent seats; the other ten are elected to two-year terms by the General Assembly. The United States, the United Kingdom, France, Russia, and China are permanent Security Council members chosen because they were the winners in World War II. Each of the five has a veto over any resolution passed by the Security Council.

The United States had used its leadership to establish international institutions capable of coordinating economic and political relations among the world's countries. This has proven farsighted for reasons U.S. policy makers did not realize at the time; namely, that one state dominance would not continue for long and a common framework had to be in place for debating and potentially dealing with the world's problems. The next three post–World War II trends have challenged U.S. leadership and have redefined major global issues.

The Soviet Challenge   Within months of the ending of World War II, differences between the United States and the Soviet Union began to surface. For example, the countries argued over what factions should come to power in Eastern European countries. By the late 1940s, the differences had crystallized into a superpower rivalry. Another geographically large, resource-rich state with a sizable multiethnic population and major military power was challenging the United States for world leadership. Two characteristics combined to make the adversarial relationship more intense and the consequences of war more threatening than earlier competition, such as that between France and Great Britain in the 1700s. First, the U.S.–Soviet rivalry introduced a new and devastating military threat—nuclear weapons. Second, the struggle was explained in terms of deep ideological divisions that gave form and focus to policy making. People used **ideologies**, sets of interrelated ideas giving meaning to events, to legitimize political institutions.

Probably because of the threat of nuclear war, the post–World War II superpower competition proved to be unlike any other historical period of intense two-state rivalry. No war was ever fought between the two main antagonists directly, which is why the term **Cold War** was used. Wars relevant to the rivalry occurred often, but they were called proxy wars because the states engaged in the fighting were clients of the superpowers. During the Vietnam War, for example, the Soviet Union supplied most of North

Vietnam's weapons. The U.S. rejoinder came when it supported the insurgents in Afghanistan who were fighting the Soviet Union. The antagonists divided Europe into two rival military alliances. The North Atlantic Treaty Organization (NATO), organized by the United States, faced off against the Soviet Union's Warsaw Pact.

With elaborate networks of alliances and aid recipients, the foreign policies of both states became fixated on each other. Both the Soviet Union and the United States interpreted everything that happened in the world in terms of their rivalry. International relations analysts have defined this period as **bipolar** because the world had two main centers of power. The enemies confronted each other for over forty years until the Soviet Union dissolved in December of 1991 because of decisions made by its own people. Its member republics became independent states without a war, a rare event historically.

Russia, the republic that controlled the largest landmass of the now-defunct Soviet Union, inherited its permanent seat in the Security Council and its status as one of the world's leading states. Yet Russia does not command the Soviet Union's economic, military, or ideological power. The fact that it cannot act as a counterweight to the United States has fundamentally changed world politics. The United States is freer to act in international conflicts when it chooses to become involved. To a large extent, U.S. and European market economics and pluralist politics have become the prevailing world standard.

The End of Colonialism From World War II on, a steady stream of newly independent states took their places in the United Nations (UN). The number of UN members grew particularly in the 1960s when decolonization spread through most of Africa. Fifty states had founded the United Nations in 1945, and by 1955 UN membership had grown to seventy-five. It increased to 117 members by 1965, 141 by 1975, 157 by 1985, 185 by 1995, and 191 by 2002. With a large majority in the General Assembly, the states in Africa and Asia, often supported by those in Latin America, began asserting their own priorities, especially their need for economic development.

The newly independent states did not see the world as bipolar but **multipolar**; that is, as comprising many power centers. The terms *First, Second*, and *Third World* were coined in part to reflect their disagreement with the prevailing bipolar perception of the international system. The First World represented the already industrialized states in the "west" with their market economies and multiparty politics. The Second World reflected the Soviet Union and its "eastern" allies with their one-party systems and government-controlled economies. The Third World referred to the rest of the world's states with their lower levels of industrialization, higher levels of poverty, and vulnerability to actions taken by the powerful countries.

Leaders in the Third World states thought that by coordinating their policies, they could become another power center. The first attempt occurred as early as 1955 at a conference held in Bandung, Indonesia. The countries attending initiated the Non-aligned Movement (NAM) to differentiate themselves from both the United States, with its allies, and the Soviet Union, with its allies. Subsequently, Third World states followed this political initiative with a coalition designed to bring their economic plight to the world's attention. This network, called the Group of 77, grew to 130 states by the 1990s. It established the United Nations Conference on Trade and Development (UNCTAD) as an organization focused solely on Third World issues.

It was not until 1973 that less industrialized states scored a success in negotiations with the First World. The Organization of Petroleum Exporting Countries (OPEC) used an embargo of oil to triple the price paid for a barrel of crude oil. In the heady atmosphere this produced, Third World states passed a series of resolutions in the UN General Assembly reflecting their interests, such as recommending more foreign aid. None of the resolutions were implemented, and by the early 1980s OPEC's negotiating position was undermined by the world's oil glut. Nevertheless, during the 1970s, Third World countries had managed to focus attention on their distinct set of problems and redirect some World Bank and IMF resources. The less industrialized states became more than just places where the Soviet Union and the United States could play their bipolar game by proxy.

Increasing Interconnections   As the numbers of states and IGOs have increased, so too have **nongovernmental organizations (NGOs)**. These private agencies link people across international borders in a wide variety of ways, such as by occupation, religion, personal interest, and issue activism. A sample listing of NGOs would include professional groups like the International Skeletal Society (with pathologists and orthopedists as members), the Catholic Church and the World Council of Churches, Rotary International, Amnesty International, Care International, and the International Red Cross. In addition, the number of businesses with overseas affiliates has exploded over the years. Currently about 300 IGOs and well over 5,000 NGOs channel international contacts among governments, groups, and individuals.

The proliferation of IGOs has greatly contributed to the complexity of the international system. Governments still engage in **bilateral diplomacy**, states dealing one on one with each other, but more and more they interact using **multilateral diplomacy** within the framework of IGOs as an established way to address issues. Common positions are negotiated, resolutions are passed, and actions are taken in cooperation with other states. Also, whether using bilateral or multilateral relations, states are no longer the primary channels for international interaction. People have created ever-expanding networks of NGOs and businesses, each with its own priorities, policies, and communication links.

The explosive expansion of international activity in the decades since World War II continues. It is a necessary reaction to the ever-accelerating internationalization of issues, institutions, and interaction processes, whether economic, ecological, linguistic, social, philosophical, or political. The pace of technological innovation shows no sign of abating and it, together with population growth, continues to shrink the psychological and actual space among people of the world. The increased speed of communication and transportation can be applied peacefully, as in e-mail, or during war, missiles for example. International decision-making networks aim to foster the former and forestall the latter. The international scope, importance, and complexity of issues facing the planet's peoples demand cooperative and coordinated responses. No longer can one state or even a small group of states manage, much less negotiate, solutions to the world's problems. One word has come to summarize all these changes: *globalization*.

GLOBALIZATION

The word **globalization** summarizes current world trends in one handy descriptive, and for some proscriptive, concept. Many people ask what globalization means, and the number of responses might well match the number of people, maybe more if some of them decide to be creative. The difficulty in making sense out of the concept, and applying it usefully to real-world events, reflects the fact that it can mean whatever the person using it wants it to mean because of the wide variety of definitions. The rest of this section should help the reader categorize the various meanings attributed to the term globalization. Like democracy and other often-used concepts, globalization's definition depends on the perspective of the person using it.

The following discussion provides four general definitions of globalization distilled from its use by policy makers, academics, journalists, and interested citizens. Since the process of globalization has ignited controversy, each of its definitions continues to attract substantial criticism. Therefore, the definitional statements are followed by an opposing argument. In this, like any other, age of transition, every trend some people think of as inevitable and dominant will engender an argument because other people identify a countertrend as better representing reality. In times of change, new and old systems of behavior and thought clash and trends collide. Intelligent people deeply disagree over the causes of current problems and which of the available alternative solutions will create a better future.

Exponential Increases in International Economic Transactions During the last decades of the twentieth century, the international movement of goods, services, and financing, as well as of people such as tourists and workers, has grown from a moderate swell to a flood. The market system of economic exchange known as capitalism, has taken hundreds of years to evolve. Industrialization has produced ever faster and bigger transportation and communication systems, from steamships to modern airliners, from the telegraph to the Internet. Medical advances plus the mechanization of food production, processing, and packaging have led to an explosion in the world's population.

Some people contradict the assumption that the expansion of interlocking economies constitutes anything startlingly new. External trade and currency flows have dominated specific local economies in centuries past. In the sixteenth century, for example, gold and silver from the New World debased currencies and caused economic dislocations throughout Europe and the Ottoman Empire. In the 1920s, the German economy became dependent on U.S. loans for the viability of its currency. These loans stopped abruptly after the September 1929 stock market crash and subsequent massive bank failures. The Great Depression hurt Germany even more than the United States. European nineteenth- and twentieth-century colonization provides many other examples of externally dependent economies.

Integration of International/Global Economic Decision Making The second way of thinking about globalization builds on the first and points out that the continual growth in the density of international economic networks has required setting international standards of behavior. Establishing rules for trade, monitoring currency values and international banking, and maintaining liquidity through loans all have enhanced the roles of transnational private banks as well as the economic IGOs, the World Trade Organization, the World Bank, and the International Monetary Fund. World economic growth has accelerated through the volume of international activity, and the number and size of international corporations have also increased.

The millions of international contacts made each day have resulted in porous state boundaries. As the one world economy becomes more sophisticated, problems arise, such as trade disputes and sometimes a crash in the value of a country's currency. Dealing with these and many other issues has become regularized through international agreements and adjudication mechanisms administered by IGOs. This international institutionalization began as long ago as 1865 with the International Telegraph Union.

The critics of this second globalization trend point out that the international agreements and organizations do not bring benefits to all the world's people. In ensuring a "free" flow of goods, financial investments, and profits, they actually foster more trade and investment by corporations headquartered in the already industrialized states. Their investments made in the less industrialized states have not lifted about a half of the world's population out of poverty. In fact, the planet's poor are getting poorer relative to the volume of wealth created by world's economic growth. To the persistent problem of a growing gap between the rich and poor, add the severe deterioration in the world's natural environment caused by unfettered industrialization.

Strengthened Political International Governmental Organizations The United Nations system of IGOs and many ratified international agreements have set international standards of behavior. Since international legal rules have become commonplace, a plausible case can be made that even the most powerful of states should act responsibly in the international community. They must learn to manage, not dominate, IGOs. Weaker states have always known the need to comply with outside demands. Now the strong must also contribute to a stable world by following agreed-upon norms for taking action. Such behavior will provide for a peaceful resolution of disputes and cooperation in solving common problems. Such political stability will also enable the world economy to expand. Thus, forging workable international political institutions flows logically from and supports global economic integration.

In contradiction to asserting that globalization is establishing an integrated political as well as economic system, many would argue that the great powers, and especially the United States, still dominate the world and determine what decisions are made by international institutions. This point of view regards international elites—that is, officials in powerful countries' governments and in transnational corporations—as doing what they want to most of the time in their own interests. They use international institutions to legitimize their actions and not as sources of governance, that is of rule making that compels general obedience. The people with this point of view say that international institutions have not eroded the sovereign state but have enhanced it.

Increases in International Nongovernmental Contacts and Communication A fourth phenomenon defined by some people as globalization recognizes the phenomenal increase in nongovernmental cross-border human activity produced by modern communication and transportation systems. The Internet is a most recognizable example. It has taken only a few years to revolutionize personal communications around the world. Also news reporting, business negotiations, and other worldwide communications conducted by governments, universities, and NGOs can take place in real time via satellite-based systems such as teleconferencing. Worldwide transportation networks move more and more people every year with relative speed, efficiency, and comfort. Some travel on business, some for tourism, some for humanitarian activities, and all gain the personal knowledge and contacts it takes to build relationships if they choose to do so. The physical movement of millions of people every year, as well as the ease with which millions more to talk with counterparts in other countries, has enabled an unprecedented level of international cooperation separate from and sometimes undermining official government policies.

Critics of this fourth view of globalization think it goes way too far and its proponents are simply taking their personal values, learned as part of their own cultural socialization process, and presenting them as universal for all humans. Because values and perceptions of what constitutes good behavior are socially learned, they all come from a specific culture. A logical case to make, for example, sees the United Nations Universal Declaration of Human Rights as not universal at all but as an elevation of Western ideas about human rights to worldwide applicability.

This section of Chapter 1 has presented four ways of thinking about globalization. They can be summarized in a general definition: "By **globalization** we simply mean the process of increasing interconnectedness between societies such that events in one part of the world more and more have effects on people and societies far away" (Baylis and Smith 1999, 7). All four trends discussed previously assume the world as one place becoming ever more interdependent and necessitating the interaction of diverse people in different states. Whichever one or combination of the trends a person thinks summarizes current world events most accurately, the word globalization has become emblematic of the current age. Like bipolarity and Cold War characterized the second half of the twentieth century, globalization exemplifies the early twenty-first century. The fact that the concept means different things to different people makes it more applicable, not less so, in this age of transition.

This introductory chapter has provided an overview of major historical trends affecting today's world, both long-term trends and those occurring since World War II. It has elaborated a definition of what many still think of as the dominant institution in the international system—the state—and noted other organizations used by people to respond to current events and issues. Finally, the chapter elaborated on globalization, the concept that has become a popular symbol of the current age.

The rest of the book describes and analyzes problems arising from four general world issues: cultural diversity, poverty and the need for economic development, deterioration of the natural environment, and political conflict. The four discussions present human beings in four corresponding contexts: cultural, economic, biological, and political. As a reminder that the four issues apply to the lives of real people, the chapter introducing each issue begins with a vignette describing how some specific persons are directly affected by that issue.

TERMS AND CONCEPTS

Bilateral diplomacy *14*
Bipolar *13*
Cold War *12*
Colonialism *7*
Culture areas *2*
General Assembly 12
Globalization *15*
Government *9*
Ideologies *12*
Imperialism *7*
Industrialization *7*
International governmental organization
   (IGO) *11*
International Monetary Fund (IMF) *11*

International system *10*
Legitimacy *9*
Most-favored-nation status *12*
Multilateral diplomacy *14*
Multipolar *13*
Nationalism *9*
Nongovernmental organization (NGO) *14*
Patriotism *9*
Security Council *12*
State *9*
United Nations *12*
World Bank *11*
World Trade Organization (WTO) *11*

DISCUSSION QUESTIONS

1. Who lived in your local area in 1350? How did they use the resources of the area? How did they govern it?
2. How does the history in this chapter differ from the history in your elementary school texts? From your high school texts? What elements are consistent?
3. What post–World War II events served to limit the power of the United States?
4. What is the situation of the world today in regard to world and regional powers?
5. What major ethnic groups appear in the newspapers on a regular basis?

RESEARCH PROJECTS

1. Prepare ethnic, physical, and political maps of North America for today and for the year 1400.
2. Collect different maps of one continent. Be sure they represent different time periods and different types of maps. Using these maps, discuss the changes that have occurred on this continent.
3. Choose a business or private organization in your area. Explore the international connections that are important to this organization.
4. Talk to your grandparents or others about their impressions of the Cold War era. How do their memories differ from your realities today?
5. What does globalization mean in your town? Report on ten important ties your town has to other countries.

INTERNET RESOURCES

International governmental organizations: http://www.library.northwestern.edu/govpub/resource/ internat/igo.html This is a good source maintained by the library at Northwestern University for finding a wide diversity of IGOs.

International Monetary Fund homepage: www.imf.org This source discusses the background and policies of the IMF.

United Nations homepage: www.un.org This is a good source of information on the member states and current projects of the United Nations and its affiliated agencies.

World Trade Organization homepage: www.wto.org Information and news from the WTO can be found at this source.

CHAPTER 2

Ethnicity and Global Diversity

To understand global issues it is first necessary to understand the vast diversity of the world's peoples. It is this diversity that often makes it difficult to resolve common world problems. Thus, an examination of the differences, or perceived differences, between people is essential to understand the world situation fully. Cultural identity is a significant underlying factor that is often overlooked by analysts who use states as their main or only frame of reference. All decisions that individuals make about their lives are colored by their cultures, ethnic groups, genders, and classes. The decisions that governments make are similarly influenced by like concerns. Therefore, in order to understand international debates completely, it is important to know what identities within a state are privileged and which are discriminated against.

All the people, both leaders and followers, in any political system are informed not only by their state imperatives, but also by their different values and views of reality. Thus, the well-educated leader of one country can diametrically disagree with an equally well-educated leader of another, and neither will yield to the other's understanding. Bitter disputes, many of which lead to war, are based upon claims to land or resources that seem insignificant to outsiders. Many will die to preserve their country's rights to seemingly trivial places or things. When contemporary people of European descent study their history they look at the children's crusades, the Inquisition, and witchcraft trials with utter bewilderment. Time has so changed European traditions that the past has become a different, and somewhat distasteful, culture to modern Europeans.

It is clear that cultural beliefs are very powerful. Some people will fight to the death to maintain them while other people will deeply disagree with these same beliefs and be unable to support them. This is the reality of the world today as it has been throughout human history. To create a peaceful and cooperative world, people must come to understand the differences that exist between cultures and respect the depth of those differences. People may not like one another but, if they are going to work together as they increasingly must, they must agree to disagree on what they cannot resolve and find solutions to their conflicts, which must be resolved or violence will result.

This chapter introduces significant cultural distinctions in the contemporary world in order to begin to explain why people will value various economic, political, and environmental issues differently. It rejects the assumptions of the Victorian theory of Social Darwinism, which still echo in some arenas. The assumptions that the most technologically advanced societies are chosen to be superior and by nature to rule the world and that less complex societies are inferior and doomed to extinction are now repudiated. Different societies are adapted to different environments and succeed or fail in those contexts.

The case of female genital surgery and the many cultural dimensions that define reactions to this procedure conclude this chapter. Many of the concepts that are defined here are used to try to explain the variety of issues that arise in the discussion of the case. It is an important case because it engages the emotions as well as the intellect of the people who argue for and against it. In the next chapter the case of the Inuit of Nunavut will also illustrate many of the concepts introduced in this chapter and provide a case for analysis using the perspectives in Chapter 3. This is also an important case because it presents the contemporary effort of one state, Canada, to deal with the ethnic variation within its boundaries without resorting to force or state disintegration. The development of a new territory with an ethnically defined legislature can offer, if successful, a new model for other states with similar ethnic enclaves.

CULTURE: THE DEFINITION OF HUMANITY

In 1990 a group of American college professors, who taught a variety of international courses, traveled to Thailand in order to learn more about the people of that country. They found themselves sitting in a rural village asking questions of the residents. The group leader asked the townspeople if they had any questions for the Americans. The first question came from a soft-spoken woman who asked: "Did you plant your rice fields before you left home?" None of these urban American professionals knew how to answer the question.

This incident in Thailand demonstrates the existence of two contrasting truths about humanity. The first is that all humans share a common heritage: a **human culture** which allows us to understand the basic needs and capabilities shared by all people. The second is that different groups of people have developed individual ways to deal with these human problems in their own environments: **specific cultures** which are shared by the members of each society. Americans and Thais both understand the need for people to provide sufficient nutritious food for their families, but the ways in which they obtain that food are radically different. "How can these people leave their fields in the summer?" the Thai woman wonders. The Americans recognize the importance of this question but ponder, "How do we explain that we talk and write in the winter and earn enough to pay for a year's food?" Each is capable of understanding the other, but the explanations are not simple, because they are embedded in complex cultural systems. Each needs to translate the questions and answers for the other not only in linguistic terms but in cultural ones as well.

As the vignette implies, culture is central to understanding human life on the planet. That is why the first concern must be to define culture, a term that has so many different meanings. Natural scientists see a culture in a petri dish. Some artists find culture in opera and classic literature but not in rap or comic books. In this book, the term culture is used as defined by cultural anthropologists. Traditionally, anthropologists begin by quoting the first academic definition posed by Edward Tylor in 1871.

According to Tylor (1871, 1), culture is "that complex whole which includes knowledge, belief, art, morals, law, custom, and any other capabilities and habits acquired by man [*sic*] as a member of society." The strength and utility of this historical definition is that it highlights the fact that cultures are complex, patterned, and learned.

Children learn the culture shared by the adults in their world. There is nothing biologically innate in culture. The Thai child learns to grow rice and learns other related social traditions, from eating habits to religion to gender rules. Reared in another culture, that same child might have adopted very different traditions and might never even eat rice. The culture that children learn involves a complex mix of skills, beliefs, and facts which allow them to function successfully as adults in their respective societies.

As cultural traits are developed, they are integrated so that they support one another. The term **holism** is used to mean that all traits of a culture reinforce all others. For example, the religious beliefs of a culture complement the economic system, and the political system is supported by the kinship system. In traditional Inuit culture, the importance of hunting and gathering as an economic system is reinforced by a political focus on consensus and dispute resolution, the centrality of nuclear families, and the importance of animal spirits in their religion. A change in any element would change the others.

While culture shapes human society, it is located in the mind of individuals and encompasses every aspect of their life. Culture, therefore, consists of patterns of belief and guides for behavior learned by individuals, as they become full members of their societies. Individuals can learn a second culture but perhaps not to the same level of completeness as the one they learned in childhood.

Culture Change

One of the most commonplace observations made about the modern world is that it changes constantly. Most people laud some changes, from new medical breakthroughs to improved technology for special effects in films, as progress. Other changes, such as social shifts in family composition or immigration patterns, are publicly condemned as destructive of morality. At the same time, the seemingly exotic areas of the world are presented as unchanging realities. This perception is not true. In fact, change is inherent in the nature of all human culture. Since culture is the adaptation of society to environment, changes in environment, both physical and social, always trigger changes in culture. Culture change, then, is necessary for continued human survival. Logically, there are two categories of change: internal and external.

Internal changes are created by people within the society. In the long run, these changes can be seen as evolutionary, but in the short run, they appear as inventions. Important inventions are new ideas or techniques that are constructed from the mass of collected knowledge and are adopted as valuable by members of the society. These can dramatically change the culture, like the invention of the airplane in the United States, or they can be less far-reaching, such as the creation of a new fashion trend. Successful innovations are those that are regarded as useful or desirable within the contexts of a specific culture. Internal changes are negotiated by the members of society and ultimately sustain the flavor of the culture itself. This is not necessarily true, however, of changes from external sources.

External changes are invented or promoted in one culture and are introduced, from the outside, to another culture. In the most benign fashion these changes are voluntary. Innovations from one area of the world are considered desirable, and others clamor to adopt them. These can be trivial, such as new music styles from the Caribbean, new fruits from the tropics, or new soft drink flavors from Europe, or important, such as new drug therapies from France or new computer technology from the United States. Exposed to new cultural traits through everyday living, individuals adapt those that fit their lives and tastes.

More broad-based and philosophical **voluntary innovations** can also be adapted. The recent adoption of the capitalist model by formerly communist countries is a clear example. After decades of foreign pressure to overthrow communist regimes, the changes came from within. Trade agreements between countries which are ideologically divergent, like the United States and China, also demonstrate the ability of vastly differing cultures to integrate their respective practices voluntarily. Such agreements represent the victory of economic needs over political dogma. Many externally originating changes, then, are the result of the open and welcome diffusion of desired ideas and material goods.

Some changes, however, are not welcomed and are not adopted willingly. Within the historic context of colonialism, it is easy to find cases in which nations with superior military technology forced their ideas and methods on colonized nations. Often these **involuntary innovations** were defined by the stronger state as being "for the good" of the colonizing nation. The spread of Christianity and British social customs in the colonies of Great Britain during the nineteenth century illustrates this well. While there is clearly no evil in the practice of Christianity or the playing of cricket, the fact is that these specific practices were impressed by the colonizer without respect for the culture of the colonized people. The traditional religions and rituals were often outlawed in the colonized nation and any practitioners were punished. Those who adopted the British customs, in contrast, were rewarded with employment and material goods. Some who adopted the new traditions also adapted them into their own culture. Today one can find variations of Christianity around the world; for example, in rural Mexico some saints are reminiscent of older gods, and in New Guinea some variations of cricket include war and sex dances.

Other social practices and restrictions were mandated as well. In the nineteenth century, several African nations allotted important political offices to women. In the state of Buganda, for example, the women of the royal family had courts with judicial roles. Under the British, who ironically were then headed by Queen Victoria, the offices of the women were eliminated while those of the men were maintained. At the same time, the military forces and punishment for capital crimes were placed in the hands of the British governor so that Europeans controlled all forms of physical force. The male leaders were allowed to remain in offices, but their powers were substantially truncated. Such imposed changes instill dependency on the colonial states.

Culture and Economic Adaptations At first it might appear that the variations among different societies and cultures are so vast that any attempt at generalization would be fruitless. It is possible, however, to group cultures into four categories: gatherers and hunters, simple agriculturalists, pastoralists, and states with heterogeneous economies. These terms describe the cultural and economic bases of most societies.

These categories can be called evolutionary in the sense that they proceed from simple technology to complex technology but not in the sense of Social Darwinism. This categorization does not assume the moral superiority of more complex stages nor does it argue that contemporary cultures in the simpler stages are backward or ancestral to their more complex contemporaries.

There are few self-reliant groups of **gatherers and hunters** left in the world today. Small enclaves can be found in the Arctic, the deserts, and the tropics, but even these exist encapsulated within a modern state. In the past, however, independent foragers thrived across the globe. This was the original way of life for all humanity. The economic base of this simplest form of human society is the gathering of wild plants and the hunting of wild animals for food. Economics within this system take the form of **generalized reciprocity**. People in bands share with one another. They give without the expectation of equal or immediate return. All benefit from the successes of any one individual. People go hungry only if no one is able to find food. Once the plants and animals of one area are depleted, the people are forced to move their camps to a new place. The only goods they can own are those they can carry. This lifestyle means that bands need large areas of land and individuals have little wealth.

The social implications of this economic system are profound and repudiate some of the assumptions held by citizens of modern state societies. Social classes do not exist in such societies since all individuals own roughly the same material goods and perform the same tasks according to their age and gender. There are no designated leaders in bands and, while some individuals may be more admired or liked than others, group decisions are made by consensus and all people are given a say. Competition within and between bands is minimal. In short, gatherers and hunters lead generally egalitarian lives in small groups in which cooperation is the key ideal.

Simple **agriculturalists** make up the second category. One of the most important innovations in the history of humanity was the domestication of various staple plants. Once established, dependence on domesticated plants allowed populations to grow well beyond the capabilities of foraging societies. Additionally, farmers can settle in permanent towns where they can own, work, and defend their fields. Outside of the family, generalized reciprocity gives way to **balanced reciprocity**, in which equal return is expected for each gift. Differences in wealth develop between those families with good lands who have access to more food and better trade goods and those who do not. Permanent homes allow for the collection and storage of material goods.

Members of simple agricultural societies, or tribes, own personal possessions, and some are wealthier and more prestigious than others. Raiding between groups is common in this type of society because of political issues as well as the fact that people have things worth stealing. Poorer clans and communities become dependent on the generosity of richer ones in times of need. This dependency often leads to differences in status and prestige. Equality is not an ideal in most tribes. Social rank becomes an issue, and some people are born to better lives than others. There is still flexibility, however. While tribes, unlike bands, recognize leaders in their groups, tribal leaders are rarely permanent, and there is no office of chief in simple agricultural societies. Outstanding individuals in war or peace are recognized and followed.

The third category consists of **pastoralists**. Whereas agriculturalists depend on domesticated plants, pastoralists depend upon domesticated animals. These animals, rather than domesticated plants, are the foci of their societies. Some pastoralists, including the Nuer, Dinka, and other people of eastern Africa, are farmers as well, but they consider farming secondary in status to herding cattle. Others, like the hill tribes of Afghanistan, the Sami of northern Europe, and the Bedouins of the Middle East, have traditionally depended almost entirely on their herds for food. In these tribes, nomadic movement is the norm. Herds, generally owned by clans, are moved over hundreds of miles to graze on ever-new fields. These groups, unlike bands, however, have the use of animals to help with transportation and heavy work. Horses, camels, and, in the case of the Sami, reindeer allow for a far different trek from that of the bands. Domesticated animals also provide security not found with hunting. Barring catastrophic accidents, a relatively stable food source can be relied upon to feed a relatively large population.

Like the agricultural tribes, differences in wealth are clear and dictate differences in status. Ownership of large herds and the rights to rich grazing areas confer high status on members of the clan. Prestige, as well as power, is an important issue here. Wealthy individuals wield both influence within their family groups as well as power in their relations with others. Raiding is common in these societies. Herds are more easily stolen and maintained than fields, and the heroics of warriors on horseback belong to the romance of human history.

The final category consists of **states with heterogeneous economies**. The development of primitive state organization with a heterogeneous economic organization, over 5,000 years ago, was a major turning point in human history, just like the creation of the modern state so much later. In this system, political organization takes precedence over economic organization as a defining feature. Most early states were dependent on agriculture as the major source of food. A major difference, however, is that even the earliest states employed economic specialization and market exchange to an extent well beyond that of any other stage of social organization. Among clans one would find farmers growing a variety of foods for their own needs with some surplus for trade. In state-based economies one is more apt to find individual farmers growing crops for the market. Additionally, bilateral nuclear families, rather than clans, become the primary kin groups. Among other things, this means that the support of a wide array of kin is gone. Individual families become far more vulnerable than ever before.

The primary legal identity of an individual in a state is based on political or geographic designation. Rather than say "I am the son of Zarn" or "I am a member of the Dingo clan," people in states announce that they are "from Sydney" or that they are "Canadians." Their rights, privileges, and obligations stem more directly from their citizenship than their personal relationships.

This does not mean that all people in a state are equal within the system. One of the hallmarks of the state is a class system. Certain groups of people are considered inherently better and more privileged than others. Individuals who are born into urban families close to the centers of power are likely to hold important offices as adults. Individuals born into peasant families are fated to be peasants. Specializations of many kinds based on education, status, gender, age, and many other factors are common in states.

The core criterion of a state is a centralized political organization. Leadership becomes defined by offices that must be filled. Laws and courts, which decide disputes, are formalized and dictate the behavior of citizens. All this must be paid for and the participants must be fed. This is made possible through taxation. Police and military forces support the order and power of the leaders.

Warfare is common in state systems. Competition for land and scarce resources between states can become fierce. Expanding populations demand new sources of food, resources, and land. Before the expansion of modern states throughout the world, primitive states could expeditiously overrun less powerful tribes. In more recent times, similarly powerful states face off with far more deadly results.

Industrialism changes the productive focus of the state system from the farm to the factory. The goods produced by urban workers and the mechanism to create those goods owned by the elite define wealth of the society. The difference in financial and social status between the urban rich and poor mirrors that previously found in the urban elite–peasant relationship.

CULTURES, SUBCULTURES, AND OTHER CULTURAL CLASSIFICATIONS

People speak about American culture, French culture, Bantu culture, Kurdish culture, and the like with a general understanding that the people in each of those cultures differ in distinctive ways from the others. More important, perhaps, is that all Americans (here meaning from the United States) identify as Americans and clearly recognize that they are *not* French, Bantu, or Kurds. At the same time, not all Americans are identical, and each has additional distinctive social identities. Some Americans are upper-class males of African heritage who use Spanish as a mother tongue while others are middle-class Navajo women who speak Diné as well as English. The United States, of course, is a state that prides itself on the wide diversity of its citizens. Still, even more culturally homogeneous nations, such as Japan and Saudi Arabia, see a significance in certain human variations.

Ethnic Groups Literally, **ethnic group** means "culture" or "cultural group," but commonly the term is used to specify cultural groups that are minorities in a larger, heterogeneous nation. Ethnic groups include indigenous people, those who first lived on this land and no longer control it, but also later immigrants to the country. Native Americans, such as the Apache or the Tlingit, then, are ethnic groups living in the United States, but so are the Amish, Cuban Americans, and Cajuns. Individuals descended from each ethnicity are American citizens and fully invested in the country. Some have left the traditions of their ancestors so far behind that they no longer identify with the group at all. Most, however, recognize a common identity with others of similar descent and share traits from language to marriage customs to food that are important to them.

For the most part, as many American towns can demonstrate, a mixture of ethnic groups enriches a community. New Orleans, New York, and Santa Fe are very different cities, owing in large part to the peculiar mixture of prominent ethnic groups making up each city. The national cultures of Latin American states enjoy dynamism based upon the blending of Native, African, and European cultural elements. The variety of foods, language, celebrations, and ideas broaden the lives of everyone who lives there.

Unfortunately, this ideal synthesis is not always the reality of multicultural states. In some cases, ethnic identities take priority over the state identity and ethnic rivalries erupt. Antagonism toward, or isolation from, citizens of different heritage ensues. Sometimes this dissension springs from events that occurred long ago in the past and far from the current city. For example, tales of the Armenian massacre or the Irish potato famine remain important issues in American Armenian and Irish ethnic communities. Often differences in religion (Jews in Nazi Germany, Muslims in contemporary Europe, and B'hais in Iran), in language (Spanish speakers in the U.S. Southwest and French speakers in Canada), or in physical appearance (African Americans and Asians in West Africa) are used to characterize the value or nature of the individuals within those groups.

In some cases, as the examples suggest, the differences between ethnic groups can cause minor social discord or minor conflicts which eventually can grow to threaten the integrity of the state, even lead to genocide—the intended extinction of a group with a specific cultural category. The relative power of those who hate and those who are hated anticipate the results. In areas where the power is not overwhelmingly one-sided and where there is no overriding authority to restrict it, long-term ethnic antagonisms like those in Eastern Europe and parts of Africa can result in civil wars with extensive bloodshed.

Indigenous Peoples

Indigenous people represent the last groups of colonized people from the era of European colonization who remain under the control of the descendents of those once foreign societies. A special category of ethnic groups, indigenous people became conspicuous in news headlines at the end of the twentieth century. For the first time, guidelines for the treatment of First Nations issues are actively being discussed in the international arena. News stories report that rock stars appear at concerts with Native Amazonian people demanding their rights, and health professionals plead their case in hopes of gaining indigenous knowledge of tropical drugs and treatments. Indigenous groups, themselves, have organized and presented their cases for redress to both national governments and international governmental organizations. The United Nations (UN) declared 1995–2004 as the International Decade of the World's Indigenous Peoples, and UN agencies have been rewriting their rules to include consideration of their unique circumstances. One goal of the decade was the development of a statement of international rights for indigenous people. While a draft of such a statement has been influential in discussions since the beginning of the decade, ratification of a definitive document has been politically mired. The other major goal, the creation of a standing entity within the United Nations, has gone more smoothly. In May 2002 the United Nations created a Permanent Forum on Indigenous Issues which should assure the continuing voice of First Nations in international debates.

Indigenous cultures, or **First Nations**, are those traditional societies that have been enveloped by a nation-state with a distinctively different cultural base. They are the original people of an area who have lost political control over their ancestral lands and do not fully recognize the moral authority of the state government to dominate them. The best recognized indigenous cultures include the Native Americans of both North and South America, the aboriginal people of Australia, the Sami of Scandinavia, the San (Bushmen) of the Kalahari, the Ainu of Japan, and Native Hawaiians. They differ from most other ethnic groups because they maintain a prior claim to the land controlled by the state. They differ from other colonized peoples because the colonizers have settled in large numbers and, after generations, have stayed. The colonizers will not return to their native land because they now define this new land as their home.

Immigration

Immigration, which is the movement of people from one state to another, is not a new phenomenon. The vast majority of the contemporary populations of major countries including the United States, Canada, and Australia are immigrants or descendents of immigrants. Attitudes about immigration vary in these countries from national celebrations of the ideal to a resentment of the social and economic roles of newcomers. With globalization the nature of immigration has changed in a number of ways. The immigrants of the twenty-first century have communication and transportation options that allow them contact with their families and states left behind—options that nineteenth-century immigrants could never have dreamed. Not all immigrants, however, leave their countries for the same reasons.

Many immigrants leave their countries of origin for economic reasons. As in the past, many immigrants are seeking jobs to increase their standards of living. Some assume that the move will be permanent, but many now consider such immigration as a temporary stage of life. Many young men and women take service work in foreign countries in order to help their parents and build nest eggs for their futures. Child-care and domestic workers from Latin America and from India and Indonesia are young women who typically plan to return home. While these immigrants are often paid at the low end of salaries in the countries in which they work, other economic immigrants earn at elite levels. Professionals and business entrepreneurs from developing countries have found more lucrative opportunities in developed countries. Scientists from India, for example, have become prominent in the American computer and medical industries. Even between developed economies, globalization has meant that individuals from one state head businesses, or branches of international businesses, in foreign states. American, German, and Japanese business leaders are now settled throughout the world.

Force, rather than economic gains, propel other immigrants. **Refugees** are those people who flee their countries of origin in fear for their lives or cannot return home for political reasons. Many, including innumerable Africans today, who have fled vicious civil wars and devastating famines, find themselves unwelcome guests in states with little surplus to support them. The United Nations High Commission on Refugees cites almost 20 million in 2002, with most coming from Afghanistan after years of war and restrictive rulers. Most refugees live in hope of being able to return home in the future, but often this is not an option.

Many modern migrants, regardless of the reason for their migration, have been labeled transnational immigrants. The goal of most nineteenth-century immigrants was to settle permanently and become citizens of their new states. States mandated assimilation, expecting the newcomers to leave the languages and traditions of their old lives behind and blend into the culture of their new state. In the current century, however, immigrants are able to maintain communication with their families and cultures. They can visit, telephone, or e-mail with relatively little difficulty. In some areas immigrants have created communities that maintain key elements of the cultures of their home states. Cubans in Florida and Middle Easterners in France have created such communities. In both cases, old traditions and languages maintain their viability. For many modern immigrants throughout the world, fluency in multiple cultures and languages is far more valuable for individuals than loyalty to the traditions of one state. As anthropologist Ted Lewellen (2002, 151) has pointed out, "Living across borders, transnational migrants break down the identification of nation and state and give rise to the paradoxical concept of deterritorialized state or, more accurately, deterritorialized space." Many modern **transnational immigrants** identify equally with two states and maintain that identity throughout their lives.

Races

Race, the category of human diversity that would be mentioned first by many people, is probably the one most poorly understood. Americans will assert that there are four, color-coded human races: white, black, red, and yellow, or four races based on geographical heritage: European, African, American, and Asian. Upon reflection, others might include people from Australians to Hispanics.

Few Americans will realize that they are echoing the "scientific" classification of race that has been widely discounted by the anthropologists and biologists who study human diversity. At this point in human development, all people from Aachen to Zimbabwe belong to the same **biological race**: *Homo sapiens sapiens*. Other races of humans, such as the recently named *Homo sapiens idaltu*, lived at the dawn of modern humanity hundreds of thousands of years ago and became extinct in the ancient past. The physical variations seen in people around the world are minor and scientifically do not have the depth of the true racial differences seen in other animals. Animals that have developed races have had geographically isolated populations which have reproduced within these isolated groups. Over time, adaptations to particular environments became dominant in specific populations and not in others. Over even more time, unique species can develop. The history of Homo sapiens is, however, such that there have never been these types of truly isolated populations. Asia, Africa, and Europe formed an extenuated, but common, gene pool with no barriers to breeding at the borders. The Americas and the Pacific have been populated in biologically recent times and did not have time to form new races before they were reintroduced to the Old World.

It is obvious that people are physically different and that some groups of people can look different from others. The scientific reticence at using categories like race is not based upon any denial of human physical diversity, but quite the opposite: the recognition of the complexity of that diversity. The popularly held racial classifications emphasize a few physical traits—largely skin tone, hair color and texture, and nose shape. They tend to ignore the more biologically significant traits such as blood types or genetic markers. Many American children would argue that dark skin (high melanin) means African, and, indeed, dark skin is often found in parts of sub-Saharan Africa. Not all people of African heritage have dark skin (see the San or Pygmies as examples), and many people among those with the darkest skin tone on Earth come from Australia or Melanesia, far from the so-called Dark Continent. Aboriginal Australians are not Africans, but many of the former have darker skin than many of the latter.

Despite the lack of biological reality, many societies do classify people in categories that are based on perceived physical differences. Most people think that these categories are obvious and do not realize that the classification of these so-called **social races** differs around the world and over time. The U.S. census questionnaires have changed racial categories several times. In the 1990 and 2000 census forms, two questions of ethnic identity were in place. One asked if the individual was of Hispanic descent and the other was labeled "race." The concept of race was further modified in 2000 when, for the first time, individuals could list more than one race in the category, if applicable. Nearly seven million, or 2.4 percent of the respondents, marked more than one. Other countries recognize a different collection of races. Brazilians are said to recognize forty different races. Under apartheid in South Africa, White, Black, Asian, and Colored were the primary categories. A person with a mother of European heritage and a father descended from sub-Saharan Africans would be called "Colored" there. If he moved to the United States he might be called "Black."

If race is such a difficult concept to concretize, how does it retain such power in the modern world? One answer may be found in a brief review of the history of racial categories. A century ago, now-discredited races were widely believed to exist in America; for example, the Irish race and the Jewish race. Popular and academic literature of the time used these races as givens. Caricatures of simian-looking Irish and hook-nosed, sinister Jews were portrayed as these types. There is no Irish or Jewish race today (outside of philosophies of extreme hate groups) because these were social categories of a particular time when a majority of Euro-Americans who held cultural prejudices against these groups wished to distance themselves from them. To label a group as a different kind of human using scientific jargon allows others to discriminate against them in a manner that social differences could not justify. Better education or equal opportunity, the argument often goes, would not make them the equals of the superior race because their inferiority is inbred and not easily modified. This argument allowed many groups to justify slavery while at the same time claiming to value the human soul or spirit. In many societies around the world, those ethnic groups most despised by the majority are categorized as inferior races.

SEX

The term **sex** might appear to be a physical universal without the difficulties inherent in the term race. As mammals, the breeding strategy of Homo sapiens is based upon the sexual reproduction of males and females. It would appear that male and female should be unified categories. Purists, however, note that normal frequencies of intersexed individuals, variety in sexual preferences, and genetic varieties beyond XX and XY are found in all populations, and therefore, an exclusive male–female dichotomy is not the full biological story. For the most part, categorizing men and women as different physically is basic biology. However, the extension of beliefs about male–female differences beyond the primary sexual ones is open to disagreements. In fact, the dispute over the importance of the biological influence of sex on behavior is widely interpreted in ways compatible with cultural beliefs. Some societies, which believe that women are incapable of particular types of work outside of the home, for example, assert that women are biologically incapable of doing such work without harm. It was this type of explanation in the United States in the mid-nineteenth century that led Sojourner Truth, a former slave, to assert in a now famous speech for women's rights that she had done all the hard physical jobs and, as she put it, "ain't I a woman?"

GENDER

Gender, as distinct from sex, is the term used in the social sciences as a cultural definition. Different societies define the proper roles and the assumed capabilities of men and women differently. In some societies there are more than two genders. In India the Hijra form a third gender category which, anthropologist Serena Nanda (1990) asserts, is "neither man nor woman." Real Hijras are either natural hermaphrodites (born with both male and female reproductive organs) or undergo surgery to remove external sex organs. Their ideal role in society is to be followers of the goddess Maia, and they are called upon to dance at weddings and childbirth celebrations in order to bring the blessing of fertility. Less ideally for the Hijras, many are employed as prostitutes in the cities. In Native America the Navajo recognize *nadles*, a third gender of people who have the blessings of both males and females and who often have special supernatural abilities. The classification of *berdache* (Williams 1986), or more properly "those of two spirits," in other Native American groups is also recognized as a (normal) third gender. While the vast majority of people around the world are labeled as men or women, additional categories are recognized in some cultures.

A more obvious variation can be found by looking at the definitions of men and women in different societies. Most Americans would identify a fully veiled woman as a Muslim from the Middle East and a figure in a football uniform as an American male. Similarly they would assume a person identified as a Roman Catholic priest is a man and one identified as a belly dancer is a woman. However, these visual intercultural assumptions are often more complex. In the nineteenth-century plains of North America, a farmer was clearly defined as a male by the Euro-American settlers. Equally clearly, the Native American residents defined a farmer as a female. In each culture the role of farmer was sex-linked but in opposite ways. Each found the gendered concepts of the other absurd and even distasteful. This became an issue, and one little understood by the U.S. government, when it attempted to "civilize" the Plains Indians by making them farmers. The resistance to farming by Native American men in this area was taken as a sign of laziness and backwardness. At the same time, no effort was made to help Native American women develop their farms because nondomestic work by women was not taken seriously within the equally culture-bound gender expectations of the Euro-Americans. Over time, such differences in gender expectations in North America often led to the disenfranchisement of Native American women in economics and politics (Klein and Ackerman 1995).

Only recently have the issues of women's rights as intrinsic to human rights been genuinely argued in the United Nations and other international bodies. The widespread impact of varying rights being granted to men and women in different states had often been ignored in discussions of global issues. However, overwhelming data demonstrate that women and children are more often found in poverty than men throughout the globe, and this mandates new research and calls for new programs. Today the UN Division for the Advancement of Women (DAW) coordinates work on issues that involve women in UN agencies, including the World Bank, World Health Organization, International Atomic Energy Agency, International Labour Organization, and two dozen others.

Classes

A final global category, and one that has no biological base but great human consequence, is social hierarchy or **class**. National and international decision makers are drawn from the upper classes and reflect upper-class understandings and goals. While as noted, bands and tribal societies maintain relative social equality, states by their definition do not. With the dominance of the state form come almost global class strata. Poverty tied to powerlessness and great wealth tied to great power prove true not only when dealing between states but within them as well.

Stratification is a difficult concept for Americans to grasp because it conflicts with the deeply held ideal of human equality and the fictive identification of the United States as a classless society. Even so, class is an element of American society, and the ideal of equality is taught to children as equal opportunity rather than equal results. Therefore, there can be rich and poor, powerful and powerless as long as all people have the right to reach the high positions. Every child, or boy it was said until recently, can grow up to be president. The fact that this is not, and has never been, true is a painful cultural contradiction that many Americans would like to ignore.

Most states do not recognize all their citizens to be equal. In fact, people are valued, paid, and respected according to the social status they hold. Some obtain their status by birth. Royalty and the wealthy elite, for the most part, are born into families that already have royal titles or wealth to pass on. This type of position is often called an **ascribed status**. The opposite, an **achieved status**, is one that is earned by the actions of an individual. For example, in England, Queen Elizabeth II holds an ascribed status, while the prime minister has earned an achieved status. The next monarch of England is expected to be the son of the reigning queen; the next prime minister almost certainly will not be a child of the current one. Some societies are more fluid with respect to social movement than others, and an individual not born into it can become part of the wealthy elite by earning vast amounts of wealth and learning the correct social behavior of the group. For the most part, however, most citizens of states change little from the status, or class, of their parents.

One of the problems in the contemporary world is the pervasiveness of underclasses. Often the underclass is linked to ethnic background. In many countries minority ethnic groups have been deprived of opportunities to rise in the social system, and they remain subservient, dependent, and poor for centuries. While slavery as an institution has been internationally prohibited, servitude remains. The roles of Indonesian servants in Saudi Arabia, Gypsies (Romi) in Europe, and Koreans in Japan all, in different ways, reflect ethnic group stratification.

REACTIONS TO DIVERSITY

As has been seen, human diversity is a reality of everyday life, and it has been an issue throughout history. This history has not been a uniformly peaceful one, however. Many countries have celebrated human diversity, but in others, it has been the reason for legal discrimination, war, slavery, and even genocide. The following concepts can help explain such events.

Ethnocentrism   The most common reaction to cultural diversity is **ethnocentrism**, or judging the customs of another culture according to the standards of your own. This can be as simple as judging others' food preferences. On a more serious level, members of one religion might declare the practices of another to be immoral or illegal. The cultural differences being condemned need not be very different than those followed by the critics. In fact, seemingly minor differences are often more severely condemned than extreme ones. For example, in largely Christian jurisdictions, laws exist against snake handling in the religious services of minority Christian denominations in parts of the southeastern United States. At the same time, law protects the use of poisonous snakes in some Native American religious ceremonies in the Southwest. Ethnocentrism, then, appears throughout societies.

Ethnocentrism is difficult to combat because there is a positive reality that helps cause the negative outcome. Universally, children are reared to appreciate and adapt the culture of their parents. As they learn they are enculturated so that they can function as full members of their society. They learn that their religion is true, their customs are good, and their political system is just. The child who does not learn this does not fit in. It should be of little surprise, then, that when they are adults these individuals regard other religions as false, other customs as inappropriate, and other political systems as unjust. In a homogeneous setting this would cause little trouble, but in a heterogeneous world it creates problems when groups interact.

Cultural Relativity   **Cultural relativity** is the term used to describe one solution to the problem of the application of ethnocentricity. Cultural relativity suggests that the actions of people within each culture should be evaluated according to the rules of that culture. The person who eats a dog in Vietnam, then, is evaluated differently than an American who might do the same in the United States. A concern often voiced is that cultural relativity taken to its logical extreme would allow for moral anarchy. Would the murders of thousands, or millions, as has occurred in recent history, be acceptable because the nation that allowed these deaths deemed them appropriate? From the perspective of most religious and ethnic systems, the answer would surely be no. Politically, the United Nations asserts that there are universal human rights that supersede any national values.

The balance between ethnocentrism and cultural relativity is a delicate one. Patriotism is an admirable trait, but it is also a form of ethnic nationalism which gives priority to your state. Is nationalism good if your government causes deaths or denies freedom to other peoples? In contrast, accepting people as different but still as human is far more difficult than popular slogans suggest. Where extreme ethnocentrism exists it may be impossible to understand people from other cultures and hence to deal with them successfully in business or diplomacy. Extreme cultural relativism makes it impossible to raise issues of human rights violations or environmental ruin beyond the boundary of one's own culture.

Racism and Sexism Racism and sexism further hinder world cooperation, within countries and worldwide. When individuals judge other individuals based on their racism—or perceived biological differences—it tends to distort their understanding of the world. Africa became the "Dark Continent" in European minds, and Africans became defined as a different and inferior type of people. As "inferior" people, they were perceived as needing the benefits of European civilization and consequently colonialism. The slavery of Africans was justified by this assertion of innate difference. Likewise, differential immigration laws, which encourage and discourage migration throughout the world, are often based on racist assumptions.

Likewise, sexism allows people to use their perceptions of appropriate gender behavior to judge other nations. The images of veiled and draped Islamic women are used by other societies as evidence of the "backwardness" of some Arab countries without understanding of the meaning of purdah or female seclusion. At the other extreme, women who traditionally wore little clothing (such as those in the Pacific Islands) and those who wear sexually alluring clothing (such as Latin or Caribbean women during Carnival) are used as evidence of the backwardness of those cultures. Even the presence of women in high political office is used by some to indicate the weakness of such a henpecked country. At the same time, countries with few women in high political office are taunted as medieval. Concerns over human rights, as noted above, are confused by sexism.

Governmental responses to human diversity within domestic borders have historically taken many forms—from acceptance to forced conformity to isolation on reservations to genocide. Recently governments have seen a need to deal with the increasing diversity in new ways that conform to international standards of human rights. This has highlighted the cultural differences between states and questions the universality of the concept of human rights. The case that follows illustrates the complexity of dealing with such diversity.

CASE STUDY   Female Genital Surgery

The practice in some African and Asian societies called either female circumcision or female genital mutilation, according to one's perspective, has become popularly and internationally disputed. In the early 1990s, this practice was brought to the public attention in author Alice Walker's best-selling book *Possessing the Secret of Joy* (1992) and in the film *Warrior Marks* (Walker, Permer, and Dorkenoo 1993). Both works presented female genital surgery to a largely previously unaware audience as a major world issue that needed to be halted by concerned individuals. Soon after, this view was supported in a personal story of living with the surgery and its outcome by a world-famous Somali model. During female genital surgery, girls have some of their external sexual organs surgically removed, or altered, in a coming-of-age ceremony. In the least invasive form, a portion of the clitoris is removed; in the rarer form, all the external genitalia are removed and the sections are sewn together, with only a small hole left open for urination and menstrual blood escape. After such surgery, the girls are recognized as women and are ready for respectable marriage. The World Health Organization estimates that from 100 to 140 million women worldwide have undergone this surgery and that it is performed on about 2 million more women each year.

Many individuals and social organizations, especially from parts of the world that do not currently have this practice, are appalled by it and call it mutilation. They argue that these practices are damaging both physically and psychologically to women. In fact, even in the cleanest conditions, the extreme forms of these surgeries have often caused serious internal infections, infertility, difficult birth, and long-term bleeding. Often, however, traditional practitioners perform the surgeries in less than sanitary conditions, which can lead to immediate life-threatening situations. This also can increase the spread of contagious diseases, most notably HIV. Beyond the physical risks, opponents stress that the procedure permanently destroys the women's pleasure in sexual relations. Both points of view contend that good health and sexual pleasure are basic human rights which are being denied.

On the extreme opposite side, some diplomats, and many citizens from countries that practice female genital surgery, argue that others are meddling in an important, private family and gender tradition. They assert that outsiders are judging them ethnocentrically. They contend that more hygienic surgeries should be the solution to health problems and point to the male circumcision performed in the West as a parallel practice. Moreover, they argue that moral behavior and female submission are important in their states and that this surgery supports proper female behavior.

A third party in this debate is often disregarded in the din of the public arguments. Inspired by individual women, who reject the custom, local nongovernmental organizations (NGOs) have formed in many of the countries that observe this tradition. They work against the extremes of the practice, using local values rather than Western arguments. They believe that internal changes, rather than externally imposed changes, will prevail. While sometimes still seen locally as Western apologists, in fact, several countries that traditionally practiced female genital surgery have now outlawed it. However, some of these, including Egypt and the Sudan, have difficulty enforcing these laws and continue to have some of the highest rates of these surgeries in the world. The Sudan, in fact, has recently begun a debate aimed at reinstating the legality of the practice. A joint Islamic University–Ministry of Religious Affairs meeting recommended not only the re-legalization of the custom but the establishment of training centers to educate people to perform the services. Some expressed a concern that a major educational program was needed since the public is losing its appreciation of the importance of this custom (English, Romano-Critchley, Sheather, and Sommerville 2003, 57).

In a world of transnationalism and globalization, this debate has spread well beyond the borders of the countries involved. International governmental organizations (IGOs), including the United Nations, have become involved by linking the practice with an abuse of universal human rights. International pressure has been put on countries to outlaw and enforce the laws against the practice. Many countries have reacted against this pressure as being unreasonable interference with their cultural values. Clearly there are very different interpretations of human rights and gender status at work here.

Issues have become even more complex because of transnational immigration. Once foreign issues have become domestic ones in many states that had never addressed them as problems. Three major concerns have become policy issues in Western countries, with significant immigrant communities coming from countries that practice female genital surgery. The first is the legality of the practice in the country. Can immigrants have female genital surgery performed in their new countries? The second is the legality of leaving the country to perform the surgery on a child elsewhere. Finally, if female genital surgery is seen as a human rights abuse, can this be the basis for asylum claims to enter the country?

Countries including the United States, Britain, Sweden, Australia, Switzerland, and France now have laws banning such genital operations. In July 2001 the Women's Rights Committee of the European Parliament called for all European Union countries to outlaw the procedure (Bosch 2001, 1178). Britain in 1985 was an early country to outlaw the surgeries, in its Female Circumcision Act. The penalty for performing the operation was set at five years in prison. However, the BBC reported on November 11, 1998, about a British Medical Association statement that 3,000 such surgeries were still being done each year. As of 2001 there had been no prosecutions based on the law.

A British Medical Association report in April 2001 reviewed the problem and provided recommendations for health care personnel. The report comes out against the medicalization of the surgery, although it might be safer than the unsanitary nonprofessional procedures since this might help legitimatize what is a "breach of human rights" (BMA 2001, 3). Unfortunately this means that immigrants are forced either to adapt to the customs of their new countries or to seek often dangerous illegal surgeries.

It is also a problem that the zeal to rid the United Kingdom of this practice has inadvertently led to inferior health care for women and children. In the United Kingdom physicians are mandated to discuss the legal and health issues of female genital surgery with the parents of any girl they consider to be at risk. They should also involve social service workers when appropriate. Since they consider this a form of "child abuse," they should protect the child from the parents if necessary while recognizing that the parents have "the best intentions for the future welfare of their child and do not intend it as an act of abuse" (BMA 2001, 5–6). Doctors are told to respect the parents and their customs but to protect the daughter in any case. This would include calling the child protection officers if they suspect the child might be taken out of the country to get the surgery elsewhere. This balance between understanding cultural differences and rigid protection rules can prove problematic, however. In a report on Australian cases, the authors discuss the discomfort that some African women feel when a physician discusses such private issues (Allotey, Manderson, and Grover 2001, 195). Such discussions made them uncomfortable in clinical settings even when their complaint had nothing to do with genital issues. The medical community's reaction to female genital surgery causes secondary problems. Clearly the threat of physicians' actions or the embarrassment of having to discuss inappropriate topics with an unrelated man can alienate the women and their daughters from needed health care.

In Australia a person performing female genital surgery can be imprisoned for up to fifteen years, and the same sentence can be imposed on a person who takes a child out of the country for the surgery (Allotey, Manderson, and Grover 2001, 192). Few other countries have similar laws, but the British Medical Association, as noted, recommends ways to remove children from parents' and grandparents' control before they can take the child elsewhere for surgery.

An additional immigration issue then arises. If the practice is recognized as so harmful, could fleeing the practice be considered a reason for refugee status? This has been highly debated in Canada, France, and the United States, among others, since this could potentially open the door to permanent residence to hundred of thousands of women who could otherwise not fit the refugee criteria. In the 1990s several cases arose in Europe and North America of individuals requesting asylum and refugee status based upon concerns about female genital surgery. In 1993 Canada granted refugee status to a Somali woman, Kahadra Hassan Farah, who based her case on her fears that returning to Somalia would end in forced surgery on her young daughter. In the United States shortly afterward, two similar cases, involving one woman from Nigeria and another from Togo, were more difficult but ultimately ended in successful pleas. One concern voiced was that since this surgery is so widespread, using it as a basis for refugee status could open the door to millions of women to migrate to North America. Given the rarity of such asylum claims, this concern was obviously overstated. Ultimately these countries have granted refugee status but have not yet seen many applicants. As all countries become increasingly heterogeneous, conflicting concepts of group and individual rights over gender can only generate more controversy.

Ethnocentrism Female genital surgery was, in fact, a practice in Europe and North America in the nineteenth century and continued to be a medical practice in the United States into the twentieth century. The surgery was performed to counter hysteria, depression, and excessive sexuality in women. It was clearly tied to a culturally specific concept of gender that tied seemingly inappropriate female behavior to their physical sex. As changes in gender concepts occurred, the medical procedure became increasingly archaic and ultimately disappeared. These local practices did not create the uproar that has been heard against foreign customs, and the history of European surgeries has been largely lost in the modern debates.

Critics who decry the European and American campaigns against female genital surgery as ethnocentric point to the lack of outcry over domestic cosmetic surgeries. While some such surgeries like face-lifts, nose jobs, body piercings, and the like have low percentages of medical problems, none are medically necessary and all carry some risks. More problematic, medically, are procedures like breast enlargements and genital cosmetic surgeries which have proved to be physically dangerous. The problem that Americans have in seeing the parallels with female genital surgery are emphasized as proof of ethnocentric perspectives.

Male circumcision is widely practiced in both Europe and North America, although not without medical dispute. Over the years the procedure has been medically mandated as a health matter and, at other times, rejected as medically unnecessary. While there are rare medical problems with the surgery, the question is whether the procedure is medically advantageous or is a cosmetic surgery. If it is merely the latter, any danger makes it medically suspect and, since the patient, an infant, cannot give informed consent, questions are being asked in the medical community. No such outrage has been seen in the public arena, however. Additionally there have been no major campaigns against the surgery in religious traditions, like Judaism, where the surgery is a religious mandate.

In both cases it is easy to assert that female genital surgery is far more dangerous and physically invasive than any of the European and American cases. This begs the issue of ethnocentrism, however. Why do the domestic traditions appear trivial while foreign traditions appear so irrational? Why shouldn't the domestic issues be argued and resolved before taking on the concerns of others?

Gender/Sex Clearly this issue has both gender and sex components. It is a cultural and physical tradition. The nature of the surgery itself is to change the sexual organs and to modify sexual sensations. The purpose of this, however, is largely culturally defined. The image of the good woman is essential to understanding the goals of the practice. If a virtuous woman were seen as submissive, sexually remote, clean, and faithful to her family, a physical modification that would assure or, at least, promote such an outcome would be clearly sensible. For cultures that, at least in recent decades, define the good woman as more autonomous and sexual than this, a surgery that lessens this outcome can be seen as horrific. Certainly a major cause of the campaign against female genital surgery is the growth of the women's movement in Europe and North America. Women's groups lead the public protests against female genital surgery and have been instrumental in changing the gender definition of contemporary women. The ideal American woman of the twenty-first century is a far cry from her counterpart of fifty years ago. Autonomy, sexuality, and public accomplishment are now commonly valued in women. With the change in gender values, the perception of traditions, like that of female genital surgery, has changed dramatically.

The supporters of this tradition also see the opposition in gendered terms. Many point to the sexuality and public persona of Western women as just the reasons for the surgery. This behavior highlights their fears about the true nature of women who are surgically unchanged. From the gender concepts of those who support the procedure, modern Western women appear to be immoral and become poor wives and mothers. Many non-Western women regard single motherhood and crimes against women in Western societies as the result of the women's movement and gender changes. They consider the loss of support and respect from men an undesirable result of increased freedom. From a cultural perspective, the gendered realities of others are seen as deeply flawed, while the failings of one's own reality are seen as unfortunate, but more minor. There is a growing movement of domestic women's groups in non-Western societies, and they work for changes in gender relations that fit their cultures. Often opposed to female genital surgery, they are frequently labeled as Western sympathizers by traditionalists.

Summary Female genital surgery is a tradition that is rejected by people around the world except for those who practice it; therefore, it provides a good case to challenge culture-based feelings of ethnocentrism, sexism, and racism and to question the limits of cultural relativity. Many people who belong to cultures that follow this practice regard opposition to it as an ethnocentric attack on a long-held tradition that upholds family, gender relations, sexuality, and cultural authority. They assert that others should look to their own customs if they want to make changes in harmful traditions. Others, who oppose female genital surgery, argue that there are limits to cultural relativity. To them this practice is an assault on women based on sexism and ignorance. They argue that some basic human rights override cultural rights. To further complicate the issue, transnational migration has brought people who value the surgery into states which outlaw it. This case challenges people to look at it with both their minds and their hearts.

TERMS AND CONCEPTS

Achieved status *32*

Agriculturalists *24*

Ascribed status *32*

Balanced reciprocity *24*

Biological race *29*

Class *32*

Cultural relativity *33*

Ethnic group *26*

Ethnocentrism *33*

External changes *23*

Gatherers and hunters *24*

Gender *31*

Generalized reciprocity *24*

Holism *22*

Human culture *21*

Immigration *28*

Indigenous cultures/First Nations *27*

Indigenous people *27*

Industrialism *26*

Internal changes *22*

Involuntary innovations *23*

Pastoralists *25*

Racism *34*

Refugees *28*

Sex *30*

Sexism *34*

Social race *30*

Specific culture *21*

States with heterogeneous economies *25*

Transnational immigrants *29*

Voluntary innovations *23*

DISCUSSION QUESTIONS

1. Is there a limit to cultural relativity? What is the relationship of human rights to group rights? Who decides what is right and wrong?
2. What are the major ethnic groups in your community? How do they celebrate their differences?
3. What is the history of immigration in your state? Are current immigrants different than those who came before? If so, how?
4. Is generalized reciprocity a means of exchange in any aspects of your culture? Do any people give without expecting a return?
5. Who are the indigenous people in your region? What is their legal and cultural standing? How do others evaluate their status?

RESEARCH PROJECTS

1. What customs and traditions have immigrants from other countries brought to your community? Have they historically been welcomed? Has their situation changed over time?
2. Choose an international story in the newspaper and investigate the cultural background of the countries involved. Does this deepen your understanding of the story?
3. Choose a Native American, or another indigenous, group and trace the history of its legal status. Have they always been full citizens of your country? Does their current legal status differ from that of other citizens?
4. Choose a controversial issue in your community. Argue the issue from more than one side. Put yourself in the shoes of those with whom you disagree and present their case as convincingly as you can. What have you learned about yourself and others?

5. Write a plan to change a social, health, or political problem in another country. What is the problem? How do people in the country involved view the problem? How would you solve the problem? What cultural differences do you have to consider in making the solution appropriate for the people you are trying to help?

INTERNET RESOURCES

Amnesty International website: www.amnesty.org This site highlights human rights abuses.

Department of Anthropology at Texas A&M: www.tama.edu/anthropology/news.html This site provides information on culture issues that are currently in the news.

UN Gateway site on women's issues: www.un.org/womenwatch

UN High Commissioner on Refugees: www.unhcr.ch This UN agency deals with refugee issues.

World Health Organization: www.who.org This UN agency coordinates international health issues.

UN Permanent Forum on Indigenous Issues homepage: http://www.un.org/esa/socdev/pfii/index.html

CHAPTER 3

Perspectives on Ethnicity and Global Diversity

"Nunavut is an outdated idea, one of the last applications of the postwar ideal of national self-determination."

—GURSTON DACKS, 1986
(QUOTED IN PURICH 1992, 79)

"Nunavut is not just an important achievement for Inuit. It will be an important inspiration for other Aboriginals in other parts of the world."

—JOHN AMAGOALIK, 1993
(QUOTED IN PELLY 1993, 29)

R easonable people can look at the same situation and come to very different conclusions. They can use the same data and interview the same people. They can use the same standards of reason and be of equal intelligence. Still they may come to different, perhaps opposite, opinions and be absolutely convinced that those who disagree with them are wrong. Such informed yet conflicting opinions are based upon the fact that people deeply hold different sets of complex, value-laden ideas about the nature of the world and the human condition: the way that things are supposed to be.

People use these fundamental notions to interpret all new situations that arise. Academics talk about paradigms and theoretical interpretations, and scholars are taught to be aware of their influence on the construction of new theories. This same situation is true of all interpreters, but most people remain unaware of the force of these paradigms on our daily opinions of world events. Since ethnicity, class, religion, and region influence the learning of values and manners of thinking, it is not surprising that similar perspectives are held by similar people.

In this book these differing sets of interpretive ideas are called **alternative perspectives**, and we shall examine the most prominent perspectives for each major issue described in Chapters 2 through 9: cultural diversity, economics, ecology, and peace and war. The point should *not* be which is the right perspective and which is wrong, but how and why sensible people approach each issue differently. For the current issue, cultural diversity, we explore three such alternative perspectives: globalism, state primacy, and cultural pluralism.

GLOBALISM

Individuals and groups who believe in the concept of globalism assert, as the term suggests, that the division of the world into specific political or economic entities is outmoded. They regard the contemporary world as one in which all peoples are joined in complex interactions and one in which all economies are tied to a true world community. It is just as easy to purchase a Coca-Cola in South Africa as it is in Hong Kong or Chicago. Americans wear clothes made in Mexico and India, while Mexicans and Indians watch American television programs and listen to American music. Development projects in Brazil and Indonesia affect the world's climate. Inventions and disasters in one part of the world are quickly felt in others. In these circumstances, according to those who believe in globalism, the only logical course is to encourage the further political integration of the world's people. Along with this goes the hope that, in this integrated system, all people will be able to share in the universal human rights promised by the United Nations Charter.

The question is, how to further this unification. There are two approaches to this goal. One response is that it is already happening, as the preceding examples suggest. There are specific cultures, which are becoming universally understood. They are the leaders who set the standards in global affairs. More isolated cultures are less significant, and the individuals who identify with them must change or continue to be insignificant. An extreme goal of such a policy would be a world governed by the "superior" cultures and populated by people who culturally resemble their most successful inhabitants. The other response perceives unification where no one existing culture dictates to the rest of the world. This new world culture would include all the best traits of the existing cultures and would eliminate those that threaten the rights of individuals.

An emphasis on external, and sometimes involuntary, changes which give priority to this new world culture is fundamental to this perspective. Societies, or ethnicities, based on gathering or hunting, tribal, or primitive state organization are outdated. They cannot share in the wealth of the world as long as they remain in their current lifestyles. Unfortunately, they do not know enough of the world to recognize this situation. Efforts focused on improving the lot of such people without changing their lifestyle to fit into the world system could be deleterious to them. By viewing isolated cultures through the globalism perspective, as evolutionary anachronisms, one would consider any encouragement of their continuation as they are now as going against historical logic and condemning individuals to primitive, difficult lives. Inherently this belief is a modern version of the theory of Social Darwinism, which was influential on American and European thought a century ago. Social Darwinism evoked the concept of the "survival of the fittest" and applied it to cultural evolution. Those cultures that were more complex had proven themselves the fittest. This logic was used to justify colonialism by arguing that the colonial powers were bringing civilization to the less fortunate. Now it has evolved to assert that the contemporary world powers with a vision of universal rights are best suited to lead us toward a successful world civilization.

Assimilation   One common view held by advocates of globalism is that the more backward cultures will disappear when individuals recognize the benefits of the more advanced cultures and voluntarily change their ways. This belief has formed the social policies of many colonial states. Called **assimilation**, it holds that, over time, all people will give up the customs of their inferior cultures to become members of the superior ones.

Many social policies are built on the awareness that the road to assimilation goes through education, especially of a culture's youth. Those who do not support assimilationist policies, however, are particularly opposed to this aspect of them. Many indigenous people complain that the national educational policies of the dominant culture are a form of **ethnocide**—the destruction of a culture. The aboriginal people of Australia, for example, have been very vocal on this issue. Thousands of aboriginal children were removed from their families at very early ages and were sent to boarding schools where they were punished for speaking their own languages or practicing their own religions. The curriculum, created for Anglo-Australians, was based upon the understandings of European heritage. When the "educated" children were allowed to return home, they were strangers to their families and their cultures.

In a strange way there is a liberal idea at the core of the assimilationist agenda. It assumes that the more "primitive" people of the world are capable of being educated and becoming part of the modern world. Their backwardness is based on their limited knowledge rather than any innate limitations. This basic idea has existed throughout the history of the United States, not only in its Native American policy, but in its immigration theory as well. The concept of the American "melting pot," even if it is not reality, is assimilationist in nature. It promotes the United States as welcoming people from all nations, though immigrants are expected to give up their previous ways in order to become Americans. Thus, while new cultures flavor the cultural melting pot, at the core it remains American. Contemporary political debate over the possibility of mandating English as the official U.S. language can be seen as a confrontation over assimilation.

Acculturation Conceptually related to assimilation, **acculturation** holds that individuals will modify their cultural upbringing by adapting to a new culture. They will not give up their original culture entirely, but they will adjust it to fit new circumstances. Assuming the desirability of a global culture, it would follow that people would wish to take on many of the superior traits they find in people of other cultures. Education plays a role, but it need not be forced and it need not replace the original culture completely. Minority groups, First Nations, and nonindustrial nations should be "allowed" to learn the political and economic systems of the successful states and the ideals that support them. Family organizations, art, religion, dress, and other cultural elements, which do not (in theory) impede modernization, need not be changed for acculturation to succeed.

Acculturation to the material traits of a popular culture is ubiquitous, as the broad international recognition of Coca-Cola and McDonald's demonstrates. The spread of Christianity, Buddhism, and Islam throughout the world through missionization, for example, is more comprehensive. However, acculturation does not aim to create an absolute copy of a cultural model. McDonald's in Israel serves kosher hamburgers. More significantly, variations in Islamic and Christian practice exist in different areas of the world. Therefore, few ideas are accepted but in a way that make sense with the existing ideas.

Syncretism Syncretism refers to the mixing of cultural ideas from different sources in order to create a new reality. Those who regard globalism as the creation of a wholly new world culture favor syncretism as the major mechanism that will form the new world culture. An example of how this has happened with religion involves the adoption of Catholicism by indigenous groups in Latin America. The religions of rural Latin America, which merge the identities of traditional local gods with those of Roman Catholic saints, are such examples. The processionals in celebration of saint days in Mayan towns echo the ancient religious practices as much as the Christian ones.

However, syncretism is not always acceptable to those who champion acculturation in other forms. Pope John Paul II has preached vehemently against this modification of the teachings of the Catholic Church but supports the use of local languages in church services. Those who believe in acculturation in the service of the centrality of superior cultures require that the key items of the superior culture be accepted. To the pope, of course, that key item is the religious understanding of his church. To those who are seeking a new universal culture, the new ways of understanding Christianity are part of the road to common understandings; the core beliefs in the faith have been accepted while the means to express them are being comprehended in a locally acceptable fashion.

Advocates of globalism recognize a difficult challenge. They look to a bright future in which all people will share in the wealth and rights possessed by only some today. The cultural difficulty is how to achieve this end without harming the rights of people to choose their own futures. The most optimistic assume that all people will share their views of the good life. Others realize that cultural differences run deep and that different people value different beliefs and customs, often more than prosperity and peace. Most advocates of this perspective recognize that the creation of a new global reality in which all share in a mutually satisfying culture is an extraordinarily difficult challenge—one that must be done carefully so as not to sacrifice the ways of life of some for those of others. They believe that this difficult challenge must be undertaken because the endpoint is so worthwhile.

STATE PRIMACY

While the state primacy perspective of the world does not define the superiority of types of systems, it does privilege a specific type of political organization. The state is viewed as the most important unit for both national and international interaction. According to those who hold a state primacy perspective, the primary political identity for all groups and individuals should be as citizens of the state of their birth or adoption. The state primacy perspective does not argue for universal similarity in cultures or centralized power between states. In fact, it gives states a tremendous amount of autonomy in deciding the nature of their own realms. Its vision of the ideal world, then, includes many different states, each of which determines the ethnic policies of its own residents.

National identity that is the same as state identity is not as common as many Americans would assume. The concepts of nation and state are quite different. A *nation* is made up of a group of people who identify themselves as a unified and unique culture. A *state*, in contrast, is a complex political structure that may include citizens from a variety of nations. When the Navajo in the United States, the Cree in Canada, or the Yanamamo in Brazil call themselves nations, they are using the term in its proper form. In fact, most indigenous peoples are, as the term First Nations suggests, real nations. Koreans, for example, control the largely ethnically homogeneous states of the Republic of Korea and the Democratic People's Republic of Korea. The nation of Korea is larger than the two states, however, and people who identify themselves as Koreans live around the world. Koreans who are citizens of either Korean state are governed by the laws of their own state, and other Koreans are not. In some states, like the United States, many Koreans are full American citizens who maintain a Korean identity; in others, like Japan, Koreans are identified as "not Japanese."

Can people be members of more than one nation or fit into two or more cultures? The philosophy of the modern state relies on the belief that one can indeed do this. Is the American citizen of Korean heritage part of the American nation? If the answer were no, then the United States would be a state without a nationality, which is clearly not the case. Americans, as a national group, share values which throughout the world are recognized as illustrating an American personality. At the center of these values is the admiration of the strong individual. Children are taught to be independent. They honor their families but are reared to leave them and set up independent homes and lead independent lives when they become adults. Material gain and competitive success gained through fair play are the parents' goals for their children.

Within the reality of this common culture, American nationality is also defined as a mixture of other cultures, each of which has added its own character to the society. Even if it is not a true melting pot, America has been described as a mosaic of different color tiles or a lumpy stew with multiple ingredients. While the United States is one of the few states that defines itself as multiethnic, many states in the modern world are currently multiethnic in composition, if not in ideal.

Patriotism From the state primacy perspective there is no inherent evil in the multiethnic state as long as the state identity takes priority over ethnic identities. **Patriotism**, the placing of one's primary loyalty in the state, is the real key. As long as individuals function first as Brazilians, Indonesians, or Russians, especially in issues of state interest, the interests of state primacy prevail. During World War II, for example, Native Americans volunteered for military service in the United States at a far greater rate than other Americans. Their loyalties to their own First Nations did not inhibit their American patriotism. In fact, the United States benefited in many ways from their cultural skills. The history of the Navajo "code talkers" of that war illustrates this brilliantly. Navajo soldiers assigned to communications sent classified messages to one another in the Navajo (Dené) language. German code breakers were never able to decipher these communications because they were not true codes, and the Germans did not recognize them as a language. Because they were Navajo, these soldiers performed unique patriotic duties as citizens of the United States.

While advocates of the state primacy point of view would likely accept and applaud examples like that of the Navajo code talkers, they maintain a deep distrust of the power of ethnicity, viewing it as weakening patriotism and creating rifts in the state system. Numerous cases can be cited to support this concern. Civil wars based on ethnicity have been recently fought in countries from Bosnia to Liberia; ethnic violence, such as terrorist incidents of the Tamil of Sri Lanka or the Irish Republican Army, and political crises, such as the threat of the Quebecois to break up Canada, have redefined their states. All these situations threaten the primacy of the state.

The solutions to these problems lie with the states themselves according to this perspective. The state has the right, and perhaps duty, to defend itself from internal and external threats. Issues concerning the distribution of rights and privileges between types of people within the state must be decided within the state. Given the nature of the state, the power to decide such issues resides in an elite which controls governmental offices. The fact that the elite is often composed of individuals from similar ethnic backgrounds is sometimes considered unfortunate, but it is unimportant compared to the need for state security. It is also asserted that the situation is best understood from the local perspective and that outsiders cannot understand the real circumstances.

Subjugation   Subjugation, an extreme authoritarian approach to unifying cultures, is rarely advocated today. It proposes that people of superior groups should control the lives of people of inferior ones. Policies of subjugation reject an active, or at least internally originated, role for members of the weaker society. As justification, it assumes that the individuals of inferior societies are themselves inferior. Racism can flourish in this atmosphere. Social practices from nineteenth-century American slavery to twentieth-century genocide in Nazi Germany or Rwanda or Burundi were justified by the practitioners using themes of racial superiority and policies of subjugation.

Paternalism   Those advocating any of the solutions suggested for ensuring the unification of world cultures often run into accusations of **paternalism**, which literally means "acting as a father." More broadly it means taking a superior position over others and trying to control their actions. Such control is done "for their own good" because the superior figure "knows better." The protected individuals or groups are treated like children. Outlawing the handling of snakes in the rituals of the Holiness churches of the American Southeast can be considered paternalism. The larger society, which does not accept the biblical interpretation of handling snakes, dictates that adults who do find snake handling an important religious act are wrong; they are endangering themselves and must be stopped for their own protection. Paternalism, itself, is illegal nowhere, but it is rarely welcomed by those treated as inferiors.

Critiques from the Globalism Perspective   Advocates of globalism reject the state primacy perspective on two grounds: first, because states are artificial constructs based on historical accident rather than natural groupings; and second, because most world problems are global in scope rather than pertinent only to the local interests of states. Cooperation is thus negotiated rather than mandated in this perspective.

A particularly troublesome issue which reappears around the world is the position of those groups that straddle state boundaries. In the state primacy perspective, the state contends that the interests of these ethnic minorities are secondary in importance to those of the state. Members of the same ethnicity in other states are regarded as different people with different citizenship. The Inuit, as noted below, live in a contiguous circumpolar land that covers four states. They have a national identity as Inuit and national identities as Russian, American, Canadian, and Danish. In the latter identities, they have clear administrative rights and privileges but in the former they do not. General Inuit issues have been championed by newly formed circumpolar and First Nation organizations. The welcoming of these organizations by international agencies, including the United Nations, as new cultural organizations with observer status and the extensive press coverage given to international meetings concern state nationalist proponents because they regard them as threats to the important primacy of the state system.

Globalism advocates see a daunting problem in state nationalists putting their faith in the rectitude of nation-states. They do not always seem worthy. There is no mechanism, in this view, to deal with the states that harm groups of people within their borders. There is no way to deal with the issue of human rights in states that do not come up to international standards. If a state defines the slavery, murder, or active discrimination of a particular group as acceptable, can outsiders legitimately help the victims?

The recent case of the former practice of **apartheid** in South Africa provides a clear example. Here, a numerical majority in the state, the original inhabitants, were legally defined as inferior, and all aspects of their lives were severely circumscribed. Nearly universal condemnation (supplemented by boycotts) was directed at South Africa; however, because of the nature of the state system, direct action was not immediately effective. If state primacy was absolute, even the boycotts were inappropriate. Many nations, including the former Soviet Union and China, have made just such assertions when other nations have condemned their internal actions. The example of South Africa can be used to justify the stand of state primacy as well. It was largely the internal changes made by South Africans themselves that overthrew the internationally despised practice of apartheid.

CULTURAL PLURALISM

Advocates of globalism prioritize a united world; advocates of state primacy prioritize the state; and the advocates of cultural pluralism prioritize the autonomous rights of individual cultures, regardless of their power. In this view, nations, cultures, ethnic groups, and indigenous peoples are the units of interest. Proponents argue that people identify with these groups, and, if one believes in human equality, then these groups too must be equal. All recognize, of course, that such equality does not exist in political or economic terms. Rather than seeing ethnic pluralism as a validation of evolutionary failure, as do the followers of Social Darwinism, cultural pluralists see this as the result of a particular peoples' history which is set in a world of institutionalized inequality. They argue that the existence of a privileging of some cultures over others should not give the system ethical authority.

Tolerance Cultural pluralism mandates **tolerance** of cultural differences without ethnocentric judgment. The fact that people are different is acceptable. People whose cultures are similar are no better or worse than those whose cultures are far different. All cultures must be granted respect and their people human rights. To tolerate some custom or belief is not necessarily to like it or to adopt it. A Jew can tolerate the practice of Christianity in the community without converting to that faith and vice versa. People of any faith can believe in the superiority of their own religion, but they can also tolerate others believing differently. A more difficult question might be raised when the basic values of the religions are inherently in conflict. Can a Christian tolerate the practice of Satanism in the community? In the United States the legal answer is still yes, but the emotional response of individuals in such a situation is often a strong no.

One question of tolerance, of course, is at what point it stops. As with the argument about cultural relativism, tolerance of the intolerable cannot be moral. Two areas of contention inevitably arise for advocates of cultural pluralism. One issue arises frequently when the rights of one culture limit the rights of another. When the Hopi and Navajo in the United States or Jews, Arabs, and Christians in Jerusalem claim religious rights over the same lands, what is the culturally diverse solution? Outsiders might believe that a compromise that dictates sharing would be fair, but the participants in the dispute might violently disagree and complain that the presence of the others corrupts the sacred area.

A similar dilemma is faced when the rights of one culture inadvertently harm others. Many simple agricultural cultures practice slash-and-burn agriculture. They burn the remnants of last year's fields in order to fertilize them for the next crops. Mayan farmers in Yucatán do this yearly. This process creates a great deal of smoke for several weeks. More recent residents in the area, including those who run the tourist areas of the Yucatán, feel the fires are deleterious to their health and economic way of life. Globally, some environmentalists consider slash-and-burn fires harmful in both causing smoke in the atmosphere and adding to deforestation throughout the planet. The Mayans, and others, believe this economic system is crucial to their survival in their cultures. Still others find it detrimental beyond the confines of Mayan lands. Where does tolerance lie?

The other issue is equally difficult. People ask what moral truths transcend tolerance. In fact, few ideals beyond the highly abstract value of human life appear in all cultures, and even this value is interpreted in different ways. Morality is an aspect of cultural learning; therefore, any definition of what should be a universal morality is inherently ethnocentric. However, to reject the idea of universal standards of morality is to accept anything as proper as long as it is done in other societies that approve of it. It would be a rejection of the idea of human rights. Neither stance in the extreme is reasonable. Fortunately for advocates of this perspective, most cases do not exist at the extremes.

Diversity Within States Individuals who hold a cultural pluralism perspective tend to advocate the acceptance of diversity both within states and between states. In the former they come into conflict with advocates of both other perspectives. Those interpreting the world through the lens of the globalism perspective hold that the superior cultures of any state and the world should dictate to, and change, inferior cultures. Those viewing it through state primacy, on the other hand, hold that diversity within a state is the business of that state. The view of cultural diversity on this issue is that states must accommodate the cultural differences within their borders. State autonomy is not sacrosanct when human lives are at stake. Mistreatment of ethnic minorities is a human rights issue and must be addressed in the domestic, as well as the international, arenas. Actions from boycotts, trade sanctions, and invasions are acceptable in order to protect cultural groups. The use of UN peacekeeping forces in Somalia and Bosnia is an acceptable breach of state sovereignty owing to the severity of the situation for innocent inhabitants. The lack of international action to protect the victims of the Holocaust in Nazi Germany is often cited as an international shame that must never be repeated. This extreme object lesson energizes international campaigns against a wide variety of concerns from female circumcision to destruction of the rain forest.

Advocates of cultural diversity perspectives strongly support the rights of indigenous peoples to establish legal rights including autonomy, self-governance over their own affairs, and even semisovereignty. They advocate for new forms of organizations that vary radically from those of historic reservations or homelands that were assigned to indigenous people in many countries in the Americas, Australia, and Africa.

On reservations, the power of administration was held strongly in the hands of individuals appointed by and accountable to the dominant state, and, in some cases, the movement of the residents was restricted outside of the reserve. The new vision of homelands, however, clearly challenges the sovereignty of the state itself by giving internal power to those with distinct national identities. Advocates claim, however, that this form of recognition of indigenous status actually strengthens the state by negating the threat of internal discord.

Diversity Between States Diversity between states is also celebrated in the cultural pluralism perspective. The fact that different states have different cultures allows for a richer variety of opportunities for all people. The opposite—a world assimilated into one culture—would be dull and relatively colorless, given the loss of the vast spectrum of arts, languages, dress, and architecture. Even scientific discovery, long assumed to reside solely in Western education, is enlivened with local knowledge drawn from traditional cultures. Searches for "new" animals in Asia and drugs from "new" plants in the Amazon are led, in part, by holders of indigenous knowledge who have long known of these animals and plants. In fact, a new legal question of ethnic intellectual property rights, or the right to this knowledge, has arisen since these discoveries have led to large industrial profits for those far from the site. Protection of such diversity of knowledge can be vital for the solution of future global problems. All states, then, should be encouraged to support fully all the cultures within their borders. International agencies should provide money for this purpose if the state is too poor to do so itself. Further communication between states that broadens knowledge of these cultures should be encouraged.

Relationships between states need also accommodate any cultural differences that might arise. Acknowledgment of differences as well as similarities is encouraged. Problems that arise from clashing differences must be mediated or resolved. Gender differences, for example, can create embarrassing problems. When Salote, the queen of Tonga, arrived for the coronation of Queen Elizabeth II in 1953, she was featured in newspapers around the world (*New York Times*, May 1953). Not only was she the sole female ruling monarch attending as part of commonwealth royalty, she was also physically quite imposing. The six-foot, three-inch queen did not seem comfortable in the fashion shows and luncheons attended by other queens. As a woman, however, she was not fully welcomed at the political meetings that were otherwise male affairs. She simply did not fit the English gender expectations of the 1950s. The ideal of acceptance of cultural differences between states can conflict with internal cultural beliefs.

Those who hold a cultural pluralism position to its extreme often are opposed to the state as an institution. Since the nature of the state is inherently hierarchical, they argue, if equality is a goal, the state, itself, is part of the problem. The natural unit of human society, they might continue, is the culture, not the state. Therefore, a world made up of smaller, autonomous cultures might be the next logical stage of human evolution. This view does not address the success of large, stable states, such as the United States, where citizens share a national, American identity but differ in individual ethnic identities. In some areas where state nationalities have not strongly developed, however, this goal of ethnic division appears to be happening. The breakdown of the Soviet Union and parts of Eastern Europe into smaller states roughly along previously held national lines caught many, who thought the state unit secure, by surprise. The mixture of ethnicities in states of Africa whose borders where created during colonialism for the benefit of Europeans, rather than Africans, cause tensions which are likely to produce future state divisions. The same appears possible in Canada, where votes by residents of the province of Quebec for an independent state status have been close to a majority in the recent past. If not accommodated within a state, powerful ethnic minorities appear ready to split off on their own.

One other possibility in this world of cultural pluralism is that members of the same cultures, isolated in different states, may join together into a new state. The Jewish state of Israel is an extreme example, where members of the same religion created a homeland in an area of their heritage but largely not their current residence. The problems of relationships with the existing residents of the area hardly make this an ideal example of putting the cultural diversity perspective into effect. Areas of the world, such as Amazon, the Arctic, and Kurdistan, where the majority of the people in each region have cultural unity (although intersected by state borders), seem more conducive to such new state creation. Even at their most idealistic, current states are unlikely to be eager to give up the lands in these potentially mineral-rich regions to ethnic groups that appear to be economically weaker and militarily unable to protect themselves. The ideal of cultural pluralists, which has not yet been reached, is a world where people do not attack others for land or economic gain.

Critiques from the Globalism and State Primacy Perspectives Advocates of globalism regard the cultural pluralism perspective as being virtually the opposite of their own. In their view global problems are universal and should be solved in a unified world. This perspective breaks the world into thousands of groups of people who all have unique interests. The possibilities for disputes are large, with no mechanism for solving them. This perspective also values all cultures as equal. Globalism proponents assert that some ways of life are more efficient or moral than others, and those should be preserved while others should be absorbed.

The state primacy view would also reject the cultural tolerance perspective. It asserts that a world of thousands of small interest groups is unworkable. The system of the state, it contends, is necessary to resolve problems in a fair and peaceful way. In the state, all cultural groups know the rules, and between states, governments are rational advocates in international debates. Disagreements between ethnic groups, without state intervention, can only lead to turmoil. The state is the defender of weak ethnic groups.

Synthesis While the three perspectives in this chapter are presented as if they are iso-lated and exclusive, individuals can, to some extent, maintain ideas drawn from all of them. Synthesis is possible and, perhaps, sensible. Some people believe in the impor-tance of human equality and personal choice but, at the same time, reason that strong state systems are necessary and can grant group rights in the real world. Others believe that the future will bring some form of political administration which will unify the peo-ples of the world. Globalism theorists can hold radically different views on human cul-tural diversity, however. Some may picture a unified world where the superior culture has prevailed and displaced all variations of the inferior type. Others picture quite the opposite: a world composed of small, independent, and equal cultural units that work to-gether for a common good through a cooperative administration model. Basically, how-ever, the three perspectives presented are common ways used by modern scholars and other thoughtful individuals to organize their views of human diversity.

CASE STUDY   Nunavut: A New Territory
for an Indigenous Nation

The case chosen for discussion in this section is that of Canada's evolving policies toward one group of indigenous people—the Inuit of the land called Nunavut. While any one of hundreds of cases could be used, this one is particularly compelling. Canada is now experimenting with a form of semiautonomy for ethnic minorities which, if suc-cessful, will create a form of governance that allows for indigenous peoples to live their own ways of life while at the same time remaining a vital part of the larger state. Nunavut may prove a model for future agreements around the world.

The Inuit of Nunavut are an indigenous people who developed a gathering-and-hunting type of culture in the Arctic, one of the most environmentally challenging areas of the world. They have maintained many of their traditions but have felt threat-ened by contemporary Canadian and territorial governmental policies. In a very short time they have demanded and received Canadian approval for and aid in establishing a new Inuit-controlled, Inuit-designed territory: Nunavut. The Canadian government and the Inuit of Nunavut have embarked on a bold experiment in cooperative cultural living which is being carefully watched by many countries.

Most Americans are familiar with the name Eskimo and have a popularized image of people living in igloos, hunting Arctic animals, using dog sleds, and rubbing noses. Many greeting card stores will sell cards with pictures of darling, round-faced, smiling children wearing fur ruffs and clutching husky puppies. What most Americans do not realize is that the Inuit, meaning "people" in their own language, as most are called today, are modern First Nation people, no more or less adorable than others, and that those who live in the eastern part of the Northwest Territories recently became the mas-ters of a new Canadian Territory: Nunavut, meaning "Our Land."

The Inuit are one of the few cultures that spread over three continents and are citi-zens of four states. Inuit live in Asia (Russia), North America (United States and Canada), and Europe (Greenland, a part of Denmark). This discussion focuses on the

Canadian Inuit of Nunavut, but it is important to note that while cultural variations exist regionally, there is a remarkable consistency of language, cultural skills, and values throughout gathering-and-hunting adaptations in Arctic environments.

Gathering-and-Hunting Cultures The adaptation to Arctic life is one of the wonders of human history. The Arctic is a dry, cold area with little permanent vegetation and extreme seasonal shifts in the amount of daylight. Summers are light, bountiful, and short. Individuals not enculturated in an Inuit society simply could not exist there. The Inuit, however, invented tools and skills that made them the masters of this environment. They also focused on the mammals of the region as their major economic resources making hunting, rather than the seasonal gathering of vegetation, central to their survival.

Coastal resources including species of seals, whales, and walrus and inland sources of caribou were augmented by fish, polar bears, and musk oxen. Season and local environment dictated the focus of the hunt. Special tools for these hunts included kayaks, harpoons, stone oil lamps, dog sleds, intricately designed parkas, and snowhouses in winter. The hunting group, usually composed of family members in difficult times, was dependent on the skill of the men, the hunters, and the abundance of natural resources. Too often families perished in severe seasons. (Balikci 1984, 424; Dumas 1984, 392).

As is common in gathering-and-hunting bands, the nuclear family was the central unit, but here, extended families played a large role in daily life as well. The husband–wife bond was vital for survival, with the men and women each having critical tasks that must be done to survive. Related nuclear families lived close together, with the elders and especially the skillful hunters playing prestigious roles. Unlike most bands, social rule dictated some inequality in that women were in some ways subordinate to men and the younger subordinate to the older, but essentially gender complementarity was the rule (Minor 2002). Food was shared, but it was more restricted by kinship relationships or partnerships than pure generalized reciprocity would suggest (Wenzel 1995).

Judging in accordance with the values of many Canadians of other ethnicities, there was a dark side to early Inuit culture. Murder and suicide were realities in Inuit society just like our own. The perceived real threat of starvation sometimes led to cannibalism and infanticide. Work was hard and often uninteresting. The menace of the environment and the potential threat of the shamans loom dark compared to the equally ethnocentric popular image of the cute Eskimos.

While the hardship of the region would not be denied, it is clear that many Inuit loved the Arctic and prided themselves in the accomplishment of living successfully there. They were part of the land physically and spiritually and knew the value of human cooperation. Canadians of European and Inuit heritages might agree on the details of the traditional Arctic lifestyle but disagree wildly on their evaluation of its worth.

Changes The development of Inuit culture was largely internal until quite recently. Areas where traditional cultural life was the norm continued to exist into the mid-twentieth century. Surely internal changes in the forms of technical and social inventions by the Inuit over the centuries allowed for an unsurpassed adaptation to the Arctic. While it is not known when Inuit ancestors first reached the Arctic, it is clear that small physical changes developed that were conducive to life there. The shape of facial features and the short, broad-chested body shape common among Inuit are well adapted to protecting the internal organs from extreme cold.

Their contact with other cultures predated their very early introduction to Europeans. In fact, the discarded term Eskimo is said to have derived from the denunciation of an unfriendly Indian Nation to the south. They were part of the first known meeting of Europeans and North Americans when the Vikings arrived in the far north. Despite this early introduction, major external changes and the beginnings of adaptation to Western ways have come late. The early interactions with foreign whalers and explorers were infrequent but produced new trade goods, especially metals which were eagerly and voluntarily adopted as improvements to the traditional tool chest. On the negative side, however, these contacts brought new diseases.

More intense external changes in most areas did not occur until the fur-trading era of the early twentieth century. A debt-driven relationship with fur companies developed in many areas. The fur companies were soon joined by the Royal Canadian Mounted Police with Canadian law and missions preaching a Christian message. Both launched campaigns against community disorder, traditional religion, and especially the Inuit religious practitioners. As communities were adapting to the new economy and losing the skills of the old, the 1930s Great Depression came and wiped out the call for furs. Many of the people who had adapted the new ways suffered greatly in comparison to those in the hinterland who had not changed. Many of the more acculturated migrated to larger, more southern communities and became dependent; others starved.

World War II brought military bases to the Arctic and with them came previously unknown wealth. New technologies, especially airplanes, brought access to the north into the realm of the common people and allowed trade to expand dramatically. Similarly, snowmobiles replaced dogs but increased the need for cash to pay for fuel. Wage labor became available, and new health facilities were built, introducing Western medicine for the first time. Unfortunately this close meeting with a new population also brought new diseases which caused epidemics among the Inuit who had no immunity.

After the war, the Canadian government heightened its civilian presence with monetary allowances, health care, and compulsory schools. That these all led to dependency is clear, but what is not as obvious is the particular problems of schooling. Canada viewed the compulsory schools as services to allow Inuit children to join in the opportunities enjoyed by all Canadians. Racism, however, meant that even individuals well educated in Euro-Canadian scholarship were not offered employment equal to others. In some places, this was far more extreme for men than women. Women acculturated at a more rapid rate than men, and they were accorded higher status in Canadian society. This caused a deep gender schism in some communities (McElroy 1976).

Even if education had allowed immediate access to a Canadian middle-class existence, there would still have been deep-rooted problems. First, the blanket assumption that this new way of life was better is ethnocentric and aimed at destroying Inuit culture. Education was conducted in English with a southern, Canadian-based curriculum. Traditional Inuit skills were either denigrated or ignored. Children spending their hours in these classes lost the opportunity to learn the extremely technical skills needed to survive in the traditional way. Second, the regulation that children attend schools in permanent communities for much of the year placed their parents in a quandary. They had to move into these towns or leave their children with others for months each year. Most chose to keep their families together in towns, and the adults took whatever employment existed there. Art provided an income to many; however, town jobs generally do not provide the satisfaction or prestige, at least for men, provided by the traditional lifestyle (McElroy 1976; Graburn and Lee 1990). As a result, problems connected with alcohol abuse grew rapidly among the Inuit. There was an approximately 30 percent increase in alcohol-related problems from the 1960s to early 1980s (Vallee, Smith, and Cooper 1984, 674).

Inuit Nationalism   One of the unexpected outcomes of the Canadian education was the emergence of a group of young, educated Inuit who used the system to demand their rights as First Nation people within Canada. It was only in 1960 that the Native people of the Northwest Territories were given the right to vote in Canadian elections. In just a decade, the Committee for Original Peoples Entitlement (COPE) was established to assert the land and political interests of Inuit and other northern First Nations. The next year an action group, the Inuit Tapirisat of Canada (ITC), was formed to pursue land claims and political rights of Inuit in particular. During the 1970s they developed a plan for a separate territory to be carved out of the Northwest Territories north of the treeline. This largely Inuit-populated territory was to be called Nunavut and was to be developed in the future into a fully Inuit-controlled province. Not all Inuit are enfranchised within Nunavut, however. Inuit in Quebec, Labrador, and the western Northwest Territories are not included. Initially the government strongly opposed a plan which treats the Inuit people as a nation, rather than as individual Canadian citizens. A 1982 plebiscite of all voters in the Northwest Territories resulted in 58 percent supporting it, and this strong support from many non-Inuit helped further the cause in Ottawa, the Canadian capital.

External forces also intervened. The strategic and mineral value of this region is important to Canada. When, in 1985, the United States sent a ship, USCGC *The Polar Sea*, through Arctic waters without asking for Canadian permission, it was considered an initial act in a potential claim over "uninhabited land." This challenge to Canadian sovereignty over these waters was answered in part by recognizing the claims of the Inuit who have long-standing international recognition to residence in the area. Nunavut as a populated and organized territory of Canada is an unassailable assertion of possession.

For the Inuit, like many other Canadian First Nations, a growing awareness of the lack of aboriginal rights in the Canadian constitution pushed them to action. Additionally the fact that the unique cultural rights of French speakers in Quebec were being taken more seriously than the claims of the First Nation worried many First Nation leaders and forced them to take action.

The Territory of Nunavut   On April 1, 1999, Canada began a new chapter in its relationship with its indigenous people. On that day the Northwest Territories split into two territories, and the Territory of Nunavut with Iqaluit as its governmental capital became a reality. Nunavut, comprising 770,000 square miles, is one-fifth the size of Canada, larger than any other territory or province. In this vast land lives a population of less than 27,000 people, about 80 percent of them Inuit (Nunavut Implementation Commission 1995). At the same time, the Inuit Federation became "the largest private landholder in North America" (Dickason 1992, 416), owning outright 18 percent of Nunavut.

The Nunavut Implementation Commission was formed to determine the final government organization. This government has the same powers as those in other territories. All citizens of Nunavut, Inuit and non-Inuit, are equally eligible for office, but the vast majority of the population are Inuit and a working language of the government is Inuktituit along with English and French. The challenge of the commission was to create a government form compatible with Inuit ideals. The outcome largely reflected a Canadian model with characteristically Inuit factors. The government is set upon a statement of principles of *Pinasuaqtavut* ("that which we've set out to do"), which includes as goals healthy communities, simplicity and unity, self-reliance, and continuing learning. The legislative assembly is composed of nineteen members, each elected every five years. There are also ten departments which cover issues from public works, to justice, to sustainable development, to culture. The challenge they continue to face is daunting. Social problems including alcoholism and violence, so common in northern communities, have been made a priority. Education, likewise, has been addressed early. Nunavut Arctic College has several campuses and programs of study. In 2001 it created the Akitsiraq Law School in cooperation with the University of Victoria, in British Columbia, to educate a group of Inuit lawyers so needed in the territory. Also in the same year the Bill and Melinda Gates Foundation awarded nearly $300,000 (U.S.) to establish computer and Internet services in the libraries of the territory. The utilization of new techniques to solve old problems and support old strengths appears to be the goal of the immediate future.

Tina Minor, in a study of the political participation of women in Nunavut, in 2002, describes the success of Inuit women in wage labor with leadership in business and professions. Despite this, only two of the nineteen legislators are women in the first group of territorial legislators. Women's responsibilities in their jobs and families are cited as reasons for their relative lack of interest. Women, however, are active in bureaucratic offices, and there is little discrimination against women in political offices.

Land ownership, unlike in other territories, remains in the hands of territorial residents. Only Inuit are recognized in the land claim settlement administered by the Tungavik Federation of Nunavut. In this settlement they own 353,610 square kilometers (136,530 square miles). They also have claim to the subsurface mineral rights on 36,257 square kilometers of that land. The remaining 82 percent of the land continues to be Crown land. Inuit also have the right to hunt and fish on Crown land and to receive a percentage of mineral development that might occur there. The Inuit also claim half of the seats on territorial management boards with the federal representatives holding the other half. The federal government will also pay these Inuit $1.15 billion over fourteen years. The major concession from the Inuit of this territory, and it is a deeply controversial one, is that they give up all future claims to land and water in Canada.

Analysis The development of Nunavut, "our land" in Inuktitut, changes the nature of Canada itself. Nunavut has a cultural and linguistic identity that is rivaled only by the French Province of Quebec. In this it affirms the multicultural nature of Canada. The Inuit, who have been seen as a racial group and treated with racism and ethnocentrism through most of Canadian history, are now addressed as equals. The road from gathering and hunting has been rapid.

Nunavut addresses cultural diversity in a new way by giving local power while retaining national unity and sovereignty. The growth of Nunavut can follow the road of internal and voluntary external change at the same time. The Inuit nation can be recognized while patriotism for Canada remains secure. It is a territory that recognizes the rights of all Canadians but privileges those whose language and culture fit the north. For example, the concept of gender equality in political power is seen as important and is being addressed in the development of territorial government. Nunavut is a huge social, political, and economic experiment for Canada which will serve as an example, either good or bad, for the treatment of less powerful ethnic groups internationally.

PERSPECTIVES APPLIED TO NUNAVUT

Matrix 3.1 summarizes the main points discussed in this chapter. To review, Nunavut is the name of the 770,000-square-mile eastern division of the Northwest Territories in Canada which became an independent territory in mid-1999. The vast majority of the population is Inuit, and 18 percent of the land of Nunavut will belong to them under a related, but separate, land claims agreement. Use of the rest of the land of the territory for traditional subsistence is guaranteed, as are a percentage of the profits for any mineral development from Nunavut Crown lands. All residents of Nunavut—Inuit and other Canadians—have equal legal standing in the territory, but population ratios, official language designation, and cultural traditions will likely favor Inuit leadership.

The development of Nunavut is a major shift in the map and organization of Canada, and it stands as an experiment in designing a new state model for the twenty-first century. The status of Greenland, in Denmark, with its large Inuit population, can be seen as a predecessor but not as a direct model. Nunavut is a contiguous part of a troubled state, and its success is important to the long-term success of Canada. Nunavut will, therefore, be part of the international news for years to come. Different perspectives will result in different analyses of the same situation.

Matrix 3.1
CULTURAL DIVERSITY PERSPECTIVES

	Globalism	State Primacy	Cultural Pluralism
Goal	Unified world system	State Sovereignty	Cultural Autonomy
Concepts	Assimilation	Patriotism	Tolerance
Strategy	Political Integration	Strengthen Present System	Increase Power of Ethnic Groups
See States as:	Artificial Constructs	Important World Peace	Artificial Constructs
See Current System as:	Overly differentiated	Good	Overly Centralized

A View from the Globalism Perspective

Clearly, this experiment is rash and unwise. It further differentiates people, rather than bringing them together into a global culture. It privileges people who are different rather than the mainstream culture. Also, rather than encouraging the Inuit to progress, it rewards them for their backwardness.

While few in this era of polite talk would speak as directly as the polemic above, the underlying attitude is widespread. The Inuit, especially those who are continuing to engage in traditional subsistence work, are often regarded as quaintly primitive. They cause little trouble so there is no great campaign against them, but they do not seem fully members of the modern world. Their language, Inuktitut, is considered, like Latin, a historic language that no longer has a purpose on the international scene. The Nunavut plan to use Inuktitut as an official governmental language would be interpreted as a crude method to keep the uninitiated on the sidelines. English, or perhaps French, depending upon the inclination of the analyst, would be the only logical language of Canada. Encouraging hunting and fishing by ensuring Inuit free access to all animal habitats will only delay Inuit entry into industrial employment.

Acculturation is slow and selective in this situation, and assimilation discouraged. Certainly, leaders of the new territory will need to learn to be effective in dealing with both government paperwork and non-Inuit elsewhere in Canada, and a good deal of Western training is envisioned as part of the transition. Others, however, should have less pressure to change. Additionally, and not to the liking of those holding this perspective, some acculturation of Euro-Canadians to Inuit culture seems likely in Nunavut. Those at the extreme of the globalism perspective, who look favorably on subjugation, of course, would find this whole situation unacceptable—an unnecessary experiment in government which is apt to be used as a precedent for still more changes empowering "inferior" people.

The problems that created Nunavut are not regarded as problems from this perspective. Nunavut is, in the old cliché, fixing something that is not broken. The troubles that individual Inuit legitimately face can best be solved with education for increased acculturation. Inuktituit language and culture study should be discouraged, and governmental aid should be limited to those who live in towns and send their children to school. When enough Inuit obtain the proper skills and goals, there is no reason an Inuk cannot lead the territory or province. This leader, of course, would work for his or her people by promoting the same interests that any good leader of Euro-Canadian heritage would advocate.

A View from the State Primacy Perspective

Clearly, this experiment is extreme and more than a bit dangerous. It decentralizes power from the traditional government elite to the periphery, but, at least, it does so in a manner that is established within the existing framework of the state. In the short run, it may help maintain the integrity of the state of Canada.

The Canadian form of government is far more decentralized than that of the United States. In Canada the provinces have far more power relative to the central government than do U.S. states. Danger to the sovereignty of the state, then, is found in the lessening of the power of Ottawa over the provinces and, perhaps, the territories. This is being seen in Nunavut. Canadian authorities have allotted Inuit representatives half the seats on a number of administrative boards generally controlled by federal officials. Also a good part of the land was removed from Crown control, and all Crown land has been open to various uses by Inuit. Control over mineral development is somewhat circumscribed by the claims of the Inuit.

A second concern, particularly acute in Canada, is the privileging of cultural groups. Given the history of French–English disputation in this nation and the increasing pressure for autonomy for Quebec, such a public recognition of another culture, Inuit, as worthy of a special status seems likely to effect Quebec's demands for autonomy. Certainly, Ottawa would argue that Nunavut as a territory is given no more cultural privilege than other areas. Land claim settlements are separate from the territorial organization, and they are based in prior First Nation claims. Nunavut territory is open to all Canadians just as the Yukon and Quebec are. Language use, as in Quebec, recognizes majority use. Many Quebecois advocates, however, believe their issue is primary and due for first settlement.

State nationalists would applaud several aspects of the Nunavut plan. First, of course, it is built on the existing state structure. It creates a new territory, not a new form of organization. That this territory looks different than the others is true, but at its heart, it is Canadian. It is open to all Canadians for residence and citizenship. In this way it does not mandate a permanent dominance by Inuit residents. While the population remains so heavily Inuit, it stands to reason that they will dominate; if that changes in the future, then so will the power base. A contrast with the demands of Quebec is clear in this and might be suggested by state nationalists as a new model.

Nunavut allows Inuit to be Inuit while also recognizing the nationality of other Canadians. It does, however, divide the Inuit from Nunavut from Inuit in other provinces. Settlements for Inuit in Quebec, Labrador, and the western Northwest Territories are legally separate from those for these Inuit. Likewise, the Inuit of Greenland and Alaska have agreements of their own. The likelihood of a circumpolar nation or even an Inuit nation as a political reality seems dimmer after Nunavut than before. Nunavut might be different, but it demonstrates a loyalty to the state.

From the state sovereignty position, the solution to the problems that led to Nunavut can be found within the Canadian system. The territory, either as the existing Northwest Territory, or the proposed Nunavut, should be run as territories are today. The nature of the population may flavor the society, but the law should not privilege any particular citizens. Rather than the Inuit language, English, the major language of Canada, should prevail here, although French, Inuktituit, and other languages should be allowed as second languages. Canada firmly retains control over this, like all territories, and the Inuit, as citizens of Canada, should prosper. With these corrections, this solution should stand as a model throughout Canada.

A View from the Cultural Pluralism Perspective

Nunavut is an exciting experiment and long overdue. Recognition of the special status of First Nations should be pursued throughout the Americas. It is only unfortunate that clearer, permanent sovereignty is not vested in the Inuit and that other Inuit cannot join in a broadly Inuit national political entity.

At the heart of Nunavut is the recognition of the importance of their culture to the Inuit. Nunavut recognizes the right of the Inuit to pursue culturally meaningful subsistence activities and to adapt whatever Western customs they find meaningful. In other words, it values the traditional culture but does not confine the people in an unchanging system.

The Inuit were active in creating Nunavut politically. The fight for the establishment of the new territory and the land claims settlement took two decades of work and compromise. While in the end they did not receive all they asked for, their willingness to negotiate a final agreement led to the creation of the new settlement. A belief in cultural pluralism includes a trust that the desires of members of the culture are what are right for them. Paternalism should have no place in the analysis and, therefore, Nunavut must be defended as an Inuit creation.

While cultural pluralists will defend Nunavut, they may privately hold some concerns. Nunavut may benefit the Inuit of the territory but be harmful to other First Nation people in Canada. The question of the future of the First Nations in the western Northwest Territories is still being debated. While land settlements can be finalized, political power in the west is more problematic. Dené, Metis, and Inuit remain important populations there, but even combined they do not have a solid majority of votes. Yellowknife, the capital, has a reputation of being a Euro-Canadian stronghold in the north, and there is no reason to assume this would change with the loss of the Nunavut population. The future of Inuit in Quebec (Nunavik) is also at issue. If Quebec leaves the confederation, what happens to them? Will Nunavut ultimately complicate this problem or provide a viable model?

Finally, there are concerns about the future of Nunavut itself. There is no guarantee of Inuit hegemony and no clear mechanism at hand to ensure it. Rules for leadership including clauses for length of residency and language restrictions may well discourage outsiders who might try to take over this mineral-rich region. The will of the Inuit people to maintain leadership in the government structure may well be key to the success of Nunavut.

The solutions to Inuit problems should rest in the hands of the Inuit, with the support of friends on the outside. Nunavut must be supported and help must be forthcoming to the other First Nations of the north. The successes and failures of Nunavut should be widely known far beyond the borders so that other First Nations around the globe can benefit from this experience. Nunavut is a culturally defined territory existing in a complex nation-state and it must be nurtured.

As in all things, history will record the benefits of Nunavut for Inuit and all Canadians. The future of the territory is yet to be told, but that it will be analyzed from a variety of perspectives is inevitable.

TERMS AND CONCEPTS

Acculturation *43*

Alternative perspectives *41*

Apartheid *47*

Assimilation *43*

Ethnocide *43*

National identity *44*

Paternalism *46*

Patriotism *45*

Subjugation *46*

Syncretism *44*

Tolerance *47*

DISCUSSION QUESTIONS

1. Are the people of Nunavut better off in the new territory? Are there other alternatives that might have been better?
2. Could the model of an indigenous territory work in the United States? Why or why not? In what other places could it work?
3. Do any of the perspectives fit your view for the future of the world's cultures? If so, which and why? If not, what is your unique perspective?
4. Can you think of any examples of syncretism in your daily life? What about acculturation or assimilation? How similar is your way of life to that of your great-grandparents?
5. Can excessive patriotism be a problem in a state? Why or why not?

RESEARCH PROJECTS

1. Chose one of the other areas in which Inuit live. Compare the political status of that group with that of the Inuit of Nunavut. What are the pros and cons of each area?
2. Apply the Nunavut solution to another indigenous group in a different country. Can it work there? If not, how would you change their present land and political status to improve their way of life?
3. Choose two front-page stories from today's newspaper. Learn the history of the issues and apply the alternative perspectives presented in this chapter. What perspective did the reporters take on the issues?
4. Choose a contemporary case of ethnic dispute, such as the one in Northern Ireland, in French and English Canada, or in Cyprus. Using the concepts and perspectives presented in this chapter, explain the dispute, describe the situation surrounding it, and evaluate the proposed solutions.
5. Choose one of the three perspectives in this chapter and apply it to three separate cultural situations. What are the strengths and weaknesses of this perspective in illuminating the situations?

INTERNET RESOURCES

Cultural Survival: www.cs.org This NGO focuses on the problems of indigenous peoples and oppressed ethnic groups.

www.nativeweb.org This is a primary resource center for Native American issues.

Government of Nunavut homepage: www.npc.nunavut.ca

A newspaper for Nunavut: www.nunatsiaq.com This site supplies updates on issues of importance to the Inuit of Nunavut.

The Universal Declaration of Human Rights: www.un.org/Overview/rights.html

CHAPTER 4

Economic Development

Modern technology offers the tantalizing prospect of enabling the world to produce enough food, shelter, clothing, clean water, and basic medical care for every person on the planet. Sadly, while this capability exists, its promise had not become reality by the beginning of the twenty-first century. Out of the world's population of over five and a half billion, at least two billion people lead debilitating lives of desperation on the margin of survival. They seem to inhabit a different world from those who enjoy a comfortable, consumer-goods lifestyle.

This chapter offers general explanations as to why a wide and growing gap exists between the world's rich and poor. This reality runs contrary to the image implied by the word "development," the concept that is supposed to provide an answer to the problem of poverty. **Development** is an economic process which enables an increasing number of people to produce enough wealth to support an acceptable quality of life. Unfortunately for those attempting to understand the process, this seemingly simple, straightforward definition masks major differences in strategy and in what an "acceptable lifestyle" actually means.

The dominant interpretation of development assumes that it means achieving a modern machine-based lifestyle, one measured by ownership of televisions, automobiles, and appliances and characterized by plenty of food and leisure time. An increasing number of people, however, are adopting another approach to development which emphasizes the fact that hundreds of millions of people on Earth have no hope of becoming part of a heavily industrialized society and experiencing a consumer-goods lifestyle. They must fulfill their basic needs for adequate shelter, food, clothing, and medical care by improving the productivity of their agriculture-based economies.

The industrial development strategy requires extensive economic growth. Such growth produces extra earnings to invest in machines, the fossil fuel energy to run them, educated people to fix them, and the constant flow of new technology to update them. With industrial development, earnings from economic growth must be ongoing because energy and new technology costs continue as well. The alternative approach to development, however, does not accept economic growth as essential. It defines the process as one of "improvement" and "enrichment" leading to a better life. Thus, achieving an acceptable lifestyle can mean having enough of life's basics without becoming part of a modern, consumer-oriented, energy-guzzling, machine-dependent economy.

The two development strategies, one calling for economic growth and the other for fulfilling basic needs, propose different answers to the problems of the poor. Yet the adherents of both strategies decry the chronic, dispiriting, debilitating poverty that can kill hope and create desperation, disease, and dehumanization. One pitfall in analyzing development issues as applied to the world's poor comes from the fact that relevant information can seem too abstract, statistical, and unrelated to the actual lives of real people. Therefore, our discussion begins by introducing an individual whose lifestyle represents the majority of the world's population.

A Local Leader

Meet Lucia. She has good looks, not the prettiness of youth, but long-lasting, pleasant features with the high cheekbones typical of Andean peoples. It takes only a brief conversation with her to gain respect for this Quechua Indian peasant woman. She has a quiet confidence and speaks articulately. Choosing her words thoughtfully, she seems self-assured and refined. In her, life's hard experiences have produced a reflective composure.

Lucia, her husband, and two children live in one of the farming sectors outside of Mollepata, a town about 9,000 feet high in Peru's Andes mountains. Most of the more than 900 town residents, and 3,000 people in its surrounding rural sectors, earn a living either directly or indirectly from subsistence agriculture. Potatoes, vegetables, grains, and some livestock are raised on slopes slanting often eight degrees or even more. The potato fields lie at the highest elevations, allowing crop cultivation, at around 11,000 feet. This food source was cultivated long before Europeans discovered it during their conquest. Dependent on what they raise themselves, Mollepata's residents remember well the drought beginning in 1982 when the seasonal rains did not come. Severe malnutrition was commonplace, and starvation for many, but not all, was avoided only by the intervention of international relief agencies.

In the early 1990s, Lucia organized a team from the women's committee in her sector to compete in a planting contest. Fourteen teams, twelve male and two female, entered the contest sponsored by the local nongovernmental development organization. It took courage for the women to compete because in Quechua society men are responsible for raising the crops. The contest required three days of work. Not only did the teams plant a crop in their designated area of a large field, but they also designed and dug irrigation channels. Lucia's team came in second. Upon receiving the prize of farm hand tools, she noted that her team's performance showed that women can contribute to the incomes of their families.

Lucia and her family are among the approximately three quarters of the Earth's inhabitants for whom physical survival is a goal, not a given. Yet our short introduction to this one peasant woman contradicts the assumption that the poor, out of necessity, always become beaten down, boorish, coarse, devoid of hope and humane feelings. If they can make decisions and meet their physical needs, low-income people can experience meaningful, useful, fulfilling lives. People in poverty statistically may not always think of themselves as poor.

Poverty, which exists in virtually every country, has common causes wherever it is found. Two worlds exist within the economies of most countries—one of privilege, the other of need. Statistics show that these worlds are moving farther and farther away from each other in terms of living standards and productivity, but they remain intertwined economically in ways most people do not realize. Even though both rich and poor live within the same state borders, the poor are often obscured in industrialized countries by a large middle class. Still, the overwhelming majority of the world's poor live in what can be called developing countries because of their desperate need for a successful development process. Industrial states, in contrast, have achieved the decades of economic growth it takes to move a majority of their people into the modern middle class. In these states, the poor live in pockets surrounded by people who, in global terms, live as part of the world's rich. Yet since most global poverty is located in states with primarily agriculture-based economies and low wealth production, tackling development as a global issue usually focuses on the situation of states in the **developing world**.

DEFINING THE ISSUE

Most people learn about the developing world through pictures of starving children in newspapers or on television. When a natural disaster, or war, or both cause large-scale deprivation, the events make the nightly news. Such news stories leave the impression that relief aid will fill the need until the unusual situation causing the problem comes to an end. The episode is treated as an isolated emergency, and little attention is focused on mitigating the underlying chronic poverty that allows one crisis to push large populations to the very edge of survival. The unspoken assumption—that such disastrous events are inevitable from time to time—is reinforced.

This sense of inevitability is strengthened by the data on global poverty, which make the problem appear so monumental that people reason that nothing can be done to correct it in the foreseeable future. Such news articles typically begin by describing the differences between developing countries and industrialized countries in terms of economic performance. A key comparison uses the per capita gross national incomes of various countries. **Gross national income (GNI)** represents the total value of all goods and services a country's economy has produced in a given year, including international transactions. The GNI then can be divided by the country's number of people to produce the **per capita GNI**. These admittedly very general figures, called macroeconomic data, nonetheless provide a common measure of the relative wealth produced by each of the world's states.

One common source for macroeconomic data, including per capita GNI, is the *World Development Report*, a book of comprehensive economic statistics published annually by the World Bank, an international government organization (IGO) described in Chapter 1. The World Bank data, shown in Table 4.1, report the per capita GNIs for selected countries in 2001.

According to the *World Development Report 2003*, sixty-five countries had per capita incomes of $745 or less in 2001 and were thus classified as low-income economies. This income represents very little purchasing power in any country. The number of low-income states in 2001 represents an increase of twenty-three over 1994 figures; however, the number of people in low-income countries decreased mainly because China moved from low- to lower-middle income; it had a per capita GNI in 2001 of $890. Out of a world population of 6,132.8 million, 2,510.6 lived in low-income states in 2001 while 955 million lived in the twenty-eight high-income states.

Table 4.1
PER CAPITA GNI DATA FOR SELECTED STATES AND GROUPS
OF STATES, 2001

		GNP per Capita (in U.S. Dollars)

Low-Income Economies
  Average:
  Examples:
	
	Tanzania
	Pakistan
	Haiti
		
		$430
		270
		420
		480

Lower-Middle-Income Economies
  Average:
  Examples:
	
	Morocco
	Egypt
	Jamaica
		
		$1,240
		1,180
		1,530
		2,720

Upper-Middle-Income Economies
  Average:
  Examples:
	
	Poland
	Hungary
	Uruguay
		
		$4,460
		4,240
		4,800
		5,670

High-Income Economies
  Average:
  Examples:
	
	New Zealand
	United States
	Japan
		
		$26,710
		12,380
		34,870
		35,990

Source: World Bank, *World Development Report 2003* (New York: Oxford University Press, 2003).

Table 4.1 shows the wide disparity in wealth between the world's poorest and richest states. Many states classified as "middle income" are actually in the "lower-middle-income" range. A few middle-income states have experienced significant economic growth: Thailand and Botswana each had average per capita GNI growth rates of over 6 percent a year from 1980 to 1993, and South Korea averaged over 8 percent during that time (World Bank 1995). Some states, such as Singapore, have moved from middle- to high-income status. While the economic growth of some countries has enabled them to move up in the income ranking, most states with small economies have not been as successful. In fact, a comparison of per capita GNIs shows that the disparity between high- and low-income countries has increased over time. Data from *World Development Reports* document the increase (World Bank 1979; 1995). In 1977 the average per capita GNI was $170 for low-income states, $1,140 for middle-income states, and $6,980 for high-income states. This meant the ratio of low income to high income stood at 2.4 percent, while the middle-income ratio was 16 percent. In 1993 the comparable figures were $380 for low-income, $2,480 for middle-income, and $23,090 for high-income states. Thus the ratio of low to high income dropped to 1.6 percent and that of middle to high income was 11 percent. The data show that both low- and middle-income countries produced less wealth in relation to that produced by high-income countries in the 1990s than they did in the 1970s.

Yet even in countries with the lowest per capita GNIs, a small percentage of the population maintains a lifestyle similar to that of the majority in high-income countries. Conversely, high-income countries, such as the United States, have pockets of poverty, some of them fairly large. Economic data for Native American communities illustrate this point: their combined per capita income in 1989 was $8.328, whereas that of the United States as a whole was $20,910. The poverty rate for Native American families was 27 percent in 1989, up from 24 percent in 1979; however, the overall U.S. family poverty rate was 10 percent in both 1984 and 1979 (Paisano 1997, 2, 3).

The *World Development Report* also includes data more directly illustrative of the poverty issue, as indicated in Table 4.2. Poor people tend to have less access to nutritious

Table 4.2
LIFE EXPECTANCY AND CHILD MORTALITY RATES FOR SELECTED STATES AND GROUPS OF STATES, 2001

		Life Expectancy (in Years)	Under 5 Mortality Rate (per 1,000 Live Births)
Low-Income Economies Average:		59	115
Examples:	Tanzania	44	149
	Pakistan	63	110
	Haiti	53	111
Lower-Middle-Income Economies Average:		69	42
Examples:	Morocco	67	60
	Egypt	67	52
	Jamaica	75	24
Upper-Middle-Income Economies Average:		71	30
Examples:	Hungary	71	11
	Poland	73	11
	Uruguay	74	17
High-Income Economies Average:		78	7
Examples:	New Zealand	78	7
	United States	77	9
	Japan	81	5

Source: World Bank, *World Development Report 2003* (New York: Oxford University Press, 2003).

food, medical care, and clean water, which is reflected in life expectancy and child mortality rates.

Macroeconomic data tend to reinforce an often unspoken resignation that little can be done to alleviate poverty in the world because the problem seems too large and continues to grow. Such a reaction could be interpreted as a contemporary version of the old aristocratic notion that "the poor will always be with us." To consider their condition as inevitable produces an attitude that is demeaning at best and debilitating at worst.

Using descriptive data to contrast the economic output of poorer countries with richer ones illustrates the problem, but it does little to explain why it exists. The concept of development, discussed in the beginning of this chapter, is most usefully thought of as a process, not an end result. The key question is whether the process should aim to produce industrialization first or whether it should initially concentrate on producing more food and other basic needs for daily living.

These objectives may not seem contradictory to development planners until they have to decide which projects to fund with chronically scarce investment resources. Should a large-scale project be built, such as a dam for electricity and irrigation, or should the money be used for projects that would enable villagers themselves to dig wells and irrigation ditches? One requires heavy machinery; the other, shovels. If the industrially based, heavy-machinery strategy is chosen, then those with access to large-scale financing get most of the benefits. If the pick-and-shovel method is applied, poorer people can both participate in and have ownership of the project.

Both types of projects can be found in most countries, but the debate goes on as to what should be the primary and immediate goal of development; that is, improving the daily lives of poor people or investing in the means to industrialize? The controversy, in turn, makes the problem of world poverty and the potential solutions to it difficult to analyze.

The dispute over development strategies exists in part because the rich, high-income countries historically have achieved their standard of living through industrialization by using an **economic growth strategy**. Thus, for many people planning and administering projects in the developing world, development means industrialization. Machine-based production may be expensive in the short term, but it is seen as a proven path to reducing poverty in the long term. However, because it requires major economic growth and large-scale investment, advocates of a **basic-needs strategy** alternative are increasing in number. These practitioners, academics, and some government and international aid agency personnel realize that, for the world's poor majority, the economic growth approach is not working. They focus on the need for a development strategy that will improve poor people's lives now rather than later, when the industrial profits of the elite "trickle down." The basic-needs strategy enables local people to produce more and better food and to provide primary medical care and literacy. These goals, it is argued, can be achieved in agriculture-based economies and are not dependent on industrial technologies.

The ongoing debate between advocates of the two general approaches to development—basic needs versus economic growth—recognize that the two billion people living in poverty face a set of interrelated problems which can be summarized as a cycle of underdevelopment. The leaders of many low-income countries oppose the use of the word underdevelopment, arguing that it implies that their societies are "back-ward." Still, the term aptly summarizes the conditions that keep so many poor people from improving their lives.

UNDERDEVELOPMENT: A VICIOUS CYCLE

As shown in Figure 4.1, a network of four interrelated, mutually reinforcing factors severely inhibit improvement in basic needs or economic growth in low-income and some middle-income countries. Breaking out of the cycle is so difficult that most low-income countries and communities have not been able to achieve a self-sustaining development process.

Dual Economy

A **dual economy** is one in which a small, "modern" elite, comprising people who live a consumer lifestyle, exists in a society where the vast majority of the population lives in poverty. The elite is composed primarily of large landowners, high-level government officials, a few business people engaged in international trade and finance, and some professionals such as physicians. A small middle class also exists, made up mostly of schoolteachers, managers, shopkeepers, and midlevel government workers. It remains virtually invisible when contrasted with the wealthy elite and the rest of the population, sometimes as high as 70 to 80 percent, who experience a very different way of life. Living in rural areas, most people eat what they grow themselves through backbreaking labor performed without machinery. They lack social programs as a fallback in hard times. Economists call this lifestyle **subsistence**, meaning people produce enough to live on and very little more.

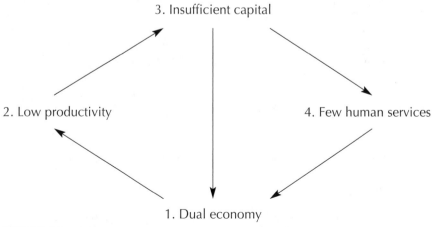

FIGURE 4.1
Cycle of Underdevelopment

Early economic growth development specialists in the 1950 and 1960s assumed that a modern manufacturing sector would expand in low-income countries, albeit slowly, as the industrialization process became self-sustaining. As it had in industrialized countries, this process was expected to bring more jobs and educational opportunities for the poor in the subsistence sector. Yet steady growth has not occurred in most of the developing world. On the whole, countries with low per capita GNIs have experienced a few years of some economic growth but not enough to change the structure of their dual economies.

Low Productivity

A dual economy typically has low **productivity**, which economists define as the output of goods and services in relation to the number of work hours used to produce them. Low productivity results in low income and little savings because not much extra is produced beyond what people consume. This, by definition, is the case with those living a subsistence lifestyle. An economy with a large subsistence sector yields very little surplus and, therefore, does not grow. Hence, low productivity limits not only future growth but also the wages workers can earn, contributing in part to what economists call the poverty trap. Industrial development requires substantial economic growth over several years. Figures vary, but the countries increasing their per capita incomes have achieved growth rates between 7 to sometimes 14 percent during a five- to ten-year period. Such growth allows for a surplus produced as income and savings to be turned back into the economy as investment in capital.

Insufficient Capital

Economies with low per capita GNIs, large subsistence sectors, and low productivity have little capital. **Physical capital**, often called infrastructure, includes such things as factories, farms, roads, railroads, telephones, banks, and machinery, while **financial capital** includes bank deposits, earnings from international trade, and money. The goods an economy produces for immediate consumption, such as food, cars, and clothes, are not capital. In sum, **capital** refers to the finances plus the facilities needed to produce wealth. Wealth means goods and more capital.

Dual economy, productivity, and capital are closely related factors. As a result, the problems in low-income economies are interrelated and structural, meaning they are built into their situation. Such a mutually reinforcing combination of deeply rooted problems does not respond to a bit of tinkering here and there. A development project or two, however effective, will not change the basic structure of the economy. A subsistence economy with low productivity and little capital thus experiences great difficulty in generating enough growth to begin self-sustained development. It struggles with the cycle of underdevelopment, as indicated by the arrow closing the cycle in Figure 4.1.

Lack of Human Services

Low-income economies have little infrastructure and, by definition, lack the educational and medical care facilities of industrial economies. Yet, as economists point out, **human capital** is needed for a successful development process. Schools, universities, clinics, and hospitals produce the educated and healthy population needed for economic initiative and improved productivity. Data reporting on people's access to education and medical care show severe deficiencies in the world's poorer states as compared with richer ones. The figures in Table 4.3 are taken from the 2001 *Human Development Report*, a compilation of statistics and explanatory narrative that is published each year by the United Nations Development Program (UNDP), an aid agency of the United Nations.

A lack of basic human services inhibits development and reinforces the existence of a dual economy. Thus the arrow that completes the cycle of underdevelopment in Figure 4.1 connects factor 4, "few human services," to factor 1, "dual economy." Without sufficient educational and employment opportunities, the middle class remains very small, leaving virtually intact the polarized pattern of two main economic and social classes—namely the high-income elites and the subsistence agriculturists. A dual economy lacks the large middle class that characterizes the industrialized world. A middle class is important because it provides not only a substantial domestic market but also new leadership and an educated voting public.

Table 4.3
PHYSICIANS PER POPULATION AND ADULT LITERACY RATES FOR SELECTED STATES

	Physicians per 100,000 People*	Adult Literacy Rates (Percent Age 15 and Above)*
Low-Income Economies		
Tanzania	4	75
Pakistan	57	45
Haiti	8	49
Lower-Middle-Income Economies		
Morocco	46	48
Egypt	202	55
Jamaica	140	86
Upper-Middle-Income Economies		
Poland	218	99
Hungary	279	99
Uruguay	193	98
High-Income Economies		
New Zealand	218	99**
United States	279	99**
Japan	193	99**

*Source: United Nations Development Program, *Human Development Report*, 2001 (New York: Oxford University Press).

**Source: CIA Factbook, 2003.

The model of underdevelopment presented thus far explains the unremitting, mutually reinforcing set of obstacles faced by developing economies. Such problems would slow development even in a society with clear-headed and incorruptible leadership choosing enlightened public policies, a questionable standard even in countries with more productive economies. Advocates of both the economic growth and the basic-needs development strategies recognize the problems associated with the cycle of underdevelopment, but they diverge over what should be done about it. Economic growth strategists generally rely on international interventions to begin the development process. Outside aid and investments, for example, are designed to make up for the internal lack of productivity and capital. In contrast, the basic-needs approach addresses the problem of a dual economy head on by attempting to change the subsistence lifestyle. Once people produce more food and other essentials of life, so the basic-needs reasoning goes, they can perhaps produce a surplus to invest. Some of the investment may well be in human services, yet some could find its way, via a reliable banking system, into the industrial sector. Either way, the central problem should not be considered as productivity and capital, but as providing a better quality of life for ordinary people.

It should be pointed out that some states classified as having low- or middle-income economies have had occasional growth years, although not reaching the 7+ percent or more over the multiple years needed for substantial development. Yet people in the developing world expect more. The model of a better lifestyle is tantalizingly flashed on television screens in villages around the world. Seeing U.S. situation comedies or soap operas, the most frequently televised programs worldwide, can raise expectations as to what constitutes an acceptable lifestyle. Many people in the developing world, as well as in the industrial world, seek answers to the question of why a majority of the world's countries are caught in the vicious cycle of underdevelopment.

THE COLONIAL LEGACY

As noted in Chapter 1, most states in the developing world were at one time ruled either directly or indirectly by an industrializing state during the age of imperialism. A strong case can be made that global European domination has contributed to the deeply entrenched dual economies of the developing world. In this context, the United States is considered as "European" because its dominant population originated in Europe. The United States dictated policies in Central American countries and Cuba for decades beginning in the late nineteenth century. It also became the colonial ruler in the Philippines and Puerto Rico after the 1898 Spanish-American War.

In many parts of the world, some of the precolonial rulers initiated economic development. In the Middle East, for example, factories and shops producing textiles flourished during the early 1800s in Egypt, Beirut, and Damascus. Great Britain at that time was the world's leading exporter of fabric and clothing. From Britain's point of view, textile making in the Middle East posed a threat to one of its main foreign policies—that is, establishing new markets for its own manufactured products. When it became the dominant imperial power in Egypt and other areas claimed by the Ottoman Empire, Britain dismantled the local textile industry.

While it may be unfair to blame colonial rulers for all of the problems facing the developing world today, colonialism did initiate some of them while doing little to mitigate others. Subsistence agriculture, for example, was not forced on an unsuspecting and powerless people. It was already the economic mainstay before the Europeans arrived. Yet colonial regimes superimposed a new elite, the flip side of a dual economy, after the precolonial rulers were removed from power. Establishing a new elite illustrates the fact that "progress," like other kinds of change, often has both positive and negative consequences. The new, European-trained elite did learn the languages, management, and communication skills essential in today's international system. However, today this elite controls governmental as well as business decisions using the language and governing style of the ex-colonial power, be it French in Senegal or English in India, for example. This results in a separation between the elite and the large majority of people. The gap is increased by differences in lifestyle and education. The elite decision makers often have earned advanced degrees in an industrialized country and live with all the conveniences available to people in high-income countries. This lifestyle gap is not simply one of quantity but of quality as well. It represents differences in culture as well as in the number of modern consumer goods enjoyed.

Many argue that colonial rule did help by providing a transition from a traditional society to a modern one and by initiating infrastructure development. Transportation systems such as railroads were built, as were educational facilities, particularly in the capital cities. Imperial powers constructed mines and port facilities, plus they made banking and other capital expenditures in laying the basis for a modern economic sector. When they left, the facilities remained in the control of the local elites, who also benefited from them.

Those emphasizing the negative legacy of imperialism hasten to note that infrastructure investments served, and continue to serve, the economic interests of the industrial states. The transportation systems linked the sources of raw materials inland with seaports. While very useful for the movement of commodities from mines in the colony's interior to the "mother" country for processing, such railroads, canals, and roads did little to develop the economy of the colony itself. They did not interconnect income-producing internal regions with each other. Angola in southwestern Africa provides a case in point. Portugal, the colonial ruler, built three railroads. Each one connected an interior region producing trade products with a port city on the coast. The northern line carried coffee and diamonds, the center line moved copper ore from the Congo, and the southern line transported iron ore. All three lines traversed east and west moving roughly parallel to each other. None of the three interconnected.

Finally, colonizers in what is today's developing world introduced new crops, not for food but for income. Literally called **cash crops**, they included sugar, coffee, cotton, tea, tobacco, bananas, and other commodities wanted in Europe and the United States. The term cash crops also includes natural resources as well as agricultural products, such as tin and tea. Economists use the phrase **primary commodities** when referring to cash crops because, unlike manufactured goods, they are traded unprocessed and in their natural state.

The imperial conquest consisted of massive land grabs by European settlers seeking to produce cash crops. They used the labor of the conquered peoples whenever possible, or turned to importing indentured servants or slaves. On English, French, and Spanish islands in the Caribbean, for example, most of the indigenous people died within a few decades of the conquest. They were replaced with slaves from West Africa. Unlike the Europeans, previous empires had not always taken over the land of peoples they ruled. China's tributary system and the Arab and Ottoman Empires, for example, extracted taxes or tribute and obedience, but often left the existing economic and social system virtually intact. Contrary to this practice, European conquest changed not only the political leadership but also the society's religious, economic, and social status practices. Chapter 2 discussed imperialism's continuing cultural impact.

Today, many developing countries still earn a large percentage of their international trade income by selling the cash crops introduced during colonial rule. As with other continuing effects of imperialism, exporting primary commodities stimulates opposing arguments over whether it has had positive or negative consequences. Copper, sugarcane, cattle, hemp, and potash, for example, provide developing countries with some income in their postcolonial eras. Yet exporting unprocessed products while importing manufactured goods produces a trade deficit. Deficits result because the prices of unprocessed products tend to decrease over time in relation to the prices of manufactured goods. Thus developing countries find themselves in an unfavorable position in trading with industrial countries.

OUTSIDE INTERVENTIONS

Economic interactions with other states, international organizations, and private corporations can assist in the development process. Such relevant outside interventions occur in four categories: trade, aid, private investment, and technical assistance. As Figure 4.2 indicates, these interventions can provide machinery, financing, and expertise, but each brings problems of its own.

Trade

Trade in primary commodities, a legacy of colonialism, can earn income for a developing state in the years when prices in the international market are high. Trade earnings, called **foreign exchange** by economists, are used to buy machinery as well as to build roads, buildings, factories, and other infrastructure. Because foreign exchange is used to buy products imported from other countries, it exists as accounts in large banks with worldwide operations. These accounts are in U.S. dollars, British pounds, European euros, or other currencies that businesses in other countries will accept in exchange for their goods. Such a currency is referred to as a **convertible** or a **hard currency**. Some development theorists believe that good planning can make up for annual fluctuations in cash crop prices. Others point out that the amount of money earned by the sale of primary commodities depends on processing and markets located outside of the developing country. Processing plants and market outlets are controlled by businesses in the industrial world, and it is in their interest to keep the costs of raw materials as low as possible. They often play one source of primary commodities against another to keep prices down.

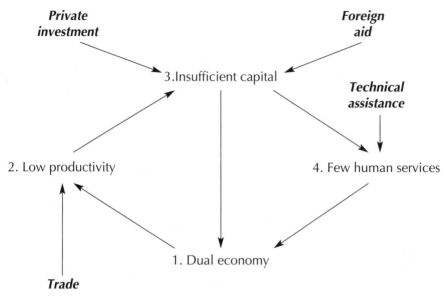

FIGURE 4.2
Cycle of Underdevelopment: Outside Interventions

Aid

The second type of international economic transaction, aid, is designed to provide capital directly in the form of loans. Official aid from public sources comes from another country's government, called **bilateral aid**, or an IGO such as the World Bank, called **multilateral aid**. In the dollar amount of aid provided, the United States ranks as the world leader; however, as a percentage of donor GNI, the United States has always ranked well behind other industrialized states, and its rating has steadily dropped since 1960. In that year, the United States provided 0.53 percent of its GNI in economic aid. By 1980 the figure was 0.27 percent, by 1993 it had dropped to 0.15 percent, and by 1999 it was 0.10 percent—the lowest among the world's twenty-eight major aid donors. The Scandinavian countries have always led in the percentage of their GNIs designated for aid. Denmark was the highest in 1999 at 1.01 percent (*Human Development Report 2001*).

Opponents of economic aid often make the mistake of thinking it is a giveaway program. To the contrary, in virtually all cases aid takes the form not of grants but of loans requiring repayment, often at commercial rates of interest. Missing loan payments affects a country's credit worthiness. Low credit ratings mean subsequent loans, needed to finance international trade for example, will cost more in interest because of increased risk.

Aid generally provides financing for specific development projects. Often a project will not produce income for some time, but loan payments come due right away. Also, the economic and political "strings" that accompany aid can be a drawback.

Most projects require the purchase of machinery, which generally must be made from companies headquartered in the country providing the aid. Thus much aid financing never leaves the donor country. Not only does this practice help businesses in the industrialized country, but it also ensures continued earnings through a trade in spare parts. Aid also produces a web of political strings, intangible but nonetheless real. Economic indebtedness brings with it political indebtedness allowing aid donors to pressure governments in aid-recipient countries for diplomatic support.

Private Investment

The third form of outside intervention, **private investment**, has the virtue of avoiding government-to-government political ties and loan repayments. Physical and financial capital invested by transnational corporations can bring income directly into a local economy through new employment opportunities. **Transnational corporations (TNCs)** are private businesses with holdings or operations in two or more countries. They are among the largest economic units in the world, as measured by a comparison of their revenues and the GNIs of states. A ranking of countries and corporations according to the size of their annual products in 1991 showed the Sumitomo Corporation as the twenty-first largest producer of wealth, ahead of such states as Austria, Turkey, South Africa, and Israel. Mitsubishi was listed twenty-second, and General Motors twenty-fifth (World Bank 1994; Mattera 1992, 704). Of the top seventy-five in 1991, twenty-seven were TNCs. Clearly many of the world's largest businesses have much greater resources than most members of the United Nations, and they operate on a worldwide scale.

The preponderant number of TNCs, and all of the biggest, are headquartered in the world's leading industrial countries: the United States, Japan, Germany, France, the United Kingdom, Canada, and Italy. A TNC can exercise great policy-making influence on the government of a low-income country, especially when the corporation produces one of the few sources of foreign exchange earnings in a country. Such corporations are often promised a favorable business climate, such as low taxes, freedom from environmental restrictions, and suppression of unions. Like trade and aid, private investment is part of the dependent relationship the developing world has with the industrial world. Private companies bring in personnel with management and other skills needed for development; however, such people focus on the work to be done to enhance the company's profitability and can be withdrawn at any time. They do not assist with projects prioritized to develop the local economy itself. Employing outside experts for this purpose is called technical assistance.

Technical Assistance

The fourth form of outside intervention, **technical assistance**, makes up for the lack of local human resources by bringing in experts from other countries. Often these specialists do the planning and sometimes help make decisions as the project is carried out. Villagers, the intended beneficiaries of many projects, usually participate only as physical laborers. As a result, the villagers, who are expected to carry on after the experts leave, do not have a vested interest in the project and often are untrained in its upkeep.

These "beneficiaries" may not even perceive the project as serving their needs because of their lack of participation in the planning. They had to do the hard physical work to build the project, which meant less time in their fields. Such disregard for the human dimension of development has accounted for the failure of a large percentage of rural projects in past decades.

OTHER FACTORS

The factors contributing to the cycle of underdevelopment create structural problems that make development difficult. Outside interventions can either help or hinder the process. They can inadvertently reinforce the problems while purporting to provide solutions. Trade, aid, private investment, and technical assistance act positively on an economy when local elites have achieved stable economic and political decision-making processes. Such stability results from a social consensus. When people agree on the basics—for example, the fact that they live in the same society and share a common future—they can develop ways of disagreeing without reaching an impasse. In extreme cases, an inability to work out problems can tear a country apart, as happened in Lebanon during a civil war which lasted from 1976 to 1989. Lebanon had achieved substantial economic growth and a relatively high standard of living, and it had become the banking center of the Middle East before internal violence destroyed its economy. Thus, in addition to economic factors, any analysis of developing world problems must account for any underlying social factors that help explain why some countries achieve ongoing growth and an improved standard of living while others do not.

Two other factors have proven important in providing a positive context for development: sufficient natural resources, either within a country's own borders or accessible through trade, and stable population growth; that is, growth that does not outrun the economy's ability both to sustain its population and to produce capital investment. One caveat should be noted before moving into a discussion of each factor. All three do not apply in the same way to every country in the industrial world. Japan, the example most often cited, was relatively resource poor when it began industrialization, and this situation continues to affect this country's policies. Japan needs to sell industrial goods in order to make up for deficiencies in fuel by importing oil. The cohesiveness of Japanese society has helped the country compensate for being located on mountainous volcanic islands with little arable land and few natural resources.

Lack of Social Cohesion

The borders of developing countries often encompass various ethnic groups with no previous history of cooperation and, therefore, with no sense of common purpose prior to their colonial rule. When Europeans drew the borders of the present-day developing countries, they often forcibly brought together groups of people who had fought each other for generations. Even among groups that had interacted peacefully, tensions arose when they were merged into one state. Where they had once been relative equals, now the European ruler favored one as the local elite. As a result, the country's identity, borders, and political institutions became sources of unresolved conflict when independence was achieved. The power of colonial rule had masked the underlying tensions among ethnic groups, but these surfaced with independence. Such countries lack **social cohesion**, a shared common identity, value system, and commitment to an established political system. These factors allow the society to achieve the stable economic and political decision-making processes needed to withstand the great stresses and dislocations inevitably produced by economic development.

The postcolonial history of Nigeria provides an extreme example of interethnic problems subsequent to colonial rule. Like the borders of many other states in sub-Saharan Africa, Nigeria's borders date from the Congress of Berlin in 1884–1885, when European states met to settle disputes over the partitioning of Africa. No representatives of Africa's indigenous peoples attended the Berlin conference, not even to provide information. Great Britain and France were the contenders for areas that now are part of Nigeria. France had moved down the Niger River, while the British had moved up the river. A boundary was drawn as a compromise between them. The British consolidated their holdings around the delta of the Niger River and inland and called the area Nigeria. It included many peoples speaking more than 200 languages and three major cultural groupings with substantially different lifestyles and a history of conflict: the Hausa-Fulani in the north, the Yoruba in the west, and the Ibos in the east. The Ibos proved to be the most adaptable to British practices and thus became civil servants and teachers, the core of a British educated elite.

Nigeria became independent in 1960. By 1965 interethnic tensions had increased and were marked by a series of incidents resulting in Ibo deaths. Other factors contributed to the conflict, such as the fact that Iboland was rich in oil and Nigeria had virtually no economic integration among its internal regions. Consequently, many Ibos attempted secession. They declared their Eastern Region as the new state of Biafra. A brutal war ensued from 1966 to 1969, ending with Biafra's defeat. It is not possible to say with certainty that British colonial rule resulted in Nigeria's bloody war so soon after independence. Yet major factors contributing to the war derive from or were exacerbated by colonial policies.

When people in the industrial world make negative judgments about ethnic strife in the developing world, they ignore the fact that it took centuries of warfare for today's major European countries to arrive at a mutual consensus about their borders. The United States also fought wars—with Canada, because it was part of the British Empire; with Mexico, with various indigenous peoples; and with itself in a bloody civil war—before its borders became unquestioned. It should not be surprising, then, that some developing countries have erupted in ethnic conflict to redraw international borders or to change which group rules within existing borders.

Some commentators link the rampant corruption and governmental mismanagement in some developing states to their lack of social cohesion. Civic-mindedness evolves from a sense of loyalty to the larger society. In its absence, rule becomes personalized, favorable to one ethnic group or the family and friends of the dictator or President. Vast amounts of capital are diverted to personal use instead of being used as investment in development projects. Mobutu, the former president of Zaire, renamed the Democratic Republic of the Congo, offers a glaring example of how a corrupt leader and his cronies can drain and impoverish a state. Billions of dollars flowed out of Zaire and into personal accounts in international banks during the more than thirty years Mobutu was in power. Such **capital flight** and corrupt government policy making have proven formidable obstacles to development in many countries.

Insufficient Natural Resources

This second factor contributing to development problems does not receive the attention it deserves. Most low-income countries lack the natural resources and moderate climates possessed by today's industrialized countries when they began a development process. Geographical location has much to do with the problems faced by today's developing nations. Almost all developing countries are located within the 37-degree latitudes north and south of the equator. Those outside this region, such as Turkey, Chile, and South Africa, are middle income. The heat in the planet's equatorial zone produces tropical, desert, or monsoon climates. Each of these climates presents problems for development. Deserts lack water, and tropical areas have thin topsoil which erodes quickly. In a monsoon region, rain comes down in destructive torrents during a short wet season, which alternates with many dry months. Such a rain pattern erodes and leaches nutrients from the soil. It contrasts sharply with the steady, easily absorbed precipitation of temperate zones. The bulk of Africa, for example, is located on both sides of the equator. Potential farmland makes up only one-fifth of the continent; 20 percent is desert, and 57 percent is reddish, rain-washed, acidic soil. High in iron and aluminum, this soil does not produce thriving cultivated plants (Harrison 1984, 70).

Explosive Population Growth

Economists agree that optimum economic growth occurs when a population grows slowly and steadily. New markets are thus created at a pace that stimulates new production. Such a balance between economic expansion and population growth is not characteristic of the developing world. Overpopulation is a problem in low-income countries where high population growth rates exist alongside low economic growth rates, as indicated in Table 4.4.

States with higher-income economies have lower population growth rates. They also report relatively low economic growth rates but, since their economies are already industrial, they do not need to sustain economic growth at rates of 7 percent and above. In the long run, major population growth and stagnant economies pose insurmountable problems for the agricultural and small industrial sectors of a developing economy. Resulting social tensions strain the social fabric of many countries. A solution could be capital investment in new machinery to increase agricultural productivity, but this is prohibitively expensive in most villages.

The problem of exploding population growth did not face the already industrialized world. During their first decades of development, the populations of Europe, the United States, and Japan grew roughly parallel to increases in the productivity resulting from the new machinery. After achieving advanced stages of industrialization, a **demographic transition** occurred. This transition, illustrated in Figure 4.3, shows the

Table 4.4
POPULATION AND ECONOMIC GROWTH RATES FOR SELECTED STATES

	Average Annual Population Change 1975-1999 (Percent)[*]	Average Annual Growth in GDP 1990-1999 (Percent)[**]
Low-Income Economies		
Tanzania	3.1	2.8
Pakistan	2.8	3.8
Haiti	2.0	−1.3
Lower-Middle-Income Economies		
Monocco	2.2	2.3
Egypt	2.3	4.4
Jamaica	1.0	0.3
Upper-Middle-Income Economies		
Poland	0.5	4.5
Hungary	−0.2	1.0
Uruguay	0.7	3.8
High-Income Economies		
New Zealand	0.8	3.1
United States	1.0	3.3
Japan	0.5	1.3

[*]Source: United Nations Development Program, *Human Development Report*, 2001.

[**]*Source*: John Allen, *Student Atlas of World Politics* (Guilford, CT: McGraw-Hill, 2004).

change in population growth that has occurred in every industrialized country. Whereas before industrialization population growth was checked by a high death rate, now it is held steady by a low birthrate.

Before industrialization, populations generally had high birth and death rates. Thus explosive population growth did not occur. This situation changed during industrial development's early stages because more food, better sanitation, and wider availability of medical care substantially lowered the death rate. Since birthrates stayed high, the population increased. As industrialization advanced, it produced a higher standard of living based on employment in the manufacturing and service sectors. Having many children became an economic burden rather than a necessity. In a subsistence-agricultural lifestyle, children provide the workforce needed to herd animals, carry wood, and take care of younger children. Industrial economies provide reasons for having fewer children as well as the technologies to achieve this result.

Unlike the population growth trends in the industrialized countries, developing countries find themselves stuck in the middle of the demographic transition with lower death rates but high birthrates. In contrast to the past experience of today's high-

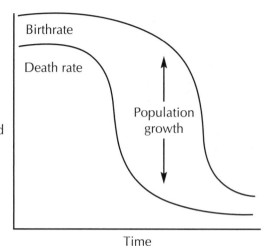

FIGURE 4.3
The Demographic Transition

income countries, economic growth in developing countries is not enough to absorb their growing populations. Colonial rule, and subsequent international aid programs, have brought lower death rates through increased sanitation and the eradication of some diseases. Ironically, the humanitarian work of missionaries and aid agencies has produced a long-term problem for the very people they attempted to help. By using new medical practices, disease was attacked as the most visible cause of human suffering and the one most susceptible to an immediate solution. However, as discussed above, long-term development was not the objective, and even if it had been it would have taken longer than it took to decrease the death rate. To put the problem in economic perspective, eradicating smallpox was relatively cheaper than building infrastructure. The present population explosion in low-income countries shows that unintended, secondary consequences can have major effects.

CASE STUDY   Namibia as a Developing Country

Located in the southern region of Africa, Namibia borders on South Africa's northwestern corner, and from there covers over 1,000 miles of Atlantic Ocean coastline until it reaches the border of Angola. Since its independence from South Africa in 1990, Namibia's experience has combined chronic development problems with a commitment to democracy. Namibia's people take pride in their progressive constitution, preserve a free press, and maintain a vibrant community monitoring human rights.

This blend of traits makes the country noteworthy, yet Namibia has slipped under the radar screen of most people studying development issues. It has a small population living in a large, arid landscape not considered strategic by the world's major powers. In an out-of-the-way place on the planet, the country's approximately 1.8 million people inhabit an area that from northwest to southeast covers the same distance as that from London to Rome.

The Namib Desert gave the country its name. Namib is said to originate from a Nama word meaning "enclosure" (*Namibia—The Facts* 1980, 5). This fits since the desert runs along the coast, forming a barrier to the country's interior. Namibia has an arid to semiarid climate, creating a dry savanna in virtually the entire country. This explains, at least in part, why it was one of the last places to become a European colony. No permanent rivers flow inside Namibia's borders. The ones that exist form international boundaries like the Kunene in the north shared with Angola, and the Orange in the south shared with South Africa. Namibia's lack of arable land compares with that in states long considered desert countries. Of its total territory, 1 percent is considered arable (Saudi Arabia has 1.7 percent). Not surprisingly, Namibia has 0 percent permanent cropland (Allen 2002, 147).

Political and Social Factors

Namibia's specific colonial history makes it unique in some ways; nevertheless, Namibia has a lot in common with other developing countries because the colonial legacy creates a heavy burden. Two colonial regimes have ruled Namibia. Germany named the territory German South West Africa and formally designated it as a colony in 1884. South African forces, fighting for the British Empire in World War I, defeated German troops in 1915, and the area then became known as South West Africa. South Africa did not leave until a settlement brokered by the United Nations ended Namibia's War of Liberation in 1989.

In important ways the two colonial experiences reinforced each other. Indigenous peoples were forced onto marginal land with the colonial government's authority enshrining and enforcing the policy. At its best, such an officially authorized and therefore "legitimate" system creates human suffering, denies human rights to the vast majority of people, and stunts their ability to learn the skills needed by a modern economy. At worst, it subjects them to punishment often accompanied by physical brutality.

German colonial policy legalized land confiscation, forced nonsettlers onto reservations, and used vagrancy laws to punish people who left their designated areas without authorization. This system was developed over time, after the crushing of the Herero and Nama peoples who had rebelled against German rule. After the main body of Hereros suffered a major military defeat in 1904, the German commander issued his infamous order to annihilate the Herero as a nation. ("Inside German territory every Herero tribesman, armed or unarmed, with or without cattle, will be shot" Dierks 2002, 115.) An estimated three quarters of the Herero died in various ways, with direct killing as the least of them. Thousands were chased into the Kalahari Desert to die as were their cattle, essential to the pastoral people. It seems the same policy extended to the Nama people since an estimated 50 percent of their population also died.

South African rule carried out German policy precedents more thoroughly. Relegating the majority of the population to reserves on marginal land produced the labor needed by the settler-owned mines and commercial farms. South Africa's government not only refined the system, making it more systematic and all pervading, but also justified it by appealing to a particularly odious, bluntly racist ideology. The assumed genetic superiority of the white "race" and the inferiority of the black "race" led to the conclusion that the two would be happier and more productive if rigidly segregated. Believers of this ideology, called *apartheid*, "separateness" in Afrikaans, made it a moral imperative to privilege settlers over indigenous people, white over black. As a result, the economy was integrated with that of South Africa and relatively few indigenous people received formal education.

The South West Africa People's Organization (SWAPO) led resistance to South African rule from the 1960s until independence in 1990. Made up mainly of Ovambo people, agriculturalists in the north of the country, SWAPO did attract many other groups peacefully resisting within the country while it also engaged in guerrilla warfare from bases outside Namibia. At independence, most people recognized SWAPO's right to rule tempered by the new country's constitution, a model of hope with its guarantees of human rights and representative governing institutions. Essentially a one-party system, it has prevailed since independence with other political parties competing at the margin. The president of SWAPO during the struggle for independence has been Namibia's only president since 1990, having been elected three times. The concentration of power, however, has not resulted in the elimination of a free press and competing political parties, nor in the jailing of judges and human rights advocates.

Economically, colonial rule has left a mixed legacy. On the positive side, some infrastructure was built, including government buildings, a railroad, and paved roads, particularly in the north to facilitate the movement of men and material during the independence war. The imperialist legacy also includes a competent white elite, perhaps 10 percent of the population, in possession of most of the commercial farms, larger stores, and privately owned tourist hotels, restaurants, shops, and travel services. The position of this property-owning class provides ongoing reminders of apartheid's recent oppression and exploitation. This explains why land redistribution remains one of the most prominent and sensitive issues in today's Namibia.

Namibia is an ethnic mosaic, as are most of the world's states. The 1988 census put the Ovambo people, the group dominating in the governing party, as the largest group at 49.9 percent of the population (*Europa World Year Book 2001,* 2839). The 2000 census, however, showed a major decrease in Ovambo relative to the eleven plus other groups: they dropped to 34.4 percent but still represent Namibia's the largest ethnic plurality with "mixed race" reported as second at 14.5 percent (*Encyclopedia Britannica* 2003, 684). Currently the changes seem to have little impact on representation in government.

Namibia has adopted tolerance and reconciliation as its official policy in response to its varied ethnic composition. The commitment to color-blind human rights protection remains, however, in tension with the recognition that past wrongs need righting. Clamor grows for a speedier implementation of the government's land redistribution policy while, at the same time, advocates of such action generally agree that the process must be lawful, transparent, and fair as possible. All in all, Namibia's multiethnic institutions, human rights community, and representative political process seem firmly established. Political life has not become polarized.

Interrelated, Structural Economic Factors

Although often overlooked, Namibia can illustrate clearly lower-income economies' underlying dynamic; namely, the interrelated factors that perpetuate large-scale poverty. Applying this chapter's structural analysis to a specific economy can highlight what developing countries have in common. Because each low-income country also possesses unique characteristics, the following description also points out Namibia's distinguishing features.

One side of Namibia's dual economy becomes apparent when a first-time visitor notices the country's modern infrastructure. Accommodations have all the comforts in the capital city, consumer goods are readily available, the telephone system works dependably along with an increasing number of mobile phones, buildings display good maintenance, and recent-model automobiles fill the streets.

A visit to the outlying township or travel to a rural area, however, reveals a radically different reality. Away from tourist hotels and the elite's city lifestyle, an observer can find ample evidence that Namibia's income maldistribution rivals the world's worst as found in many other countries in sub-Saharan Africa and in Latin America. In 2001 Namibia's poorest 10 percent of the population had a 0.5 percent share of the national income whereas the richest 10 percent had a 64.5 percent share (United Nations Development Program website). This means that the country's per capita GNI, reported as $1,960 in 2001 by the World Bank (World Bank 2003), glosses over a very wide disparity between the country's rich and poor.

Not only lifestyle but also language differentiates Namibia's upper and lower classes. The majority of the population lives in rural areas and interacts using one or more of Namibia's indigenous African languages; however, the business and governmental elite speaks English as the official language. At least learning English has one egalitarian element; almost everyone in Namibia must learn it as a nonnative speaker. Many in the capital also use Afrikaans because it was the official language under South African rule less than fifteen years ago. In addition, a small German-speaking community exists among higher- and middle-income Namibians.

Low productivity and capital accumulation characterize Namibia as they do most countries of the developing world. Agriculture provides a living for the largest percentage of the population according to the 1991 census: "agriculture, hunting, forestry, and fishing" engaged the largest category by far of economically active people at 48 percent of the total 394,341 employed. The second category related to tourism with 9.6 percent working in "restaurants and hotels." Manufacturing came in third with 5.8 percent. Fourth was construction at 4.7 percent, and mining took fifth place at 3.7 percent. The official unemployment figure amounted to 20 percent of the labor force, another reality typical of developing countries. (Percentages were calculated from data included in the *Europa World Year Book* 2002, 2839.) These employment data reflect the fact that Namibia has a primary-commodity-based economy which emphasizes livestock raising, fishing, and mining. Tourism augments these sectors because the country's government and private parks offer access to an impressive variety and volume of African wildlife.

Yet these figures tell only part of Namibia's employment and underemployment story. A visitor to the country's rural areas observes extensive subsistence agriculture.

This lifestyle maintains a sizable proportion of the population since urban dwellers are reported at only 31.4 percent (United Nations Development Program website).

As usual with a primary-commodity-producing economy having a large subsistence sector, Namibia's economic growth rate remains low; for example, in 2000–2001 it stood at 2.6 percent. Often development analysts compare the economic growth rate with the population growth rate, which for Namibia averaged 2.4 percent from 1990 to 2001 (World Bank 2003). Comparing these figures indicates that Namibia may be maintaining current overall living standards, but the economy produces little domestic savings and investment.

Developing countries desperately need human services, as demonstrated by Namibia's experience. South Africa's apartheid rule denied the vast majority of Namibians opportunities to develop the knowledge and skills needed to manage a modern economy. The scarcity of human capacity also hampers Namibia's responses to its daunting challenges in health and education. The country's mortality rate for children under the age of five illustrates its need for medical services. According to the World Bank's 2003 *World Development Report*, for every 1,000 Namibian children born in 2001, 112 died before their fifth birthday; however, the United Nations Development Program in its *Human Development Report* 2001 gave the Namibian child mortality rate as 70 in 1999. While the data discrepancy seems large, both figures place the country in the low-income country range even though Namibia's per capita GNI locates it decidedly in the lower middle-income category. Clearly problems persist in providing medical services and basic nutrition.

Currently a major health crisis directly threatens Namibia's economic progress and social fabric. HIV/AIDS dominates an already taxed medical system. Estimates abound that about 25 percent of the sexually active population have contracted or come down with the disease. The epidemic has affected so many people that it has produced a decrease in the country's aggregate life expectancy, causing it to go down from 58 in 1992 to 44 in 2001 (The World Bank Group website). Namibia's formally reported AIDS cases illustrate the rapid spread of the disease even though they reflect only a small proportion of the country's actual sufferers: 430 cases were reported in 1992 but by 1998 the number had exploded to 5,158, almost a twelve-fold increase (*Statistical Yearbook 1998* 2001, 83).

In the field of education, Namibia must deal with major problems, including one central to the system: the country needs thousands of primary and secondary schoolteachers. With higher education for blacks stymied under eighty-five years of South Africa's colonial rule, Namibia has had to play catch-up in its fifteen years since independence. The government has tried by budgeting the equivalent of 9.1 percent of the country's GNI on education during at least part of the mid-1990s, the second-highest rate in the world (Allen 2002, 138).

Namibia's lack of water may well preclude much growth in manufacturing in spite of the fact that the country has most of the other needed factors of production. Land costs relatively little compared with other countries, and a workforce is being educated. The country has reliable electricity at current usage levels as well as a dependable telephone system. Other infrastructure is well maintained, such as paved roads. On the negative side, however, Namibia's need to import all its fossil fuels is another major inhibitor to building a manufacturing sector. Also, geography creates the need for costly travel not only from Namibia to international markets and sources of supply but often inside the country.

Namibia's natural environment limits the country's range of development options, a situation it shares with virtually all lower-income countries. No magic formula exists to tackle the country's mutually reinforcing set of interrelated problems at a supportable cost. The needed applications of modern technologies require larger and larger amounts of capital.

External Sources of Capital

Trade and tourism provide Namibia with needed foreign exchange, but imports gobble up all that is earned and then some. Namibia's trade profile illustrates clearly the problem faced by low- and lower-middle-income developing countries. Predictably, Namibia has a chronic trade deficit given its pattern of primary commodity exports and manufactured goods imports. International Monetary Fund data show trade deficits from 1992 through 1997. In 1997, for example, exports amounted to U.S.$1,359,200,000 while imports that year totaled U.S.$1,675,000,000, leaving a deficit of U.S.$315,800,000 (*Namibia Statistical Appendix* 1998, 31, 34). Primary commodities totaled 88.6 percent of export income in 1997. At 60.3 percent, mineral exports accounted for the most export income with diamonds as the dominant commodity. Cattle, meat, and fish plus animal products, such as wool and hides, brought in 28.3 percent. Manufactured products, listed as canned fish, fishmeal, and fish oil, brought in only 11.4 percent of export income. (Percentages were calculated from data published in *Namibia Statistical Appendix* 1998, 31.)

Namibia's import categories also reflect those of other developing countries. Food, generally processed and including beverages and tobacco, headed the import list at 24.1 percent in 1997. Machinery and electrical goods listed at 15 percent, then capital goods, noted as vehicles and transport equipment, at 14.7 percent. The rest consisted of chemicals, plastics, and medical supplies at 11.2 percent, textiles at 7.5 percent, metal and metal products at 7.5 percent, fuels at 5.9 percent, and wool, paper, and furniture at 5.5 percent. The "other" category stood at 8.5 percent. (Percentages were calculated from data printed published in *Namibia Statistical Appendix* 1998, 34.)

In a relationship typical for developing countries, South Africa, as the ex-colonial ruler, remains Namibia's most significant trading partner. In 1997 South Africa supplied 84 percent of Namibia's imports (calculated from data in the *Namibia Statistical Appendix* 1998, 35) while ranking second to the United Kingdom as receiving the most Namibian exports (*Europa World Year Book* 2001, 2842). Namibia also retains tight economic connections with South Africa in other ways. First, both are members of the Southern African Customs Union (SACU), an organization made up of South Africa and its neighbors all with much smaller economies. Namibia's share of SACU receipts in 1997 amounted to U.S.$327 million (*Namibia Statistical Appendix* 1998, 30). Second, the Namibian and South African currencies are tied together so the value of the Namibian dollar fluctuates directly with that of the South African rand.

To some planners, tourism offers promise for Namibia's economic growth because the country has world-class wildlife in well-established public and private game parks.

The number of visitors continues to increase; for example, the growth between 1996 and 1998 amounted to 21 percent, with a total of 559,674 arrivals in the latter year. A comparison with tourism in South Africa indicates that there is room for continued expansion; in 1998, 5,898,256 tourists visited South Africa (United Nations *Statistical Yearbook* 1998, 750, 755). Namibia earned U.S.$200 million from tourism in 1998, the difference between U.S.$288 million in income and U.S.$88 million in expenditures (calculated from data in the *Statistical Yearbook* 1998, 764). Yet tourism based on wildlife management presents problems, given Namibia's arid and fragile landscape. Also, an expanding human population creates conflicts because animals break out from the game parks every now and then. Elephants have demolished villagers' hard-earned food supplies and lions have killed livestock.

Namibia receives capital from both aid and private investment, as do most developing countries. Namibia received U.S.$177.6 million in official foreign aid in 1999. This constituted U.S.$104.4 on a per capita basis, higher than that for any other African state except Djibouti (*Human Development Report* 2001, 192). Direct foreign investment in 1997 totaled U.S.$125.2 million (*Namibia Statistical Appendix* 1998, 30). As a point of comparison, the two together add up to less than Namibia's trade deficit in 1997 of U.S.$315,800 million, as noted earlier. Given the country's needs, the question remains as to whether the flow of outside capital will make a significant long-term impact.

Summary

Namibia fits the economic profile for a large majority of developing countries. Its primary-commodity, trade-dependent economy produces little savings and a need for external capital. Its vast gap between rich and poor limits domestic markets and exacerbates social and political tensions. In the constrained economic context, Namibia's government has had to develop its institutions and legitimacy. At the same time it must wrestle with the legacy of flagrant past injustices which are prominently reflected in the current society. Given all their problems, the country's leaders and people deserve acclaim for sustaining a stable society and maintaining political freedoms.

TERMS AND CONCEPTS

Basic-needs strategy *66*

Bilateral aid *73*

Capital (physical, financial, human) *68*

Capital flight *77*

Cash crops/primary commodities *71*

Demographic transition *77*

Developing world *63*

Development *61*

Dual economy *67*

Economic growth strategy *66*

Foreign exchange *72*

Gross national income (GNI) *63*

Hard/convertible currency *72*

Multilateral aid *73*

Per capita gross national income *63*

Private investment *74*

Productivity *68*

Social cohesion *76*

Subsistence *67*

Technical assistance *74*

Transnational corporation (TNC) *74*

DISCUSSION QUESTIONS

1. Given their historical role, what case would industrialized states make about economic development during the age of colonialism? What case would developing states make?
2. What factors account for world poverty? How could development strategies bring about constructive change?
3. Why are the following indicators used to differentiate levels of "human development": literacy rate, infant mortality rate, and life expectancy? What other indicators would make sense?
4. Do outside interventions provide substantial capital, enabling the typical developing country to improve its per capita GNI? Why or why not?

RESEARCH PROJECTS

1. Choose a country and make an assumption about its level of economic development. Then do some research to find the country's macroeconomic indicators (some good sources of information include the *World Development Report*, the *Human Development Report*, and the *Almanac*). Use the data to write a brief economic profile of the country. Do the data support your initial assumption?
2. Survey the media's coverage of the developing world for a month. What images are conveyed? What, if any, information is provided on the underlying economic and social problems in developing countries?
3. Compare and contrast the population growth rates and economic growth rates for several countries in the low-income and lower-middle-income categories in various years over the course of at least two decades. What trends do you find?
4. Visit a local mall or department store. Choose a category of goods and systematically determine the percentage of goods that is imported. Repeat this procedure for another category of goods. Compare and contrast your findings.
5. For a country with low-income indicators (such as per capita income and economic growth) but high human development indicators (such as literacy and infant mortality rates), discuss the factors that may account for this seeming anomaly.
6. Choose a low- or middle-income country and, using the Namibia case study as a prototype, write a report summarizing the chosen economy's present economic development status and relevant development issues.

INTERNET RESOURCES

Care: http://www.care.org A development NGO, Care provides information about its projects, data about major world issues (such as hunger, poverty, health, environment, and education), and maps and other information about the countries in which it works.

Central Intelligence Agency Factbook: http://www.odci.gov/cia/publications/nsolo/factbook/global.htm This CIA site has maps, economic data, and some demographic data about all the world's countries.

OXFAM: http://www.oxfam.org.uk This visually helpful and colorful site includes summaries of this NGOs work as organized by country and themes, such as "emergencies," and "fair trade." It also has "success stories" and external links.

UN Development Program: http://www.undp.org Some data from the annual *Human Development Report* are available at this site.

CHAPTER 5

Perspectives on Economic Development

"The ideas of economic liberty, a free market open to the world, and private initiative as the motor of progress have become embedded in the people of Chile."
—NOVELIST AND POLITICIAN MARIO VARGAS LLOSA (QUOTED IN GOODWIN 1996, 74)

"Creating a sustainable society will require fundamental economic and social changes, a wholesale alteration of economic priorities and population policies."
—ENVIRONMENTALIST LESTER BROWN (BROWN 1981, 8)

Reasonable people with different perspectives can come to very different conclusions about the same events. Adequate explanations as to why an international problem exists must, therefore, include an analysis of the alternative perspectives people use to decide on viable responses. In the case of development as a global issue, three perspectives offer contrasting explanations of how the international economy operates and what should be done about its problems. The liberal economic, dependency, and participatory perspectives organize the debate over how to respond effectively to poverty and economic downturns.

LIBERAL ECONOMICS

Liberal economics prevails as the leading economic theory in the world today. Otherwise known as **market economics**, this theory's core concepts, such as supply and demand, free trade, and laissez-faire government, were formulated in the late eighteenth century by Adam Smith and refined by his successors. Today, at the beginning of the twenty-first century, liberal market prescriptions have become the main economic policies of most governments and international governmental organizations (IGOs), while their main competitor, socialism, has become marginalized. In general, socialist strategies prescribe a significant role for government in the economy.

Liberal economists generally respond to the problem of worldwide poverty by advocating economic growth strategies. They agree that economic expansion produces higher incomes, which in turn generate more demand for products, greater growth, and more jobs. This pattern of mutually reinforcing supply and demand produces an upward growth spiral which enables an economy to break out of the cycle of underdevelopment. Economic growth is best achieved with a minimum of government intervention and a maximum of people willing to invest their capital.

Comparative Advantage

Applying market strategies to the international economic system is accomplished through the concept of **comparative advantage**. An economy has a comparative advantage in the production of a good or service when it can produce that good or service at a lower cost than its competitors. Any state's economy should aim to export those products in which it holds a comparative advantage and import those which other states can produce for less. Figure 5.1 illustrates the concept by using a simple trading system—two products (wine and cloth) traded by two countries (Portugal and England) to compare labor costs (one of the factors included in a product's price). This classic example reflects the international system two hundred years ago, developed by an early nineteenth-century economist, David Ricardo.

A cursory look at the figure may result in an obvious question: Why would Portugal trade with England when it could make both wine and cloth at a lower cost than England? The answer comes from a closer look at the figure. The phrase *relative comparison* provides the clue. If, on the one hand, Portugal were self-sufficient and traded for neither wine nor cloth, where would it get any savings? If, on the other hand, it specialized in wine and traded it for cloth made in England, Portugal would save ten labor hours. Then it could use the surplus to invest in making wine more efficiently and become more competitive with, for example, the French wine-making industry. In response, the French would have to reduce the cost of making their wine. Due to such competition over time, the price of wine will come down and consumers in all free trading countries will benefit. The same reasoning will produce lower consumer prices and growth in the cloth-making industries in states within the free trading system.

Needed Policies

Comparative advantage leads to the conclusion that people in every economy will benefit from the policies of **free trade** and specialization. Liberal economists maintain that imports and exports should be unrestricted by tariffs and other barriers. Yet states enact

FIGURE 5.1
ILLUSTRATION OF COMPARATIVE ADVANTAGE

	Portugal	England
Wine (y barrels)*	80 hours of labor/year	120 hours of labor/year
Cloth (x yards)*	90 hours of labor/year / 10 hours of labor/year	100 hours of labor/year / 20 hours of labor/year

*y barrels = x yards

trade restrictions, called **protectionism**, to keep foreign companies from competing effectively with their own businesses. If governments impose regulations artificially increasing the cost of imported goods, the benefits of competition in bringing down prices for consumers will disappear. Also, the protected domestic producers have no incentive to become more efficient by updating their plant and management practices. Over time they get further and further behind their competitors in other countries.

So economic policies should encourage **specialization**. States should emphasize producing and trading those products in which they have a comparative advantage, not block imports, and not subsidize exports. Specialization encourages cost efficiencies because of **economies of scale**. This economic principle refers to the fact that the per-unit cost decreases when a company produces more of a given product since the plant, personnel, and other overhead costs remain about the same. Also, specialization produces efficiencies through reinvestment and increasing knowledge about the production process.

In disagreeing with protectionist policies, liberal economists point out that mechanisms designed to enable a state to sell more than it buys cannot work in the long run because some countries inevitably have to be on the short end of the trade equation. Every economy in the system cannot sell more than it buys. Government policies to protect their own businesses and markets have the effect of reducing the amount of goods flowing worldwide and thus limiting global economic expansion. Markets become constricted and economies of scale cannot be attained so prices rise. On the other hand, if states adopt free trade and specialization policies, competition lowers prices for all consumers.

All economies can benefit from comparative advantage policies, albeit not always equally. In the wine and cloth example illustrated in Figure 5.1, England will benefit more initially because it can save twenty labor hours, while Portugal will save only ten hours. Yet, for both countries, specialization produces savings that can be reinvested, thereby further increasing efficiency. The resulting lower prices increase demand for the products of both countries and, therefore, stimulate further growth in imports and exports. As more and more states adopt policies encouraging comparative advantage and specialization, liberal economists assert that the international economy will grow. Consumers worldwide will purchase more goods at lower prices which, in turn, will stimulate further growth. Policies inhibiting free trade, based on the goals of self-sufficiency and isolationism, stifle growth and harm all states in the trading system.

In summary, liberal economic theory prescribes economic growth through trade as a development strategy. Every country, whether developing or industrialized, should lower tariffs with the ultimate goal of eliminating them and other trade barriers (such as quotas and subsidies) entirely. This also means that the government's role in economic decision making will be reduced as much as possible. Some developing countries that have adopted free trade and other liberal economic policies have achieved substantial economic growth. Such policies include privatization of government-owned economic enterprises and freeing the economy of restrictions on trade and financial flows. Chile provides an often-noted example of the potential success of such strategies. In the 1970s, Chile's military government opened the economy to foreign investment, emphasized exports, and greatly reduced health and social welfare programs. By

1995 the Chilean economy had grown for eleven consecutive years, often with an annual growth rate of over 7 percent, such as in 1988 (Goodwin 1996, 72).

DEPENDENCY

Dependency theorists contend that liberal economic theory ignores the particular problems faced by poor economies. Brazilian economists Raul Prebisch and Fernando Cardozo, who developed dependency theory in the 1950s, were at the time responding to an increasing gap in earnings between primary commodities producers and manufactured goods producers. These economists turned descriptive information into a theory by formulating general principles derived from the relationship between industrial- and agriculture-based economies.

The core principles of dependency theory directly challenge those of liberal economists who conceive of the international trading system as capable of benefiting all through free trade and specialization. In contrast, dependency analysts argue that free trade is in the interests of businesses in the industrial world and that they use their size and wealth to keep primary commodity prices low by playing suppliers in various countries against each other. Dependency advocates accept the necessity of using developing world governments to counter the established power of the industrial world's firms. A government's policies can help its citizens compete with foreign companies by limiting imports and subsidizing exports. A government also should redistribute at least some income within its society so that the poorest, most dependent citizens can improve their lives.

Structural Inequality—Neocolonialism

Dependency theory assumes that the structural inequalities between the industrial and developing worlds result from conscious policies followed by the already developed countries because they benefit from the inequitable relationship. Decisions made by businesses and governments in the industrial world affect the developing world more than the other way around. This inequality is referred to as **neoimperialism** or **neocolonialism** because developing world countries have achieved political independence but not economic independence. Poor countries need the rich much more than vice versa. Developing economies depend on the industrial world for markets, capital and capital goods, consumer goods, refined fuels, processed food, and just about everything else that characterizes a modern economy.

Industrial economies, in contrast, import mostly primary commodities from the developing world, which adds only a small amount to their total production costs. This unbalanced economic relationship has international political implications. A developing world country does not have much of a bargaining position when negotiating with the government or a business in the United States, for example. Nor do its interests figure prominently in the actions and policies of IGOs, such as the World Bank. In fact, the World Bank and the International Monetary Fund (IMF) invariably adopt liberal economic policies, thereby revealing themselves to be agents of the world's dominant industrialized countries, especially the United States. As pointed out in Chapter 1, both of these IGOs have weighted voting in which the already industrialized countries constitute a majority.

One attempt to redress the developing world's sense of powerlessness was the formation of new IGOs in the late 1960s and early 1970s to coordinate the production of and trade in primary commodities in order to negotiate higher prices. Most were not particularly successful. The Union of Banana Exporting Countries (UBEC), for example, tried to take on the three U.S. companies dominating about 70 percent of the world's banana trade: United Brands, Del Monte, and Castle Cook. Facing a concentrated control of marketing and transportation systems, as well as possessing a perishable food product that cannot be withheld from sale for long, UBEC's members could not gain a decided negotiating advantage.

Dependent economic relationships also exist *within* countries. In a developing state's dual economy, the subsistence sector is dependent on the modern consumer trading sector for jobs, consumer goods, fuel, capital, and markets—the same list that determines the dependent relationship in the international economy. Similarly, chronically poor urban and rural areas within industrial states are dependent on the state's high-income economy. Native American reservations in the United States, for example, bear the burden not only as losers in the colonial struggle but also of economic dependency.

Because poverty means having very few choices, the poor tend to act like dependent people. The well-to-do often think they are unwilling to work hard to better themselves and are either excessively deferential or too demanding. However they are perceived, their condition, relative to that of the wealthy, has humanitarian, economic, and political consequences that cry out for action.

Government Intervention

Dependency theorists oppose using the liberal economics prescription to break out of the vicious cycle of underdevelopment. Free market advocates advise developing economies to open their local markets and allow foreign investment as well as imports of manufactured goods. Also, according to liberal economists, the production of cash crops in which the developing economy has a comparative advantage should be encouraged. They are needed to pay for imports and investment. Dependency theorists counter that such prescriptions will only increase dependency by perpetuating the unequal relationship with the industrialized world, which uses the developing world as a source of raw materials and cheap labor.

The liberal economics and dependency perspectives share at least one common development goal: economic growth leading to industrialization. To this, dependency adds the goal of decreasing the power gap between the industrial and developing worlds. Substantial economic growth cannot be achieved by mainly primary-commodity-producing states without some wealth redistribution and shared decision making, both internationally and within the developing states. This goal implies a positive role for governments to act together within IGOs, such as the United Nations and the World Trade Organization. Dependency theorists realize that developing countries face an uphill struggle even when they work together.

Concerning internal economic policies, developing world governments should establish tariffs, quotas, and other trade restrictions to protect their infant industries from unfair competition with established transnational corporations (TNCs) headquartered in industrialized states. Developing world governments can also provide some funding for plant, equipment, and infrastructure, such as transportation and communication systems. Subsidies may be needed in the fragile early stages of development.

Dependency theory recognizes that large companies with multiple sources of raw materials and markets plus large amounts of capital often employ a common business practice: They lower the prices of their products below costs in one of their markets in order to drive out competition. They can sustain losses in this market because they charge higher prices in markets where they control a large market share. New industries, with only one or even several small markets, cannot match the giant company's low prices and are driven out of business. After the demise of their smaller competitors, the large company can raise its prices.

The international economic context has changed significantly since the late nineteenth and early twentieth centuries, when most industrialized countries began their major growth process. Today, huge multinational corporations dominate the international market and are serious competitors to small businesses in newly developing economies. Whereas a small nineteenth-century operation could make a profit, the present-day international economy requires multiple markets and access to worldwide transportation and communication systems. There are many ways in which a small, local company can be cut off and driven out of business. In this context, dependency analysts argue, it is impossible to create through free trade any semblance of a level playing field in the way advocated by liberal economics theorists.

International Economic System

Positive government action can occur externally, in the international economic system, through resolutions passed by IGOs. Developing countries recognize that they share interests and often cooperate with each other in international trade negotiations by adopting common negotiating positions (for example, by withholding support for international tariff reduction treaties until they include decreases in the tariffs industrial states can impose on primary commodity imports from developing states).

In the 1970s, the developing world attempted to effect a major change in how the international system functions. As noted in Chapter 1, the year 1973 was a banner year for developing states. Because of the oil embargo, members of the Organization of Petroleum Exporting Countries (OPEC) had negotiated with the industrial world as equals. Partially as a result, a 1974 special session of the United Nations General Assembly passed a series of resolutions which, together, were called the **New International Economic Order (NIEO)**. According to the developing countries, they constituted an attempt to level the international economic playing field. The required two-thirds majority vote occurred because, during the 1960s, most of the countries in Africa had gained their independence and joined the United Nations. A total of forty-two developing countries were admitted into the United Nations during the 1960s. Thus the poorer states outnumbered the industrialized states by three to one.

Two of the 1974 proposals show how the NIEO reflected the dependency model. The first proposal set a target for the amount of foreign aid industrialized states should provide to the developing world; the second, called *indexation*, attempted to fix primary commodity prices in relation to those of manufactured goods. The aid resolution proposed that industrialized states earmark 0.7 percent of their annual gross national incomes (GNIs) for foreign aid. Since imperialism was one of the main reasons the less-developed countries became trapped in the cycle of underdevelopment, the wrong could be redressed through increased aid. Added to this reasoning was the fact that the already industrialized states had used outside capital during their early stages of development (for example, British capital helped finance railroads in the United States and Canada). Indexation addressed the core of the dependency perspective's analysis; that is, why the world trading system works against developing countries, resulting over time in declines in the prices of primary commodities in relation to those of manufactured goods. The NIEO aimed to establish an index each year combining the prices of specified manufactured goods. When the index rose a certain percentage, then the price of primary commodities would automatically increase by the same percentage. This mechanism was designed to stabilize the income developing states would earn for their primary commodities.

The NIEO resolutions never went into effect because they had to be implemented by the industrialized countries. This result was predictable, given dependency theory's basic assumption that the industrial world has much more power than the developing world. Today, dependency is used less as a strategy for change and more as a critique of the existing world economic system and the economic plight of developing economies. Open-market competition makes sense if gains are possible at least once in a while, but, according to the dependency perspective, the cards remain so stacked against developing economies that they have little hope of making gains.

It may be something of a surprise to realize that industrialized countries, the most fervent advocates of free trade, still impose tariffs and other restrictions on imports. They also subsidize local production of some products, particularly agricultural commodities. **Subsidies** make up the difference between the farmers' cost of raising the agricultural product and the world market price for that commodity, which most years is much lower. Industrialized states use agricultural subsidies to make their farmers' products internationally competitive. The United States, European countries, and Japan buy selected agricultural products from their own farmers at a high enough price for the growers to make a profit. Then they sell these products in other countries at the lower world market prices dictated by international competition. The taxpayers take the loss. In effect, subsidies shut developing countries' products out of lucrative markets in the already developed countries. Subsidies also often make a commodity's price so low in the developing country itself that its own farmers go out of business. Developing countries' governments cannot afford such payments.

The United States provides a good example of agricultural subsidies. The U.S. Department of Agriculture's price support program includes cotton. This subsidy puts U.S. cotton farmers in a highly favorable position as they compete with many developing countries, including Egypt and Tanzania. While cotton represented less than 0.5 percent of total U.S. export earnings in 1993, it accounted for about 6 percent of Egypt's and 11 percent of Tanzania's exports (*International Trade and Statistics Yearbook* 1994). European, American, and Japanese subsidies for their own agricultural products severely curtail the markets available to development countries. A bloc of developing countries has formed within the World Trade Organization to publicize and oppose agricultural subsidy policies by industrial world governments.

Current industrial governments' financial support for their own producers violates the free-trade principle. Such policies are not new. Economic development in the United States during the nineteenth and early twentieth centuries used tariffs as a way to protect domestic markets. Also, the U.S. government provided generous subsidies in various forms; for example, free western land seven miles on either side of the tracks was given to railroad companies in the nineteenth century.

Dependency theorists point out that examples of free-trade hypocrisy on the part of the industrial world may undermine its propaganda but not the pressure it exerts on the developing world. The dominance of industrialized states occurs in bilateral negotiations with developing governments as well as in multilateral governmental organizations such as the International Monetary Fund. To receive an IMF loan, a government must sign an agreement to open up its domestic market to foreign imports and investment, increase its exports, privatize, and reduce governmental budget deficits by spending less on social programs. In other words, developing states must adopt liberal economic policies that will enable businesses in the industrial world to take advantage of what they call "emerging markets," an apt phrase given their projected role. Thus dependency is not only perpetuated but expanded by IMF policy.

Critique from the Liberal Economics Perspective

Free-trade advocates point out that activist government economic policies, such as protective tariffs, provide artificial assistance which, over time, will discourage new businesses in developing countries from becoming competitive. Free trade is necessary for comparative advantage to lower consumer prices in all economies. When governments intervene in economics they make mistakes, whether they are in industrial or developing countries. Economic efficiency is not their main purpose because political demands take precedence, such as pressure from subsidized companies and their workers to continue subsidies long after they could compete in the free market. Such political pressure makes it extremely difficult to maintain flexible pricing policies in response to changing market conditions. Therefore, subsidized companies and industries react sluggishly, remain uncompetitive, and even worse, discourage growth. States that subsidize the price of bread, for example, undermine their own farmers' ability to grow wheat at a profit. Farmers have no incentive to increase wheat production since they cannot earn more money. Sometimes they cannot even earn enough to meet increases in the cost of production, so they turn to other crops or occupations. For years, Egypt has had to use scarce foreign exchange or aid credits to import U.S. wheat because of shortfalls in its own production. When it attempted to reduce bread subsidies in the late 1970s, street riots ensued. Introducing free-market remedies is always politically unpopular in the short run but needed for a healthy economy in the long term. Liberal economists generally say that the already developed countries should practice what they preach and drop their own impediments to the free movement of goods, services, and financing.

Liberal economists concede that over years many primary commodity prices do fluctuate in the international market, sometimes severely, and that they often are not a solid basis for raising development capital. Yet, this cannot be seen as a sufficient explanation for why poor countries face the insurmountable problems that put them permanently at a disadvantage. It is true that agriculture-based economies do not have the purchasing power needed to industrialize quickly. They must gradually build a reliable basis for economic growth and accept investment and advice from the industrial world.

Sustained free-market policies will work in the long run. Unfortunately, most developing world states have had to change strategies abruptly, making stable growth difficult. Many had socialist policies exacerbated by mismanagement, mistakes, and chronic corruption. Only recently have sizable numbers of developing countries begun dismantling their elaborate, inefficient, and corruptly bloated government bureaucracies. It is possible that many of these countries will experience positive growth in the future. Some states which recently achieved years of substantial economic growth were once mainly primary commodity producers. Thailand, for example, in its early stages of development, earned large percentages of its foreign exchange through the sale of rubber and rice. In the mid-1980s, however, its liberal economic growth policies have paid off in GNI increases of often more than 10 percent a year.

The need for foreign investment remains obvious. In the case of Thailand, billions of dollars in Japanese investments spurred economic growth. Outside capital has been a catalyst in the development of many industrial countries. It can help today's developing world as well if allowed to move freely from state to state. In attracting such investment, developing economies have a comparative advantage in several product categories, not just in primary commodities. The production of textiles, for example, is labor intensive; therefore, clothing manufacturers are attracted by the lower wages in developing countries.

PARTICIPATORY DEVELOPMENT

Advocates of participatory development argue that relying on economic growth and industrialization to alleviate the problems of the world's poor has not worked for the vast majority of developing countries. The focus should be on directly raising their quality of life using strategies available now, rather than waiting until industrialization produces a trickle-down effect. Often termed a basic-needs approach, or sustainable development, participatory development produces more and better-quality food to reduce malnutrition, and it improves primary medical care, education, and housing. While economic growth may occur as a result of meeting basic needs, it is not the goal in and of itself. In fact, making growth the primary objective has often reduced the poor's quality of life because scarce resources are redirected and invested in increasing the production of cash crops instead of food.

Since industrialization requires very high levels of capital investment, participatory development advocates question why it is viewed as a goal. It sets a standard that invites failure, given the overwhelming problems developing economies must overcome. Why emulate the process used and advocated by the already rich, one that enables them to become richer by creating investment opportunities in developing economies? Ordinary people can improve their lives without industrializing first. The definition of **participatory development** has emerged from practical experience by noting through trial and error what factors account for success. First, development projects are designed to meet basic needs. Second, local people who will benefit and maintain the projects must participate by making decisions as well as providing labor. Third, locally available resources and technologies that do not cause harm to the natural environment must be used.

Local Decision Making

Local people not only determine what development projects to undertake, they also make daily organizing and allocation decisions. By participating in project planning and implementation, local leadership becomes established, which is needed to make the change permanent. To be most effective, outside aid workers act in support of local initiatives. The outsiders make recommendations, provide technical expertise, and secure outside funding. If the project is completely designed by outsiders, its permanency may well be doomed from the beginning. It may take months or even years longer to complete a project when committees of local people make key decisions, but this process greatly increases the chances it will continue after the external support stops.

Available Technology

Village-level projects are more likely to become permanent when locally available tools, fuel, knowledge, and skills are used. The less that has to be imported, the better. Beneficiaries will have to know how to run and repair the needed technology and afford the resources it requires. Often this means using picks and shovels instead of heavy earth-moving machinery. Labor-intensive technologies take more time but cost less and can be used in repair work.

The road to economic development is littered with failed projects which did not last past the first few years after outside financial and technical expertise ended. One oft-cited example is said to have occurred during development's early stages in a west African country. Tractors financed by loans from the United States ended up unused and rusting. Large tractors built in the United States need acres of relatively flat land to be cost-efficient. Such terrain exists in few places outside of the American Midwest. Also, fuel to run the tractors and their spare parts had to be imported. The repair manuals required an ability to read English at a fairly sophisticated level. All these factors meant continued use of the machines depended on a constant supply of outside expertise and financing. Even if all these factors had been in place, there was no guarantee that markets existed to return enough profit to pay for all the expenses of a capital-intensive production process. Often enough profit cannot be made because domestic markets are small in developing world countries. The international market cannot be relied on either, because cash crop prices fall just as often as they rise.

Environmental Compatibility

In any given village, the natural environment dictates what lifestyles can be sustained over long periods of time. To maximize the chances for success, grassroots development projects should maintain an equilibrium with available resources. Because expensive oil imports, well beyond the earnings of most villagers, are required to operate machines, participatory development strategies often apply **labor-intensive technologies** using human and animal power, wind, or water instead of modern machinery. Pick-and-shovel technology poses less threat to the natural environment—a problem that faced most developing world villages at the end of the twentieth century. Growing domestic animal and human populations have produced chronic erosion and deforestation. Labor-intensive answers include planting trees to replace those used for firewood. Also, villagers can raise fodder for their animals instead of letting them forage and destroy the plants needed to retain soil during the rainy season.

Participatory development advocates do not decry all of an industrial economy's technologies. Those based on renewable resources can prove useful, such as solar collectors for heating water and providing electricity. In addition, improved seeds and organic fertilizers produce more food. Technologies for controlling human fertility provide another example. These illustrations demonstrate the fact that technology by itself cannot work unless the local people decide to use it; for example, technologies limiting population growth will lower the birthrate only in those villages where there is a good chance children will survive. This is not the case where infant mortality rates remain high. Therefore, birth-control methodologies must be introduced as a part of a total, holistic strategy emphasizing improvements in primary medical care and food production. Such multifaceted programs in Bangladesh and India have proven that development can happen, and on a large scale, without industrialization. Kerala, a region at the southwestern tip of India, has carried out participatory development strategies for over three decades. The result has been an improvement in the region's quality-of-life indicators to the levels of high-middle-income countries: literacy has reached 100 percent, life expectancy stands at seventy years, and infant mortality has declined by 37 percent. These achievements have occurred even though Kerala's per capita income has remained very low, lower even than that for India as a whole, at around $330 in 1991 (Franke and Chasin 1994, ii).

Critiques from the Liberal Economics and Dependency Perspectives

Liberal economic theorists point out that, unlike machine-age technology, village-level sustainable development has not demonstrated the capacity to produce ongoing improvements in the standard of living on a countrywide basis. Economic growth projects will prove necessary at some point. Single village or even regional improvements in daily living are limited in their ability to distribute benefits and could lead to an economic dead end. In the long run, local needs and products must become part of a large-scale, ongoing, demand-and-supply cycle in which increased demand stimulates greater production thus lowering costs which, in turn, increases demand. So far, participatory development has proven to have local benefits only here and there. It can help if it does not detract from major investments. It will not produce the needed economic expansion in and of itself and, therefore, will take too long to improve the lives of people in large numbers.

Dependency perspective proponents applaud the goal of improving the poor's quality of life. Yet they hasten to point out that it is not possible to escape, in the long run, the world market economy's negative effects. Limiting the goal to providing improvements in daily living village by village constitutes a cop-out. It ignores the basic reason why the poor can only marginally improve their quality of life. The main problem is the stranglehold of the world's rich and powerful elites on local markets.

Sooner or later the products of local self-help projects, whether handicrafts or surplus food, will be undercut by multinational corporations that can use their size to charge lower prices in selected local markets. One example of how international firms can drive out locally produced goods occurred in Peru. For centuries, Andean women have used large squares of cloth to carry everything from babies to firewood. Village women wove the material with wool from their animals. The most energetic would supplement their families' incomes by selling the products of their own work in local markets. Now the vast majority of these carrying cloths consist of brightly colored acrylic material produced by a Japanese-owned subsidiary. This has resulted in further dependency on the industrialized world.

Matrix 5.1 summarizes the main points discussed in this chapter. The matrix and the discussion so far contrast the three perspectives. They also complement each other in explaining reasons for the success or failure of specific development projects. The following case study of Mollepata's irrigation channel provides an example.

CASE STUDY   From Peasants to Farmers—Development in the Peruvian Highlands

The successful irrigation project described here took place during the 1980s in four of the agricultural sectors outside the town of Mollepata, Peru. Lucia, who was introduced at the beginning of this chapter, lives in one of these sectors. The project shows how peasants took responsibility, made decisions, worked hard, and changed their lives for the better. It also illustrates that outside financial assistance and technical expertise can be effective when development professionals work with village people as partners and not as experts who make all the decisions. The peasants participating in the project seem to have changed with their experience. Assertive and proactive in meetings, they project confidence in their own decision making. They no longer wait for fate or some outside power to take action, such as a rich landowner or the government. In assuming responsibility for their own future, project participants have changed from peasants to farmers.

A Tale of Two Irrigation Channels

In 1981 the Andean Center for Development, Education, and Promotion (CADEP) began work in Mollepata. A local nongovernmental organization (NGO), CADEP had been working with peasants in several Andean towns since its founding in 1968 by the Archbishop of Cusco. As in other locations, CADEP workers began by organizing peasant committees who decided on actions they would take to improve their daily lives. CADEP leadership then located international NGO funding for the planned project.

Months of peasant meetings in Mollepata finally crystallized into a decision to rebuild *La Estrella*, "The Star," an irrigation channel that had been built in the early years

Matrix 5.1
ECONOMIC PERSPECTIVES MATRIX

	Liberal Economics	Dependency	Participatory Development
Goal(s)	Economic growth	Self-determination and economic growth	Quality of life improvements
Key Concept	Comparative advantage	Dependency	Sustainable development
Strategies	Industrialization, private funding, free trade	Industrialization, some public funding, stabilization of primary commodity prices and aid	Labor-intensive rural develop-ment, locally controlled; self-sufficiency; equilibrium with natural environment
"Best" Technology	Capital intensive	Capital intensive	Appropriate
Major Problems of Existing System	Mistaken policies, over-population	Maldistribution of wealth and power domestically and internationally	Blind use of industrial technology, maldistribution of wealth and power domestically and internationally
Sees Current International Economic System As:	Potentially benefiting all countries	Favoring the already industrialized economies	Favoring the already industrialized economies

of the twentieth century by a local hacendado, the owner of a large estate. La Estrella had brought water to some of Mollepata's agricultural sectors from a rapidly falling stream several kilometers away. The Committee to Rehabilitate La Estrella, called CORES, was organized with CADEP assistance to plan and make decisions about the project. CORES was made up of the men who would do the actual work because they lived in the agricultural sectors downhill from La Estrella and would benefit directly from its rebuilding.

The La Estrella rehabilitation project addressed the central factor of the cycle of underdevelopment—that is, the existence of a large subsistence sector in developing world economies. As a basic-needs development project, it focused on food production.

The CORES committee members worked hard and long because they clearly saw the connection between rebuilding La Estrella and improving their daily lives. In addressing subsistence directly, the project was less entangled in the cycle of under-development's other interrelated factors. It did not try to change one while the rest remained constant.

The La Estrella project avoided another pitfall inherent in the cycle because increasing productivity was not taken to mean producing products for international trade. The CORES committee began the project to produce more food to avoid famine. If enough extra food were grown and could be sold, so much the better, but rebuilding the irrigation channel was not specifically intended to increase productivity for market-ing purposes. This point may seem too fine a distinction since solving the food prob-lem would produce more crops from the same land and thus increase productivity by definition. Development projects focusing on increasing agricultural productivity, how-ever, often target cash crops, not food. Cash crops require favorable circumstances well beyond the villagers' control, involving the country's elite and the international market. The state's elite, such as exporters and the makers of government trade policy, affect the cash crop prices paid to villagers. Also, price fluctuations in the international mar-ket can have a direct effect on the livelihoods of local cash crop producers.

The La Estrella canal suffered from years of disuse and severe deterioration. Many sections were buried by landslides, a common occurrence in the rugged Andes. Previ-ously, the hacendado had paid for the canal's upkeep. This ceased with his "retirement" when the new leftist military government carried out a land reform policy after coming to power in a 1968 coup. Peasants benefiting from La Estrella had tried to keep it clear and repaired on their own but finally gave up. They needed to cooperate with one another but lacked practical experience in making decisions and taking action together for their mutual benefit, having lived for so long under the hacienda system. They also had no resources.

Mollepata's residents had suffered through a severe drought in the early 1980s. Given this fact, the decision to rebuild La Estrella may seem obvious with the clear vision of hindsight. Yet put in the context of when it was made, it took courage and more than a little desperation. Ahead were years of extraordinarily backbreaking labor, even more than the CORES committee members anticipated. Their work on the chan-nel was in addition to that already needed for sustenance, such as raising crops.

The decision was made more difficult by the dismal failure of another canal proj-ect in Mollepata, this one sponsored by the Peruvian government in the 1970s. Called *Canal Nuevo*, or "New Canal," this previous project had squandered years of peasant time and effort. Originally it was to have been bigger and better than the old hacendado channel. Canal Nuevo symbolized the progress promised by the new Peru. Unencum-bered by a feudal past, the government would ensure a bright new future. The new canal would be wider, at about four feet across, and straighter, enabling it to carry water at 1,000 liters per second, contrasted with La Estrella's 200.

Funded by a $5 million Inter-American Bank loan, Canal Nuevo was built using modern heavy equipment moved from the coast at great expense, as well as peasant labor. The contractor chosen to design and construct the project came from Lima,

Peru's coastal capital city, and had no prior experience in the mountains. Work, which began in 1974, was to take fifteen months. Six years later, Canal Nuevo was completed, but within three weeks water ceased flowing after a landslide. After two more years of futile efforts to clear rubble and repair damage from landslides, the government quit the project.

La Estrella's peasant planners and workers started from where they were with their own skills and technology. When outside technical assistance and aid were brought in, they supported what already was available. In contrast, the Canal Nuevo, while having increased agricultural production as its aim, was designed not by the people who would have to use and maintain it. Canal Nuevo was planned and built as a capital formation infrastructure project by outsiders. It was defeated by the next factor in the cycle of underdevelopment, the human services factor, because the construction firm from the coast had no experience in building irrigation channels in the Andean highlands. The firm did have heavy equipment and well-educated engineers, but this human and physical capital proved ineffectual.

Local Initiative

In 1984 the 105 families committed to rebuilding La Estrella began the task. They negotiated how much work time each person was to contribute using Andean cultural practices dating from before the Spanish conquest. Called *ayni* in Quechua, this mutually agreed upon reciprocal work arrangement applied when cooperation was needed, such as during harvests. Each month a group of men would climb to over 13,000 feet where the canal began diverting river water. This took about eight hours. They carried hand tools and enough food for the three days or more they would spend away from home. The men slept in the canal itself, their only shelter from cold Andean nights.

By 1985, after months of work, the men of CORES decided the undertaking was too great for them to complete on their own. In 1986 CADEP found funding from AGROACCION, a private German international aid organization. Jan Hendricks, an irrigation engineer who spoke Spanish and had built irrigation projects in mountainous regions, was hired to design and work on the La Estrella rehabilitation project. Unlike Canal Nuevo, several varying construction techniques were used, given the differences in terrain; for example, in one section unusually susceptible to landslides, large pipes were connected and buried underground over a 400-meter stretch. Getting each pipe to the site required tying it on logs and having it carried uphill several kilometers by twenty-four or more men. Another technology, in this case Incan, provided the precedent for braking the destructive force of rushing water in those sections where it plunged for hundreds of feet. Large rocks were set in the canal bed and held in place not by cement, which would erode, but by moss. As a result of such traditional construction techniques, some Incan canals are still functioning elsewhere in Peru.

An additional factor affecting development, social cohesion, depends on mutual respect among a society's multiple ethnicities. That such respect can help development is illustrated by the importance of traditional Quechua cultural practices to La Estrella's success. They clearly and concretely illustrate that applying traditional methods can prove positive in an effective development strategy. Proud of their Incan heritage, the villagers used their ancestors' canal construction techniques, which were appropriate in the Andes. *Ayni*, Quechua work-sharing practices, also proved necessary since it took years of labor to complete the project. Canal Nuevo, in contrast, was designed and built by Peru's Spanish-speaking elite with Mollepata's residents supplying only hand labor. Treating the local people like peasants and ignoring their fears of landslides contributed to the New Canal's failure.

As work continued, men from two additional local sectors were asked to join CORES. Because their fields lay downhill from the planned route, they too could benefit from the completed canal. After much discussion, one sector accepted while the other cited the failure of Canal Nuevo as its reason for refusing. The mostly pick-and-shovel project took until 1990 to complete, and since then La Estrella's water has never ceased to flow. Two farmers from each of the four sectors in CORES have been trained as technicians to clear and maintain the canal. They also regulate the water's increased volume during the rainy season by opening sliding outlet hatches built into the sides of the canal (an engineering design not built into Canal Nuevo). For the first time, the farmers of CORES produced two crops in 1993 because they had a source of water lasting throughout the growing season.

The Mollepata case study illustrates points made in the previous chapter, but with a positive twist. Previous information and concepts explained why development remains so difficult to achieve in many parts of the world by pointing out the factors contributing to the cycle of underdevelopment. However, applying the same concepts to the rehabilitation of La Estrella can explain its success. In the context of local decision making, outside aid and technical assistance proved vital to the project. Rebuilding the canal became a full partnership between CORES, CADEP, Jan Hendricks (the European engineer), and a German-based international NGO which provided the funding. The fact that the technicians have kept La Estrella in repair years after the canal began functioning shows the effectiveness of a local, regional, and international partnership.

Summary

The La Estrella case study illustrates the fact that a basic-needs strategy can result in effective development projects. Clearly the economic growth strategy has worked over time in high- and some middle-income economies. Yet in the contemporary context of poverty characterized by underdevelopment's multiple factors, a strategy designed to meet basic needs provides viable, low-cost options. As Canal Nuevo shows, technologies that work in the industrial world must be applied selectively, with caution, and only on a scale appropriate to the local context. In contrast, CORES and CADEP used outside help as needed, such as the huge pipes to carry water underground in a landslide prone section of the canal. This example illustrates that industrial technology is not necessarily incompatible with a basic-needs strategy, but the case study also crystallizes differences between the two approaches to development. Understanding economic growth and basic-needs development strategies provides the basis for the contrasting perspectives people use in responding to the global issue of economic development, as explained below.

THE THREE ECONOMIC PERSPECTIVES APPLIED TO THE CASE STUDY

The case study describes villagers' different experiences with two irrigation projects in Mollepata, Peru. One produced a failure and the other produced more food crops. The first project, Canal Nuevo, was a failure due to the misapplication of resources, which is common in all too many development projects. The other, La Estrella, demonstrated that major accomplishments can result from the combination of effective local leadership and dedicated development workers, supported by outside funding and technical expertise. As the remainder of this chapter will show, the three economic perspectives—liberal economics, dependency, and participatory development—provide varying explanations for the success in Mollepata.

A View from the Liberal Economics Perspective
La Estrella illustrates how effectively privately designed and organized projects can work without government regulation and intervention; however, the canal does not provide a model for countrywide development. Large-scale industrialization remains the only proven method for lifting whole populations out of poverty.

Free-market principles could explain the success in Mollepata by pointing out that its rewards went directly to those residents who took the initiative and worked hard for years digging the irrigation channel. Now that the steady supply of water enables them to produce a surplus, they can sell it in the Cusco city market at a price they negotiate themselves. Thus, those who did the work on the canal are earning the profits. Since the land they work is their own, they had an incentive to invest in it and build the channel. It was not a government project. La Estrella's success emphasizes private, individual intiative without government interference. The supply-and-demand principle determines the price for Mollepata's surplus potatoes and other products and thus their producers can make a profit. An observer should question, however, whether to invest scarce investment capital for many local projects while there is such a need for large-scale development.

A View from the Dependency Perspective
The irrigation project avoided the debilitating effects of cash crop production, which benefit the rich and powerful both domestically and internationally. It proves the poor are capable and competent, thus dispelling the myth that elites are needed to provide leadership.

Dependency theory highlights the fact that the village of Mollepata is relatively isolated. It lies in the Andes, a three- to four-day drive up winding roads from Peru's port city of Lima. Its residents are not enmeshed in producing cash crops for sale overseas, nor are they heavily in debt to a local large landowner. The two local hacendados moved away as a result of a leftist government's policies in the 1970s and, after a failed attempt at communal ownership, the land was turned over to its residents. Therefore, the negative effects of a domestic dual economy do not apply. Neither does its parallel in the international economic system based, as in a dual economy, on the unequal exchange of cash crops for industrial goods. Mollepata's residents experience less of the oppressive polarization between the powerless and the powerful than elsewhere in the developing world. In the context, outside help was directed by and in the interest of the villagers themselves. International NGO financing and technical assistance supported decisions made by CADEP and the project beneficiaries. Inequality did not distort the relationship between those who did the work and those who received the benefits.

A View from the Participatory Development Perspective
The contrast between Canal Nuevo and La Estrella shows that basic-needs projects are the only kind that make sense for the majority of the world's people. Industrialization with its long-term promise of trickle-down benefits has not and will not solve the problems inherent in global poverty.

Mollepata's experience fits all participatory development principles; that is, beneficiary decision making to improve their daily lives, available technology, and environmental compatibility. CADEP, a nonprofit private development organization based in Cusco, helped organize the residents of the agricultural sectors into a decision-making committee. They argued, debated, decided, and carried out their own plan, advised all along by CADEP development workers. Local leadership emerged from this process.

For a project to remain in operation, village people will have to maintain it without outside help. Therefore, the second principle of participatory development emphasizes using technology currently available to villagers. This applies to La Estrella since most of the work was done with picks and shovels. In addition, ancient Incan building techniques were used; for example, large stones were dug into the channel bed to break the fall of water when it cascaded steeply downhill. This was vital because fast-flowing water will erode the sides of even concrete-lined conduits.

The irrigation canal's success can also be attributed to participatory development's third principle: it was designed to have a minimum impact on the natural environment. Upkeep of the canal does not require pumps or other machinery that need fossil fuels. The technicians, village people trained to monitor and maintain the canal, regulate the flow of water by using sliding overflow hatches. The hatches are operated by pulling up on a handle. The overflow outlets diminish the danger during the rainy season of fast-flowing water that could erode the channel.

To summarize, each of the three perspectives highlights different reasons for La Estrella's success. Some of the reasoning overlaps, such as the point that the people who planned and worked on the project also received the benefits. Advocates of all three perspectives would see this as a reason for success but would have differing explanations: participatory development emphasizes local decision making; dependency aims to redress inequality; and liberal economics assumes the efficiency of personal financial incentives and private, nongovernmental decision making. The analysis indicates that the design of development projects would benefit from taking all three perspectives into account.

TERMS AND CONCEPTS

Comparative advantage *88*
Dependency *90*
Economies of scale *89*
Free trade *88*
Labor-intensive technologies *97*
Market economics *87*

Neoimperialism/neocolonialism *90*
New International Economic Order (NIEO) *92*
Participatory development *95*
Protectionism *89*
Specialization *89*
Subsidies *93*

DISCUSSION QUESTIONS

1. Which perspective do you think best explains the success of the irrigation project in Mollepata, Peru: liberal economics, dependency, or participatory development? Give reasons to support your answer.
2. What do the liberal economics and dependency perspectives have in common? The dependency and participatory development perspectives? Explain your reasoning.
3. Choose a current problem facing low-income states, such as indebtedness or population growth. How would each of the three perspectives discussed in this chapter explain its cause? What would each suggest as a solution to the problem?
4. List some of the common assumptions about world poverty made by people you know. Which perspective does each assumption reflect?
5. In your opinion, should U.S. development policies be based on liberal economics, dependency, or participatory development? Why do you think so? What assumption does your view reflect about the U.S. role in fostering world development?

RESEARCH PROJECTS

1. Read several articles about world poverty and determine which perspective each author takes on the issue of economic development.
2. Write a short list of questions about the causes of world poverty from the point of view of each perspective. Pose the questions to at least five people and record their answers. What perspectives do the respondents seem to take?
3. Research the position of the United States on a current trade issue, such as copyright ownership. Which perspective does the U.S. position reflect?
4. Choose a country and gather some information about its trade pattern. What are its major trading partners? What does the state import and export? Given the trade patterns and economic interests of the state, which perspective would its people be most likely to support?
5. Find several examples of development projects (successful or unsuccessful). Which perspectives do they reflect? How can you use the perspectives to explain the success or failure of each project?

INTERNET RESOURCES

Japan International Cooperation Agency: http://www.jica.go.jp The Japan International Cooperation Agency, a unit of Japan's Official Development Assistance Program, provides an extended explanation of participatory development in its report "Participatory Development and Good Governance."

U.S. Agency for International Development: http://www.info.usaid.gov In addition to providing maps, charts, and other data, this colorful site includes information on the agency's projects.

World Business Council for Sustainable Development: http://www.wbcsd.org This site presents a wide range of explanatory material discussed from a business point of view and thematically organized under topics such as "Energy and Climate." It has case studies under the topic "Sustainable Livelihoods."

Third World Network: http://www.twnside.org.sg/ The site includes articles on current development issues written by people in the developing world.

Society for International Development: http://www.sidint.org This NGO site includes brief descriptions about local NGOs in many countries and their activities.

CHAPTER 6

Human Ecological Sustainability

Homo sapiens is one of the most successful species on Earth in a number of respects. Members of this species can live in virtually all climatic zones—from the Arctic to the tropics and from deserts to swamps. They are omnivorous and have developed technologies, or tool kits, that allow them to build shelters, process foods, and provide elaborate health care. Consequently, the number of people on Earth has grown to a historic level, but population growth is not the only consequence of this success. The human race has also changed the planet. The human impact on the natural environment has effects not only on the biological reality of humans, but also on their cultural, economic, and political realities. With this awareness, the research of biologists, chemists, and geoscientists becomes key to understanding these new issues.

This chapter discusses typical human adaptations to nature in order to analyze their effects. People, in their respective adaptations, can either use the land without using it up or work the land and cause a myriad of problems. Pressing problems of health, food, and pollution, which have plagued the last century, have caused widespread human misery. The case study involving the Amazonian rain forest in Brazil, presented at the end of this chapter, illustrates and defines many of the world's ecological concerns. It must be remembered that humans are very much part of their environments.

ECOSYSTEMS: THE NATURE OF ENVIRONMENT

In 1859 Thomas Austin, an Australian farmer, imported twenty-four rabbits from his native Britain. These common European animals are placentals, meaning that they give birth to developed young. Placentals were unknown on the Australian continent, which is home to an entirely different form of mammal, the marsupial, which give birth to immature young that grow in external pouches. Soon Mr. Austin's rabbits were loose and breeding "like rabbits." With the local predators, dingoes and eagles, decimated by European hunters, the descendents of Mr. Austin's rabbits spread throughout the southern half of the continent, killing small mammals and much of the plant life in the semi-arid areas that had been damaged by the sheep (also imported). Foxes, brought from Europe for fox hunting, also went free and followed the tasty rabbits. Soon the region was denuded of much of its plant life, birds, tortoises, and small marsupials, leaving a decimated landscape behind. In the twentieth century myxomatosis, a virus fatal to rabbits, was spread throughout the continent as a means for control. While this limited the population for a while, the disease spread to Europe and killed valued rabbits there. Currently Australian government scientists are experimenting with new biological controls, including the virus RCV (rabbit calicivirus), which is quickly deadly to infected rabbits, but offers concerns for long-run consequences and efficacy. (Vandenbeld 1988, 252–55, Anderson and Nowak 1997, 34–37)

This oft-told tale of nineteenth-century Australian history illustrates several important concepts of ecological importance. First, Mr. Austin did not set out to destroy the ecosystem of southern Australia with rabbits. He was merely trying to re-create the environment of his birth in this new world, and it never occurred to him that the small, nonaggressive animals could be an environmental threat. More important was the fit of the rabbits within the existing environment, which was either unknown to or not considered by Mr. Austin at the time. These rabbits found a niche that was virtually void of predators and filled with food. They thus became aggressors in this particular setting. Most important, however, was the concept of system or interconnectedness, in that the rabbits became a particularly dangerous threat to the plants. Similarly, the rabbits were protected from predators, since farmers had killed off the dingoes and eagles which, they believed, were killing their domesticated, and economically important, sheep. The increasing loss of plants allowed rapid erosion, further threatening animals and plant life in the area. Then the solution to the problem created new problems, spreading disease to other areas which became connected to the previously isolated continent through human development. The introduction of the twenty-four seemingly harmless rabbits upset an ecosystem and had far-reaching consequences.

Interrelationship of Environmental Systems

All environments are composed of complex interconnections, called **ecosystems**, between plants, animals, and physical and chemical factors. The most important part of the word ecosystem, as the term implies, is the interrelatedness of the elements within the system. When one element changes, others may be modified in turn. For example, a change of the acidity of the water in a stream will affect the plants that depend on that water, the animals that depend upon those plants, and the people who depend on the plants, animals, and water. The interrelationship of all plants and animals and their physical and chemical environment within a region is a specific ecosystem. In the larger sense, the Earth is also an ecosystem since no part of the world is truly isolated from the other parts.

Many of the changes in ecosystems are begun by human agency but end in consequences well beyond human expectation or control. In some places, populations appear to be nearing a critical level and, perhaps, their **carrying capacity**—the number of people who can be supported indefinitely in a given environment with a given technology and culture. For example, in India or Bangladesh, where huge populations have decimated forests, polluted waters, and consumed soils, poverty and disease are uncontrolled, and the capacity to feed and house the number of people who are born is seriously strained.

The world resources are finite, yet all people share the resources. We know that the **commons**—areas publicly owned and open for general use—are not typically well tended. Often individual interests override the common good. Environmental changes which bring short-term benefits for individuals or communities can often lead to long-term devastation for many more people. Biologist Garrett Hardin described this trend in the article "The Tragedy of the Commons," published in the journal *Science* (1968). People using public land for grazing animals or similar economic gain, for example, will overuse these areas while protecting the lands they privately own. In this view, individual self-interest triumphs over communal good, and the common areas of the globe steadily degrade. The full impact of such a view is most vivid in the use of the oceans as a dumping ground for garbage and the atmosphere as a recipient of chemical pollutants. A more complex issue is the need for the conservation of areas, such as temperate and tropical rain forests, which are located within individual states but whose environmental stability is crucial to the well-being of people well beyond the borders of those states. Clearly, abuses of all these commons have become global issues.

HUMANS AND THE ENVIRONMENT

The major cultural and economic adaptations used by humans to survive in their environments include foraging, pastoralism, agriculturalism, and industrialism (see Chapter 2). Each of these adaptations has advantages and disadvantages in terms of its ecological effects on Earth's environments.

Foraging

Foraging depends primarily on the hunting of wild animals and the gathering of wild plants. As the sole means of human survival for more than a million years, it has been a successful form of adaptation. It is also successful ecologically, since its form of human food procurement is in balance with the natural environment.

The traditional strategy of the Inuit, the San of the Kalahari, and aboriginal Australians, among others, foraging is characterized by low populations which are dispersed over large areas. Foragers are constantly moving and, therefore, cause little disruption to the natural environment. There are no centers of pollution since there are no permanent houses or garbage dumps. People have simple forms of technology and use little energy because humans provide most of the labor themselves. Shortly after foragers move their camps, the actions of other animals and natural forces remove what they have left behind. While there is little permanent damage to the natural environment through this way of life, foraging cannot support large populations, and many such societies have been forced to practice infanticide in order to stay below the carrying capacity of their environments.

Pastoralism

Pastoralists—people who focus their economies on specific domesticated animals—include the Bedouins (camels), the Nuer (cattle), the Sami (reindeer), and the Kurds (sheep and goats). These cultures can support larger, more dense populations than foragers, but the numbers are still far below those of agricultural societies. Pastoralists are often migratory, leading their animals to new pastures. Compared to foragers, their technology is more specialized but still not complex, and their energy use includes animal power as well as human labor. Their environmental uses, however, are more demanding in an ecological sense: herd animals exploit plants and pollute water, and large animals demand abundant quantities of land to survive.

Agriculturalism

People who focus on domesticated plants are horticulturalists or, if they use complex technology, agriculturalists. They share in kind, if not degree, the exploitation of the environment and the susceptibility to diseases that come with plant cultivation.

An essential element of agriculturalism is the ability of the group to develop large, dense, sedentary populations. A large number of people can live using a much smaller region than foragers. Horticulturalists, using slash-and-burn techniques, can destroy large areas of forests, leach the nutrients out of fields, and pollute the air with smoke. Agricultural techniques increase the yield of fields and can feed far more people in smaller areas, but there are environmental costs. The use of fertilizers and plow animals increase the pollution of the lands dramatically. Denser human settlements produce more garbage and human waste, which must be disposed of to prevent health disasters. Water is also an issue, and irrigation techniques often pollute water supplies just as they increase crop yield. Technology in these societies can be quite complex, and some of the new tools, from metallurgy to fossil fuels, create their own forms of pollution.

Industrialism

Industrialism is the primary subsistence strategy of the world system today. While many still live in less technologically complex societies, millions of people live in industrialized societies. All people, however, are influenced to some degree by industrialism. It is the only known economic strategy that can support the current population of the world.

This form of the subsistence strategy depends on the production of goods through the use of fossil fuels. From the coal that fueled the beginning of the Industrial Revolution to the petroleum base of contemporary industry, carbon-based fuels have allowed technological advances previously thought impossible.

One social result of the development of industrialism is that a vast inequality exists between those who can use fossil fuels and those who cannot. This is true both within industrialized societies and between industrial and nonindustrial countries. In either case, a significant percentage of the population must still be involved in intensive agriculture or agribusiness in order to feed the large population of people maintained by this type of society. A broad societal difference between rural and urban life is created. Between countries, the nonindustrialized states are generally poor and dependent upon industrialized states for technological improvement. While there are signs of serious problems in parts of the world, the upper limits of the carrying capacity of industrialism as a world strategy have not yet been reached.

The long-term sustainability of industrialization, as it is currently practiced, is a serious concern. The ecological threats include extensive pollution from fossil fuel use, high-density human waste, and chemical contamination. In addition, as finite amounts of oil and coal are depleted, the extraction techniques bring more environmental change. Parts of the world appear incapable of growing enough food for their increasing populations. The rush to economic growth through industrialization and cash cropping has increased the use of agricultural lands for other purposes, such as housing developments, shopping centers, and light industry.

THREATS TO CRITICAL RESOURCES

As mammals, humans cannot survive without numerous basic environmental resources, including breathable air, potable water, and arable lands. Without these resources, humans and other animal life on Earth would die. Humans also need heat, clothing, and the plants and animals of the planet. Some animals and plants are used directly as food, while others are vital to the continuity of the ecosystem. Industrialism has improved the lives of millions of people, allowing increases in food, population, and technological goods. This has a cost, however. Globally, industrialization has threatened all of the ecological essentials of human life. When looking individually at issues of specific environmental domains, it must be made clear that each is interlinked with the other. Earth's ecology does not respect state boundaries. Air, water, land, plants, and animals exist throughout the globe, and environmental threats to any one of these resources are carried from one state to many others.

Air

The air, perhaps, is the ultimate common, but it is often taken for granted. The atmosphere that envelops the globe is essential to the survival of all living things. This unique blend of elements has no barrier walls and so the modification of any part of it can alter all its other parts and negatively affect the whole world. Air pollution comes from industry and urban life, from automobile emissions, factory outflows, and oil-, coal-, and wood-burning fuels. National and regional laws restricting the type of fuels that can be used and limiting the amount of allowable discharge of pollutants are now common in industrialized states. Most of these rules look at the local environment and react to immediate problems since there are higher concentrations around, and downwind of, sources of emission. However, global issues that threaten the future of the world's environment remain largely unchecked. Increased levels of carbon dioxide and other gases in the atmosphere, as well as the depletion of ozone, are among the long-term challenges to the well-being of the planet.

Carbon Dioxide **Carbon dioxide** (CO_2), is a colorless, odorless gas which makes up over 350 parts per million of the atmospheric gases. A natural part of the atmosphere, it is used by plants as a necessary part of their respiration. The mere existence of CO_2 does not pose a problem; in fact, the world as we know it depends on this gas. The relative increase in CO_2 in the delicate mix of the environment, however, is a problem. The burning of carbon-based fossil fuels in factories, automobile emissions, and power plants spews massive amounts of CO_2 into the atmosphere. Chemists estimate that there has been a 30 percent increase in CO_2 concentrations in the atmosphere since 1800 (Hileman 1995, 19).

An additional factor is the loss of plant life from the mass destruction of rain forests, decreasing the rate of breakdown of carbon dioxide into oxygen and carbon. More CO_2 is produced and less is removed from the atmosphere through photosynthesis. Therefore, the percentage of carbon dioxide in the air has increased. One major threat of CO_2 buildup is the greenhouse effect, which many scientists fear will advance a climatic change involving increased global temperatures.

Global Warming **Global warming** refers to small but regular and significant increases in the temperature of the Earth. Atmospheric gases, including CO_2, methane, ozone, and chlorofluorocarbons, which scientists call **greenhouse gases**, allow the short-wavelength radiation from the sun to pass through the atmosphere and reach the Earth. Like the glass in a greenhouse, short-wave radiation passes through and warms the inside. The greenhouse gases, however, absorb and trap the infrared radiation that is emitted from the planet. With increased amounts of greenhouse gases in the atmosphere, less energy escapes back into space. The buildup of this increased capture of light energy warms the general atmosphere. Scientific models largely support an increase in this phenomenon in the foreseeable future if fossil fuel emissions continue at the present or increased levels (Hileman 1995, 18). The **United Nations Environment Program (UNEP)**, the **World Health Organization (WHO)**, and the World Meteorological Organization (WMO) issued a joint report in 1996 which warned against a "wait-and-see approach," since health problems from increased heat waves and insect-carried diseases could quickly follow global warming. They estimate that from three to six times as many deaths from severe heat in cities like New York could be expected by 2050 (Cushman 1996, 2).

To the average person, an increase in three or four degrees Celsius in a century hardly seems cause for alarm. After all, humans have survived through the ice ages with far less complex technology. It is humans' dependency on technology, however, that has made this a serious concern. Not only has industrialization caused the problem, but it also makes the human consequences far more severe. The estimated change in temperature within the complex climatic system would also trigger a rise in sea levels (flooding low-lying lands), severe heat waves, and the disruption of agriculture in tropical and subtropical areas (Hileman 1995, 19). An International Panel on Climate Change (IPCC) document, "Climate Change 2001" (Watson 2001), reports a 0.6 degree Celsius increase in average temperature during the twentieth century. The warmest decade of the warm century was the last, supporting the scientists' models. Further, a 0.1 to 0.2 meter increase in sea level was noted.

While the potential effects on glaciers in the north and ice packs in Antarctica, on storms and prevailing wind streams, on changes in ocean circulation patterns, and on particular periodic climatic events, such as the Pacific "El Nino," are still being debated by some climatologists, evidence is growing in support of the theories that anticipate such changes. To be sure, the rise in sea levels will threaten some urban regions, such as New Orleans and the delta of Bangladesh, and other densely populated areas, causing the dislocation of millions of people. The loss of agricultural potential would also be devastating in a heavily populated world, as would the destruction from more frequent and more violent storms and other severe weather patterns.

Virtually all of the proposed solutions to global warming lie in the realm of prevention. International guidelines limiting the release of greenhouse gases into the atmosphere and the use of fossil fuels in industry and automobiles are advanced as essential first steps. It is a truism of science that putting any system that has been modified back into a former state takes both great skill and good fortune. Once a system as complex as global warming is fully under way, it would be nearly impossible to reverse it. Carbon dioxide released into the atmosphere will remain there for decades, and sea levels will fall only with the refreezing of water into glaciers. Modifications in plants, landforms, and waterways would create their own climatic events. Clearly, in a systemic change like this, using technology to fix individual problems as they arise will not do much to reverse the pattern of global warming.

Restrictions on the use of fossil fuel, then, seem necessary, but such limits would restrict the economic growth of the developed and developing world. The vast volume of such fossil fuel emissions comes from the developed world, particularly the United States. The United Nations in 1995 reported that the United States was the world's greatest polluter, emitting four times as much CO_2 as Japan. Russia, the second most polluting country, emits 73 percent of the U.S. total, and China, the third, emits 52 percent (United Nations 1995, 37, 91, 154, 194). Since restricting the use of fossil fuels would mean a significant slowdown in U.S. industrial growth, neither global warming nor the necessary solution will be easy for the world.

Some progress has been made in developing international limits on the emission of greenhouse gases. The 1997 Kyoto Protocol on Climate Change, which came out of an international meeting held in Kyoto, Japan, sets emissions targets for the developed nations. Between the years 2008 and 2012, the industrial powers are mandated to decrease their emissions of six greenhouse gases, including carbon dioxide, to an assigned percentage below their 1990 emissions levels. The U.S. goal was set at 7 percent. The protocol also encourages the development of such projects as reforestation which will clean the atmosphere. To date the United States has not agreed to be a part of the protocol, and its CO_2 emissions have not decreased. European countries, however, have supported the protocol and are showing success in decreasing emission. While the results will be less far reaching than many environmentalists want, the conference establishes an agreement that global warming is a critical world problem that needs international action.

Ozone Depletion   Another major international concern is **ozone depletion**. The depletion of the ozone layer is a second atmospheric issue that has captured headlines in recent years and has been the subject of important international agreements. While high ozone levels in the atmosphere often cause health care officials in big cities to announce "ozone alerts" and recommend that people with respiratory problems remain indoors, the opposite problem exists higher above the Earth. The ozone level in the lower stratosphere has thinned dramatically, especially in the most outermost areas of the world, near the poles. These decreased concentrations are described as "holes" in the ozone. These holes have begun to form in this protective layer which protects life on Earth from destructive ultraviolet rays. Without protection, radiation can cause skin cancers, cataracts, problems in the immune system, and increased mutations in animals. It can also disrupt photosynthesis in plants. This problem is of particular concern in very sunny areas, such as much of Australia. Maintaining the ozone layer is necessary for the continuation of the contemporary pattern of life on Earth.

Scientists Mario Molina, Paul Crutzen, and F. Sherwood Rowland shared the 1995 Noble Prize in Chemistry for their work in explaining the process of ozone depletion and predicting the repercussions. Chlorofluorocarbons (CFCs) chemically break down ozone (O_3). The ultimate proof of the problem has been the expanding hole in the ozone layer first noticed in 1985, over Antarctica. More recently, a similar weakening in the north has also become quite severe.

Many world leaders, scientists, and politicians, believe that damage to the ozone layer is happening and that it has potentially deadly results. Once again the solution seems to lie in the prevention of further damage. In 1987 the industrialized nations signed the Montreal Protocol on Substances That Deplete the Ozone Layer. The treaty mandated the end of the production of CFCs, which account for over 70 percent of the chemical damage, by 2000. In 1992 the date was moved up to January 1, 1996. In the developed world, CFCs had been widely used in refrigerants and aerosol-spray propellants. It has been estimated that the United States, alone, would spend about $100 billion to end CFC use (Alder, Cazamias, and Monnack 1995, 428). The ban on CFCs has been very successful. While a steep decline in CFCs in the atmosphere has not yet occurred, the Scientific Assessment of Ozone Depletion in 2002 announced that it appeared that the Montreal Protocol was working since CFCs were no longer increasing in the atmosphere and that within fifty years, the normal protective concentrations of ozone would be regained.

Water

In addition to clean air, human survival depends on abundant, clean water. More of the surface of this planet is covered with water than dry land; consequently, the Earth is seen as a blue sphere from outer space. The problem is not the quantity of water on Earth, but its quality and distribution.

Oceanic pollution and overuse are a first concern. The oceans are an integral part of the human commons, covering about 70 percent of the Earth's surface. A healthy ocean is important for climatic stability, adequate food supply, healthy tourist industries, and access to new sources of minerals and other resources for potential medical cures. According to Sylvia Earle, a former chief scientist of the National Oceanic and Atmospheric Administration, "The *living* ocean drives planetary chemistry, governs climate and weather, and otherwise provides the cornerstone of the life-support system for all creatures on our planet, from deep-sea starfish to desert sagebrush. . . . If the sea is sick, we'll feel it. If it dies, we die." (1995, xii).

Two major and conflicting problems stand out: (1) the oceans are being used as dumping grounds for industrial wastes, and (2) oceanic resources are being overutilized. The oceans serve as dumps for the world's wastes both incidentally and intentionally. Incidentally, runoff from urban regions located near ocean shores and from nearby farms and industries goes into the oceans and creates pollution in the coastal regions. Some of the urban-area beaches in New York and New Jersey have been closed to summer swimmers due to high fecal contamination of the waters or dangerous medical wastes on the shores. These problems endanger the health of millions and the economic livelihood of many others as well. Oil spills from accidental tanker collisions and leaks in drilling operations add to the pollution.

Intentional dumping of hazardous wastes, sewage discharge, and garbage from coastal cities into the seas has long been practiced under the mistaken notion that the vastness of the oceans would allow relatively small amounts of waste to dissipate and harmlessly disappear. Until recently, coastal sludge has been dredged and redeposited farther out at sea on the assumption that this would protect the shore. Obviously, the fact that the ocean is a complex ecosystem dooms such actions to failure. Some parts of the Atlantic, just east of the New Jersey shore, have been labeled "dead" as a result of dumping practices that were outlawed in the United States in 1992. Even nuclear wastes have been discarded in the ocean by such industrial countries as Russia and the United States.

The United Nations, through UNEP and the International Maritime Organization, has taken a lead in promoting rules of the uses of the oceans and advising on techniques for limiting pollution (Carroll 1996, 46). The Regional Seas Program of UNEP has enabled states that share ocean resources to work together to protect them. The United Nations declared 1998 the International Year of the Oceans in order to highlight the problem and call for increased research and awareness. The overall 1994 treaty that addresses these and other problems unique to the oceans is called the UN Convention on the **Law of the Sea**. This long-debated UN-supported treaty established general rules for conduct in the oceans. It also codified the definition of a twelve-mile limit of state control over coastal waters and an exclusive economic zone in which the state has rights over natural resources. As with all such international agreements, however, the goodwill of the signers is essential to the success of the mission, and few sanctions exist that fully counter national interests.

A second major concern is the availability of sufficient **potable water**. Clean drinking water is the problem that comes closest to home. Life cannot continue without access to usable water. Not all water can be used, however, and most water on Earth can be found in the oceans or frozen in the poles. Available non-saltwater is found in rain, lakes, rivers, and underground in aquifers. Rain, which replenishes streams, reservoirs, and underground reserves, provides most of the potable water that people drink. Acid rain and air pollution can taint the water before it ever reaches the ground. In the rivers and lakes, this water can be further contaminated by industrial wastes, chemical and biological fertilizer runoff from agriculture, human wastes from urban communities, and numerous other pollutants. Illness, and even death, can result from drinking such untreated water.

Aquifers, caches of water found in rock cavities underground, provide the spring and well waters which are valued for their purity. For most of human existence, aquifers have supplied a seemingly endless source of drinkable water. Today, however, the same types of pollutants that affect surface waters seep into the earth, and wells in many parts of the world have become toxic. Another threat to the aquifers is overuse. The demand for water for industries, irrigation, and urban populations has ballooned since World War II, and water shortages are becoming commonplace even in the wealthiest areas. Irrigation water is rationed in part of the western United States. Also, demand for water from the Colorado River, which flows through the southwestern United States and northern Mexico, has caused disputes between the two countries and between U.S. states, including California and Arizona.

Acid rain is a third major issue. Rain is a major source of freshwater. Evaporation and rain are two aspects of the natural recycling of water, as runoffs from melted snows join with rain and replenish lakes and streams. When the rain turns toxic, the entire system is in trouble. A variety of pollutants have tainted rainwaters, but one of the most commonly discussed is sulfuric acid, which causes acid rain. Sulfur dioxide (SO_2), an acidic chemical, is emitted from factories burning sulfur-containing coal and from diesel fuels. The sulfur dioxide in the smoke chemically reacts with the water in the atmosphere to create sulfuric acid (H_2SO_4). This is maintained in the clouds and falls to Earth in the form of acid rain. The high acidity of this chemical can weaken or kill any plants and animals that are adapted to a less acidic environment. Additionally, fish and other aquatic life can be endangered by increasing acidity of the water in small lakes. In the 1970s, the Adirondack Mountains of New York were plagued by dying trees and lakes with dead fish, both poisoned by acid rains. Similar incidents in Germany, Russia, and Canada made this one of the first ecological issues brought to international attention.

Solutions to acid rain were sought in the industries producing the sulfuric acid. One solution factories had used to protect the areas surrounding the plants from the dirt and pollution of coal burning was the construction of extremely tall smokestacks, but these only intensified the problems of acid rain (Odum 1993, 121–22). Mandates for the use of alternative fuels, or so-called cleaner coals, sprang up in regions, and expensive refitting of plants did take place. In the 1980s, Western Europe restricted levels of SO_2 emissions, and many factories in the former Soviet Union switched from coal to natural gas or oil. Within a decade, reports of decreased pollution in the Arctic seemed to reflect success (Facts on File 1993, 1).

Land

While dry land covers a minority of the Earth's surface, it is the home of virtually all humanity. It also provides the breeding ground for most human food and the resource base for most industry. With the growth of the human population and industrialization, demands on the land have increased exponentially. Most land, unlike the oceans, is not commonly owned. Private and state ownership of specific land has become the norm, despite global implications of land degradations. The destruction of land through erosion, including deforestation and desertification, and toxic pollution continue to affect the world's climate and productivity.

Erosion is a primary concern for environmentalists. While poets have seen the Earth as eternal, scientists see the destruction of large parts of it through overuse or inappropriate use. Although it does seem to be increasing, this ecological devastation is not an invention of the twentieth century. Erosion, from deforestation and intensive agriculture, in inhabited parts of the American Southwest had already occurred by the thirteenth century. In Chaco Canyon, ancestors of the contemporary Pueblo people moved away from their cities and irrigated fields in the canyon after a dry spell made their modified environment too difficult.

The most vivid picture of devastating soil erosion, however, is that of the Dust Bowl of the American Midwest in the 1930s. Photographs, works of literature, and individual life histories remind us of the human pain caused by these environmental changes. The drought and loss of soil in one of the world's most important grain-growing areas caused population dislocations and added grief to the already stricken Depression years.

Fertile soils are delicate. The organic materials in soil are easily eroded by water and wind. Overgrazing, inappropriate farming techniques, and other disruptions leave land open to erosion without protection of the vegetation that could rebuild the fertility. The fact that the grain fields of the United States once again have become bountiful should not be taken, however, as proof that past harm can be easily overcome. Fertilizers can make up for soil depletion, but they create new problems of their own. Many scientists believe that the long-term health of the U.S. Midwest is threatened by the destruction of the aquifer, overuse of fertilizers, and urban growth. At this point, by nature and by human intervention, only one-quarter of the Earth's soils are suited for modern agriculture without intensive irrigation and fertilizer (Odum 1993, 139).

A major threat in many parts of the world today is **desertification**. Areas of the great deserts, including the Sahara, are growing, and grasslands, and similar marginal areas, are becoming arid. UNEP reported in 1984 that 35 percent of the Earth was in danger (Amstutz 1995, 438). Ten years later, the UN Convention to Combat Desertification (UNCCD) was established. The UN Food and Agriculture Organization (FAO, www.fao.org) estimates that more than 250 million people are harmed by this and as many as a billion others could be affected in the near future. The reasons for desertification include overgrazing and changing weather patterns after deforestation. The extensive grazing of cattle, or other herd animals, on such grasslands has destroyed the protective vegetation. In some areas, these lands can be purchased cheaply, used intensively for a finite amount of time, and abandoned by, often foreign, enterprises such as cattle ranching. Similar damage is done with **deforestation**, in which tropical forests are cut in order to create grazing areas for animals. In parts of Asia and South America, this has accounted for major soil degradation.

Environmentalists are also concerned about **toxic pollutants**. The pollution of the air and seas extends to the land. Modern industries, which by their nature create extensive amounts of potentially dangerous wastes, must be able to dispose of those wastes. In the past, landfills or waste dumps were widely employed. The garbage was simply buried in out-of-the-way lands and left to disintegrate.

The problems with this practice are evident today. Many of these wastes do not fully disintegrate, nor do they necessarily stay in place. Frequently, chemicals from these materials leach into the water supply and pollute areas far from the original dumps. In addition, many out-of-the-way areas are no longer remote with the extension of urban or suburban areas.

Laws in many wealthy countries now mandate that industries assume responsibility for the proper disposal of their pollutants. Cleanup is now the price of doing business, if the laws are enforced. In poorer nations, however, local and international industries function under no such laws or have no means of enforcing the ones they enact. Consequently, this can lower the price of doing business in these countries and attract foreign corporations. In at least one case, this did not free a multinational corporation in the face of an extraordinary disaster. Union Carbide paid about $0.5 billion in compensation for the deaths of more than 2,000 people in 1984, in Bhopal, India, following a leak in an insecticide plant. Despite this occasional reckoning, the pollution tragedies of the past in the industrialized world continue largely unabated in today's developing world.

Plants and Animals

Extinction, the complete loss of a biological species, is normal in the world ecosystem. The nature of evolution argues that animals and plants that fit in a particular environment continue to breed; those that have changed and become unfit, or those that have not changed in a changing environment and have become ecologically unfit, do not successfully reproduce and eventually become extinct. While each extinction might be a loss, each is not a threat to the world or an unnatural occurrence. The fate of most species that have existed on Earth is eventual extinction. The loss of dinosaurs, mammoths, and giant sloths is part of the natural history of the world. The contemporary ecosystem would not exist if extinctions had not occurred. Obviously, this does not mean that extinction is inherently good, but it clarifies that extinction, in its nature, is not inherently bad. The problem of the contemporary era is that human actions have created an artificial world environment that has dictated a broad and massive loss of plant and animal life without replacement. In other words, human interference with natural systems has created the world as it is now. It is the diversity of life on this planet that is threatened, and this type of extinction is both new and frightening.

A major focus of this concern involves deforestation, especially in the tropical rain forests, which are decreasing at an alarming rate. The loss of trees negatively affects the soil. In tropical regions, the soil level is particularly thin and fragile. The trees and the ecosystem supported by the soil are themselves very important. Temperate and tropical rain forests in the Americas, Asia, and Africa have been called the lungs of the Earth. They absorb huge amounts of carbon dioxide from the atmosphere as part of normal photosynthesis. Conversely, when the forests are burned, as they often are in clearing for agriculture, they release CO_2 back into the atmosphere. The relationship of the tropical rain forests and the greenhouse effect is well documented. It has been calculated that 45 percent of these forests have been lost to deforestation (Amstutz 1995, 438).

Another international need for the preservation of these forests has recently been recognized. The plants and animals of the rain forests are not well known by most people outside of their environs. In many ways, they represent an unknown library of new knowledge. The application of Western science and technology to these new raw materials may well produce discoveries valuable to business and health. Questions of the ownership of these materials and the importance of knowledge of them have raised questions about ownership and intellectual property rights. The United Nations is currently establishing principles for the recognition of and payment for use of these rights. Some nongovernmental organizations (NGOs), such as Cultural Survival, have taken the lead in demanding that the rights of indigenous rain-forest people be taken seriously. Some businesses, such as the cosmetic firm The Body Shop, have negotiated with local people for the use of the tropical goods that have been used by the firm. They have also found it good business to advertise themselves as a multiethnic business.

One important recent discovery came from the temperate rain forest of the Pacific Northwest, where the bark of the Pacific yew tree was found to be a source of taxol, an effective treatment for ovarian cancer and perhaps other cancers. In 1991 Bristol-Meyers Squibb contracted with the U.S. government for yews on federal lands. Since Pacific yews are the only known source of natural taxol, and these trees are found in old-growth forests, the rapid reduction of old-growth forests in Oregon, Washington, and British Columbia nearly destroyed this rare, and now very valuable, resource, even though semi-synthetic taxol is now produced.

A final important issue concerning the rain forests is a local one. While much of the world regards these forests as resources, people and endangered animals think of them as home. Many of the last horticultural and hunting people of the world live in these forests. The destruction of the forests inevitably means ethnocide as well. The cultures of Yanomamo and Bororo, among many other groups, cannot be relocated elsewhere. These people lack power in the national and international political scene. The reason their plight has reached the international press is due largely to the publicity that musicians, including Sting, have brought to them through rock concerts and other benefits.

Other people are affected as well in different, but important, ways. Rural women in many parts of the world spend hours each day collecting firewood for cooking and heating. As the forests recede, the women are forced to go farther. The United Nations (1995, 55–56) figures confirm this, showing that in some tree-poor areas in Africa, Asia, and Latin America women spend from two to four hours a day collecting wood for their homes.

Extinctions are no less a problem for animal species. Every year animal species become extinct. Most go largely unnoticed; others, like the dodo bird and the carrier pigeon, become metaphors for finality. In the contemporary era, the plight of tigers, elephants, rhinoceroses, spotted owls, and the great apes have been addressed in national legislatures; international accords regulate hunting them, destroying necessary territories, trading in animal parts, and the export of animals out of their natural areas. While all continue to be endangered, and some undoubtedly will become extinct in the wild, public interest and the growth of ecotourism have shown governments the importance of these resources.

Many endangered animals live in the sea, and the issue of the commons is a complicating factor. The endangerment of two types of sea animals illustrates the interaction of economics and politics in the preservation or destruction of natural resources. One prominent call of ecologists is to "save the whales," and clearly, the awe of the great whales is very real. One of the authors remembers being in a small boat crossing a strait in southeastern Alaska when she noticed an island she had never seen before. As she pointed it out to a friend, her "island" moved, spouted water, and dove under the surface. A local naturalist told her that she had seen a blue whale that was being tracked in the area. Her island, this animal, can weigh one hundred tons. A whaling factory ship could process this animal in an hour.

The story of the exploitation of whales is historically enlightening. Before 1860, whaling was a major industry in the United States and Europe, with whale oil and bones being lucrative products. As whales became harder to find, substitutes were developed, including new oils, steel bones for corsets, and gas lighting. The decline reversed at the turn of the century, with a demand for oils for soaps and margarines. In 1900, 2,000 whales were taken, and a decade later, ten times as many. By the end of World War II, Norway and Britain, using technologically advanced factory ships, became the leaders of the industry. At that time, the International Whaling Commission (IWC) was formed to research the situation of whales and recommend limits. By the 1960s, Japan and the Soviet Union had become the titans of whaling, with whale meat becoming the main economic product. In 1967, the IWC completely protected blue, right, gray, and humpback whales, and quotas on others followed. In 1983, it mandated, despite the objections of Japan, Norway, and the Soviet Union, an end to commercial whaling by 1986. Iceland and Norway have withdrawn from the IWC to resume whaling, and Inuit and some others take some whales for cultural purposes; however, the pressure on the whale populations from hunting is well reduced. The products of the whale are no longer in high demand, and the reputation of the industry is bad. The gray whale population has increased to the point that it is no longer defined as endangered. Many coastal communities have turned to tourism using whale watching as a main source of recreation to compensate for the losses in the fishing industry. Today, the pollution of the oceans presents an increasing threat to whales.

Fish are less romantic than whales, but far more important economically. Seafood is the major animal protein for many millions of people (Carroll 1996, 43). Until World War II, fishing was largely a local, low-technology industry. More recently, however, fishing has become a high-technology industry, with drift nets and factory ships able to harvest vast areas of the sea far from their harbors. Some of the most productive food-fish areas of the world have become overfished. The outer banks of Newfoundland, which provided cod and Atlantic salmon for hundreds of years, are essentially fished out. A shocking study conducted in 2003 found that 90 percent of the large predatory ocean fishes had been lost in fifty years (Myers and Worm 2003, 280). Strict restrictions on fishing off Canada have led to disputes between that nation and the European Union. Likewise, the depletion of many Pacific salmon runs has caused serious political disputes between indigenous and nonindigenous fishers, between Alaska and Washington, and between Canada and the United States. Similar international disputes center on fishing areas off South America and Africa. Aquaculture, especially fish farming, has been promoted as an answer to the wild fish shortages and is well established in parts of Asia. It is not equally successful, however, in all areas or with all species, and disease and serious pollution appear to be growing problems. Recently in Washington State, escaped farm-raised, nonindigenous salmon were declared a "pollutant."

Resources in Balance

It should be clear that all of the issues discussed in this chapter are interrelated. Carbon dioxide affects land, water, and plants and animals. Deforestation, erosion, desertification, plant and animal extinctions, and atmospheric pollution are interrelated. A change in one element causes changes in others, and the cycle of environmental deterioration continues. They all also illustrate the reality that scientifically it is far easier to prevent environmental problems than to fix them with technology. The focus remains on the importance of environmental changes for people. A personal and profound attack on human well-being by an environmental system out of balance is disease.

HUMAN HEALTH

One of the great wonders of the twentieth century has been the improvement of health care. A child born in an upper- or middle-class household in a high-income country can expect to live about eighty years. Never before in history has this been true. Much of this good health results from improvements in medical knowledge and technology joined with improved nutrition and safer working and living conditions. Unfortunately, this is not a universal reality. Another child, born into a poor, rural household in another part of the world, faces much bleaker prospects. Poverty creates an environment of poor nutrition, lack of health care, unhealthy living conditions, and dangerous or unhygienic work conditions. Additionally, in many parts of the world, overpopulation has caused intense stress on available resources, and a lack of pollution regulations has fostered deadly environmental conditions.

Diseases

Many diseases that were considered deadly at the turn of the century now can routinely be cured by Western medicine. Also, vaccines can now prevent many diseases. Smallpox, a previously deadly disease, has disappeared completely. The technology of Western medicine, led by the discovery of antibiotics and the lessons of sanitation, has increased the normal life span of people in high-income countries. Two major difficulties, however, come with this good news: this progress has not been universal, and the nature of development has created new health problems and allowed older ones to spread widely.

The health concerns of gatherers and hunters are quite different from those in more complex cultures. Accidents including food poisoning and hunting mishaps, infanticide, and childbirth are major causes of death. Lack of pure water and malnutrition can also be problems in some environments. Chronic and epidemic diseases, however, and diseases spread by pollution are rarely of concern since the small populations and regular movements do not provide conditions for the survival of such diseases. The major health issue for foragers is their lack of health care technology so that, despite often extraordinary knowledge of the medicinal herbs of their region, serious ailments are often disabling or fatal.

Health issues among pastoralists differ from those of foragers. While accident and childbirth are still killers, there is an increase in deaths from diseases. The hardship of a migratory lifestyle is difficult for the elderly and the extremely young. Humans are susceptible to many diseases carried by animals as well. For the first time in human history, then, epidemics and plagues are introduced in pastoralism.

Health in farming communities is conditioned by sedentary living. Accidents are less frequent, but injuries from violence are more numerous. Illness from pollutants in the water supply and food are common, and epidemics become constant threats with both dense populations and settlements contaminated by wastes and pests like rats. Health care may slightly improve, but the diseases often overwhelm the capability to cure. The Black Death of 1348–1352 in Europe illustrates the depths of disease and human suffering that such societies could reach.

Issues of technology take center stage as both the cause of illness through pollution and the preservation of health for people in the industrialized world.

Sickle-cell disease (sicklemia) and malaria are different diseases with different symptoms and causes. Human changes to the African environment, however, have spread both diseases and brought them into a symbiotic relationship. This case demonstrates the complex set of circumstances that might be set off by human design without any understanding of the outcome.

Sickle-cell disease is a genetic condition in which the red blood cells take a crescent, or sickle, shape and produce severe anemia. Without recently developed and expensive treatments, sickle-cell disease proves fatal before the victim reaches adulthood. Victims of sickle-cell are homozygous for this trait, which means that they have inherited this abnormal feature from both parents. What is peculiar about this disease is that it occurs at far too high a rate for such a deadly disease. Normally, a fatal genetic disease of this sort kills its victims before they have children or before they have many children. Such diseases continue as a very rare condition in the population. This has not been true of sickle-cell disease, which has become rather common in some populations. This observation led researchers to search for the cause of the high incidence of the disease. As it happened, the map of its distribution was a clue: areas of sickle-cell turned out also to be areas of uncontrolled malaria.

Malaria, a parasitic disease, is spread by mosquitoes. It has been estimated that between 300 and 500 million people get malaria every year and that about 1.5 to 2.7 million people die annually from the disease (Wade 1997, 4). The majority, who survive, may live with symptoms of ill health throughout their lives. Conditions that spread malaria have blossomed in the modern world. In the parts of Africa where sickle-cell is most severe, deforestation and irrigation have been used to increase agricultural production. These areas have proven to be prime breeding grounds for the malaria-carrying mosquito.

Thus, those who are most prone to sickle-cell are also highly endangered by malaria. The relationship between the diseases is somewhat complex. People who are born with sickle-cell traits have a natural immunity to malaria. Unfortunately, people with sickle-cell disease die of that malady. Those who inherit sickle-cell traits from only one parent, however, do not have that disease and are immune to malaria. This explains the high incidence of sickle-cell disease. The abnormal trait is beneficial in areas where malaria is common.

Responses to the problem of malaria have focused on insecticides that can kill the mosquitoes, but these leave their own health consequences. The draining of wetlands, which will kill the mosquitoes, modifies the general environment; and preventative medication, which works in many cases, is now being rendered ineffective by new resistant forms. If the malarial mosquitoes became extinct, the disease would follow, and after many generations, without medical intervention, there would be no advantage to those with sickle-cell genes, and sickle-cell disease would follow and become extremely rare. This complex interaction of disease, development, and environment would finally become harmless, but at an environmental cost.

Better known are the diseases and illness caused by industrial pollution of the air, land, and water. The Bhopal disaster mentioned earlier epitomizes the worst nightmares of ecologists. The sudden and gruesome deaths of thousands of people made news headlines around the world. Most disasters of this kind, which are slower and less photogenic, are more difficult to prove to the industrialists and local residents alike.

Health Care

While the most complex successes of modern health care are found in the industrial world, many people around the world have been introduced to Western medicine. Governments and NGOs have built clinics in poor and rural areas. The WHO has been involved in organizing worldwide research and care since 1948. Many NGOs, including numerous medical missions, have focused their work in developing areas, opening clinics and educating people. The most important successes of these clinics have related to local sanitation. Teaching mothers how to care for their children by giving them clean water and food and protecting them from contamination has saved millions of lives. One of the largest killers of the world's children, diarrhea, can usually be overcome with a little knowledge, clean water, and inexpensive foods. Similarly, the use of vaccinations and antibiotics prevent or cure diseases that could have become epidemics in developing states.

The clinics' missions are based on the most easily accepted elements of Western life: people wish to be healthy and to see their children thrive. However, two factors can discourage peoples' use of the clinics: money and culture. Many people cannot pay the slightest amount for medicine or even to travel to a clinic, and successful cures are only the ones that make cultural sense in ethnic communities.

Malnutrition

The major underlying condition of poor health worldwide is **malnutrition**, which is caused by insufficient caloric intake and a poorly balanced diet. While starvation is a reality that has made the international news often in recent times, there is a much broader problem. Poor diets make people increasingly susceptible to a wide range of diseases they might otherwise have avoided. The relationship of homelessness to tuberculosis is a clear demonstration of the problem. Likewise, the death of children from diarrhea is largely the result of diet deprivations. Why, in such a rich world where food production is at an all-time high, are so many people deprived of healthy foods?

The answer to this question lies in an understanding of the economic world. The world's wealth is unequally distributed. The wealthy and middle class in the world live healthier, more comfortable lives than their ancestors, while the poor do not. In fact, some of the economic innovations that have led to increased wealth have had negative effects on the poor. One example is cash crops. Farmers and ranchers who had formerly grown food for use by their families and communities are now producing food for sale. Moreover, they produce one or two crops for this market, rather than the broad variety of crops needed for a healthy diet. Many grow major cash crops, such as coffee and sugar, which add nothing in the way of nutrition to a diet. Furthermore, if the world price of a crop falls below the amount the farmers need to feed their families, they cannot keep the crop as food for their own use. In earlier generations, rural farmers may have produced less, but fears of poor nutrition or starvation were dependent on such things as severe weather patterns and insect infestations that could destroy an entire crop. Today's farmers still fear these things, but they also must deal with the caprices of a world market over which they similarly have no control.

The modern economic situation has also had an impact on the most basic of human foods—mother's milk. In many parts of the world, men migrate to cities in order to earn money for their families, and women remain in the countryside to run the farms, rear children, care for the elderly, cook food, and do everything else that has to be done at home. In addition, because it has become increasingly difficult to obtain firewood in parts of Africa and Asia, women must walk long distances to gather fuel, adding to the physical toll of this way of life. As mothers who value large families, they work while pregnant and while nursing to ensure the survival of their families. Nursing is a problem, however. The physical condition of the mother affects the quality and quantity of her milk. Young children are left with older ones, and their mothers often cannot be available for regular feedings.

Some corporations see these situations as areas of opportunity. In a now famous case that occurred in the 1970s, the Nestle Company used hospitals in Africa to promote its dry infant formula. Mothers were encouraged while in the hospital to use the free formula with their newborn babies. When the women left the hospital, many had no breast milk to feed their infants and no money to purchase the formula. Often mothers used too little formula for good nutrition and used unsterilized bottles. Many children suffered. An international boycott of Nestle and censure by the WHO followed. Nestle changed its policy, and UNICEF (United Nations Children's Fund) and other organizations advocated breast milk as the best infant food. The larger issue—that of a mother's ability to feed her child in the contemporary economic situation—was never fully addressed, however.

It is also important to recognize the political reality of hunger. The displacement of millions in Africa during the 1980s and 1990s, which produced heartbreaking pictures of children scarred by malnutrition and dying of starvation, was a result of both natural droughts and political turmoil. People fleeing genocide in Rwanda and Burundi, for example, were unable to feed themselves. Their farms and possessions were left behind as they fled for their lives, and they had no surplus cash to buy food. International relief agencies meant the difference between life and death for thousands, and some international workers were driven away by death threats. The crossing of international boundaries by starving refugees causes a host of political problems; some states, including the Democratic Republic of Congo in this case, have attempted to close the borders to limit political turmoil within their own countries.

Many people throughout the world are hungry. Not all of them die, but millions suffer. Environmental disturbances, including drought and severe storms, are temporary problems that have been aggravated by human interaction. The destruction of productive food lands in the interests of cash crops and urban sprawl has been another important factor. The politics and economics of food distribution have sometimes pitted the rich against the poor.

CASE STUDY   Brazil and the Tropical Rain Forest

The complex relationship between people and their changing environment is played out in all societies. In rare cases, however, one state can control a unique environmental region that is necessary for the health and well-being of people around the world. Brazil is such a country.

Brazil is one of the largest, most modernized nations in the world. Beginning on June 3, 1992, the Earth Summit, a global assembly of states, was held in Brazil. Here 178 countries met to consider the world's environment and agree on regulations to protect it. Brazil made a statement by hosting this meeting. Earlier, at the 1972 Stockholm Conference on the Human Environment, the Brazilian delegation had been one of the least interested in ecological protection (Stone 1985, 155). In the twenty years following the Stockholm conference, the expense of ecologically destructive development became evident with the collapse of the so-called Brazilian Miracle and massive international censure. The Earth Summit thus represented Brazil's public commitment to ecological responsibility. It is a significant commitment because Brazil is a nation of vast resources, some of them with worldwide importance and monumental ecological problems. This also makes it an important case to illustrate environmental threats and related concepts.

Brazil is an enormous country, the fifth largest in the world. It is also highly urbanized, with 81 percent of the more than 172 million Brazilians living in cities (United Nations 2001, 29). The rest of the people live in thinly populated regions. Almost half of Brazil is located within the Amazon Basin, one of the last remaining great tropical rain forest terrains. In this region lies Brazil's future and its greatest problems. It is a region of global interest since it contains countless rare and unknown species of plants and animals and has great stands of trees which, given their role in the carbon cycle, are vital to the health of the Earth's atmosphere. Furthermore, the fires of burning timber, resulting from slash-and-burn agriculture, are associated with the depletion of the ozone layer. Consequently, an important national resource is also a critical international resource. Clearly, in the Amazon, issues of state sovereignty and global interests often clash.

Amazonian Environment

The Amazonian rain forest is an area in which thousands of plant and animal species interact, creating a complex matrix. The sheer numbers of species of plants and animals in the forest overwhelm those in temperate areas. The most obvious plants are the tall trees that form a high, dense canopy which shades the rest of the rain forest. The lumber from these trees, including cedar and mahogany, are obvious commercial resources. In addition, rubber trees, which made part of the Amazon a boom area at the start of the twentieth century, and coffee trees have provided significant Brazilian exports. Major mammals found in the forests include howler monkeys, tapirs, capybaras, and jaguars. Innumerable tropical birds and insects join the amphibians and reptiles, creating a mosaic of animal life. The loss of an individual species immediately threatens the long-term existence of many others.

Within this plentiful environment it seems odd that the forest could be so fragile, but it is. It is one of the most delicate environments on Earth. In the dark on the forest floor the soil has been slowly eroded by rainfall over the centuries. A lack of rocks in the forest means that there are no new minerals eroding into the soil. New nutrients come largely from rain carrying minerals from the rich rivers. Insects and other life forms in the forest use the dead vegetation that enriches temperate soils. Little is left to form rich soil (Denslow 1988, 33; Buckley 1992, 4–5).

From a distance, Europeans and Americans see global prosperity, and even survival, in the maintenance of the forests. These plants and animals of the rain forest, left undisturbed, protect and regulate global climatic and atmospheric conditions, promise resources to improve the health and well-being of people throughout the world, and protect the cultures and lives of the indigenous people who first inhabited this area.

Although Brazilian environmentalists and indigenous people work for the protection of the Amazon, many other Brazilians—from entrepreneurs to cattle ranchers and the urban poor to rubber tappers—see their future prosperity, and even survival, in the development of the Amazon. Many consider the destruction of parts of the forest necessary to produce timber, create pastureland for cattle, and open lands for settlement. Highways and railroads are cut through the forest to move people and goods far into the Amazon. Miners, by the tens of thousands, seek to make their fortunes in the extensive mineral reserves. In some places, unrestrained gold-mining areas resemble historic pictures of nineteenth-century California and the Yukon. Just as national and international goals clash, so do those of the people who need to preserve the Amazon and those who seek selectively to destroy parts of it.

Economic Uses of the Amazon

The first rush to exploit the Amazon was not for gold or timber, but rubber. During the 1850s, rubber tapping became an Amazonian industry when the international market for rubber exploded with the advent of rubber bicycle tires and, soon after, automobile tires. The rubber trees of the Amazon were the sole supply of rubber at the time. The town of Manaus, which is the most inland port for access to large ships, became the capital of the rubber region. In the rubber boom days of the early 1900s, Manaus had a population of nearly 50,000 and an international reputation. European companies performed in the ornate opera house that was the city's pride. The rubber boom also brought to Manaus roads, polluting ships, unsanitary urban sprawl, overexploitation of rubber trees, and abuse of the local indigenous people.

The bust that followed the boom came to Manaus soon after Amazonian rubber tree seeds were smuggled to Malaysia and cultivated there. It rapidly became cheaper and more efficient to use Malaysian rubber. Manaus reverted to a smaller community, and rubber tappers worked for subsistence wages rather than great wealth. Since 1967 Manaus has been a free-trade zone and today is full of factories and shops. However, this economic strategy has not been completely successful in improving the standard of living. By the end of the twentieth century, Manaus, a city of nearly 2 million, was polluted, had no sewage system, and had an unemployment rate of 30 percent (Dostert 1996, 58).

Rubber tapping has continued, and many tappers are now active in environmental protection. Rubber trees, if treated correctly, can produce rubber for extraction without harming the trees. Indeed, the clear-cutting of forests to obtain other trees in the forest means the destruction of this renewal resource, and rubber tappers are aware of the danger to their industry. One union organizer, Chico Mendes, became an international voice and ultimately a martyr in environmental conservation. He reached out to the indigenous people of the Amazon to join in common interests. On December 22, 1988, Chico Mendes was murdered by local landowners. In a century, rubber tappers had changed from being symbols of environmental destruction to heroes for environmental survival.

Cattle ranching is another industry that has concerned ecologists. The chief opponents to Amazonian environmentalists are the developers of the interior. The Brazilian government has actively encouraged Brazilians from coastal cities to relocate into the interior. The building of the national capital, Brasília, in the southern interior symbolized this internal movement. In 1970 the then military-controlled government designed the Program of National Integration, which would build roads and settlements in the interior for the new inhabitants. The plan envisioned that 75 percent of the migrants would come from the northeast where drought was severe, but only 30 percent came from there; the others came from cities and knew nothing of rural life or farming (Moran 1988, 157). The Transamazon Highway was built in 1971, and other highways were built later to encourage migration (Prance 1990, 61). When the rural population did not grow as anticipated, the government used the infrastructure for other purposes, especially cattle ranching (Stern, Young, and Druckman 1992, 70). Annual rural population growth from 1995 to 2000 was −1.6 percent while urban growth was +2.0 percent (United Nations 2001, 29).

Until the mid-1980s, the government offered loans and tax incentives for entrepreneurs to clear sections of the Amazonian forest to create pasturelands for beef-cattle raising. The incentives were so lucrative that individual investors could make the success of the cattle operation a secondary concern. This was important since, owing to poor soil conditions, most of the pastures that were created became unusable for cattle in a few years, and many areas were soon after cleared and then abandoned. According to author Bob Reiss, "Of the 135 million cattle in Brazil, half lived in the Amazon, eating the place to death. Each bull needed one hundred times more pasture to live here than in the South of Brazil where the soil was better" (1992, 131). Without the government's financial encouragement, then, the industry would not have grown because it was not an economically sensible or desirable industry in this area. The cutting and burning of the forest for pastureland contributed significantly to depletion of the rain forest.

Another governmental plan for Amazonian development involves dams. Over seventy dams are scheduled to be built in the Amazon by 2010 (Reiss 1992, 20). Dams are needed for electricity to run the industries and light the cities throughout Brazil. The environmental impact of such dams is of great concern. The flooding of lands would kill plants and animals alike and, in some cases, destroy the traditional lands of indigenous people. Further, the acidity of the water is expected to corrode the machinery and make the dams difficult to maintain. The Balbina Dam, built with World Bank support, north of Manaus, illustrates the potential threats: rich forest lands were flooded, the lands of the Waiami-Atroari Indians were destroyed, and little energy was produced (Prance 1990, 62).

Mineral extraction is also a factor of the new Amazon, where gold, iron, bauxite, diamonds, manganese, copper, nickel, and other minerals are available in commercially viable amounts. The control of such wealth has been important to the Brazilian government. Mines have recently been developed with environmental safety in mind and are run cleanly (Stone 1985, 140ff).

Gold mining, however, remains a problem for the government and the people alike. Gold rushes are notoriously rowdy, and the Brazilian case follows suit. Stories of murders over claims were reported daily in Brazilian newspapers in the late 1980s and early 1990s. The clash of gold miners and indigenous Brazilians also elicited scenes reminiscent of the American Old West. Miners and Indians both died from homicides, and Indian massacres were also reported. The Brazilian government legally barred gold miners from Indian-reserved lands, but implementing the laws was difficult and it was frequently ignored. In all mining areas, the customary practice of using mercury to separate gold from waste metal has poisoned miners, local residents, and the plants and animals of the rivers. In 1993 nineteen Yanomamo, indigenous people from the Venezuelan-Brazilian border, were reported killed by environmental mercury poisoning (Sponsel 1994, 43).

Indigenous Peoples

The role of Indians in Brazilian society is a complex one which goes beyond the Amazon and beyond environmental factors. Amazonian Indians, however, are important in the environmental understanding of the region. These people have adapted so well to life in the Amazon that any environmental change would immediately challenge their ability to maintain their cultures, and a catastrophic change would threaten their very survival. Indigenous people, more than anyone else, understand the resources and dynamics of the healthy Amazon. Globally, their knowledge is important, and this is being lost. Their ability to hunt, gather, and farm for subsistence is threatened in many areas. Dams and roads cut into their lands. Outsiders steal their lands and kill them by bringing pollution, diseases, and violence. A road across Yanomamo lands brought epidemics of influenza, tuberculosis, and measles in 1974, killing large numbers of Yanomamo and destroying several villages (Commission for the Creation of the Yanomamo Park 1989, 45).

The Brazilian government's agencies that deal with Indian problems have been notoriously ineffective. Today, reserves are set aside for individual indigenous nations, but the government vacillates on protecting these regions from outsiders. One notorious case occurred in 1988 when two Kayapo men, including leader Paulinho Paiakan, traveled to the United States to speak at a rain forest symposium. They expressed their concerns about rainfall development in general and about a proposed dam in particular. While they were in the United States, they were invited to visit Washington, D.C., to speak about their concerns to members of the World Bank and the U.S. government. On their return to Brazil, both men and Darrell Posey, an anthropologist who acted as an interpreter, were indicted under a Brazilian act that forbid "foreigners" to denigrate the Brazilian government. Although the charges were eventually dropped, the status of Indians in Brazil and their relationship to the government were made clear to the world, to Brazil's embarrassment.

The health conditions that plague inhabitants of the Amazon include those of new diseases introduced to the Indians, among others. Pollution problems, such as the lack of urban sanitation and mercury poisoning, mentioned before, are severe impediments to basic health. Malaria is widespread and an increasingly severe threat in areas where the forest has been cut and the waters made stagnant. The increase in standing water reserves allows malaria-carrying mosquitoes to breed in areas where previously they had been less of a threat. Reiss reports that in the Amazon "health officials watched the number of reported cases grow from eighty-nine thousand in 1975 to seven hundred thousand in just the first six months of 1989" (1992, 113). By the beginning of 2000, concerns about malaria, and especially drug-resistant malaria, in this region became international concerns. In 1999 the Pan American Health Organization began a program, Roll Back Malaria, which involves all the Amazonian states. In 2001 USAID followed up with a five-year Amazonian Malaria Initiative and pledged $2 million annually to the cause. Diseases and deaths connected to development lifestyles also plague the inhabitants of the region. Sexually transmitted diseases spread with prostitution. Alcohol abuse, homicide, and other crimes exist at high levels throughout the new communities of the Amazon.

Analysis

The Amazon is an example of the wealth that a large, healthy region can offer a growing nation. At the same time it reflects the harm that ill-considered development can afflict upon plants, people, and other animals. The Amazon is important to the future of the people of Brazil and to people around the world. While the rate of deforestation decreased in the last decade and the government of Brazil, and specific state governments, most especially Acre, have increased their oversight and use of the regions, in June 2003 a report from the government of Brazil caused immediate concern. Using satellite photographs of the Amazon region, scientists announced that there was a 40 percent increase in deforestation compared with the previous year. This was the worst loss since 1995. Reasons from unique weather conditions to increased soybean production were suggested, and the government of Brazil immediately ordered increased study and commissions to recommend new programs and laws. It appears that the views of the Brazilian government and international public opinion on unchecked development are changing and that the importance of this international treasure is being recognized. The future will tell if this change is sustainable and in time to save the Amazon's wealth.

The Brazilian Amazon provides a laboratory for understanding the complexity of an ecosystem. The relationship among trees, soil, animals, water, and human health is quite clear. Even the ordinary practice of road building has brought deforestation, plant and animal extinction, soil erosion, water pollution, and disease. But this ecosystem is globally important inasmuch as the Amazon is a necessary part of the world commons. The burning of forests has not only added CO_2 to the atmosphere; it has also reduced the number of trees on Earth that take in CO_2 from the atmosphere. The stand of trees in the Amazon is therefore essential for the good health of the atmosphere, and the conservation of the Amazonian ecosystem is a priority for all the world's nations.

TERMS AND CONCEPTS

Acid rain *116*

Carbon dioxide *111*

Carrying capacity *108*

Commons *108*

Deforestation *117*

Desertification *117*

Ecosystems *108*

Extinctions *118*

Global warming *112*

Greenhouse gases *112*

Law of the Sea *115*

Malnutrition *123*

DISCUSSION QUESTIONS

1. Celebrities often campaign for ecological causes, raising money to support rain forests or local rivers through a rock or folk concert. What issues are raised by these celebrity campaigns? What additional questions should be asked?
2. What are the major ecological problems in your region? What is being done about them?
3. What are the more important problems to solve: those that are long term like global warming or those that are immediate like water or air pollution? Why?
4. Why are NGOs and IGOs so active in ecological issues? Should they be?
5. Can the commons be cared for in a responsible way? Why or why not? What are the local commons? Are they healthy?

RESEARCH PROJECTS

1. Choose another rain forest area of the world. How do the issues and problems there compare to those of the Amazon?
2. Choose one IGO that works on environmental issues. Discuss the methods it uses and the specific problems on which it focuses. Where does it get its funding?
3. Choose two front-page stories from today's newspaper. Are environmental issues discussed in the stories? Should they be?
4. Choose one area of the world and evaluate the health of the climate and the people who live there. What are the three most pressing problems you discovered?
5. Choose one item that you own. What materials are used in the item? What are the costs to the environment related to these materials?

INTERNET RESOURCES

www.amazonia.org.br/english/ This webpage on issues of the Amazon is run by the NGO Friends of the Earth.

www.worldbank.org/ This is the homepage for the World Bank, which supports development projects throughout the world.

http://www.brasilemb.org/ The Brazilian Embassy in Washington, D.C., is a good source for information on the Amazon.

www.fao.org This is the official webpage of the Food and Agriculture Organization of the United Nations.

www.unccd.int This is the webpage of the Secretariat of the United Nations Convention to Combat Desertification.

CHAPTER 7

Perspectives on World Ecology

"Both epidemiologists and the general public now understand that, with respect to infectious disease, we live in a global community in which the health of developed and developing nations is intertwined. In this global community, infectious diseases can spread rapidly around the world, making the global surveillance of emerging infections vital to world health."

—FELISSA R. LASHLEY AND JERRY D. DURHAM (2002, XVI)

"Although SARS took advantage of conditions in a globalized society to spread rapidly and cause wide-ranging disruption, control efforts bene-fited greatly from the world's interconnectedness. Communications technologies were used effectively—from web alerts to daily electronic reporting of cases to support for 'virtual' laboratories—to amplify avail-able resources and accelerate progress in both the generation and dissemination of knowledge."

—CONCLUSIONS TO WHO GLOBAL CONFERENCE ON SEVERE ACUTE RESPIRATORY SYNDROME (SARS): WHERE DO WE GO FROM HERE? *WEEKLY EPIDEMIOLOGICAL RECORD* (AUGUST 22, 2003), 303

The Earth is home to all people. No one wants to destroy it. Having said that, it is clear that there is a wide discrepancy among the views of intelligent people about how the resources of the Earth should be used and conserved. It is equally clear that everyone cannot live the conserving life of gathering and hunting. It would not satisfy most contemporary people, nor do they have the skills to survive in this way. More globally, the technology of foragers has a low carrying capacity and could not accommodate the current world population. At the same time, it is possible that mixed forms of subsistence may comfortably coexist on this planet and that different environments may be better suited for some rather than others. As Chapter 4 demonstrates, it is equally true that the pressure for full industrial utilization is strong, and growing, throughout the world.

This chapter focuses on three perspectives which describe how different people view the world and how they respond to issues that seem to place conservation and progress in economic conflict. Called the high-technology, shared-technology, and appropriate technology perspectives, each presents a different view on how people and governments can best approach development (see Matrix 7.1 on page 139).

HIGH-TECHNOLOGY PERSPECTIVE

Advocates of the high-technology perspective are optimistic about the ability of humans to overcome obstacles through their intelligence, technological innovations, and hard work. Humans are in this view the masters of nature. Moreover, nature exists for the use of people and provides the raw material for progress. There is little romanticism about the nobility of nature, nor about the people who live closely attuned to it. Proponents share a pragmatic view that is supported by economic development over the centuries.

The basis of the high-technology view is that human creativity is equal to any challenge. Problems can be solved and new technologies can be created to overcome any obstacles to progress. Progress, furthermore, is viewed as inherently good for all people. Visions of hunger cured by genetically created crops, diseases eradicated by vaccines, polluted waters cleaned by new chemicals, and the atmosphere purified by technological manipulation are all hailed by advocates as future realities that will make the concerns of today short lived and insignificant.

Problems not only will be solved, but the fact that problems are noticed by concerned people will hasten their solutions because of the nature of the market system. There is a lot of money to be made or saved in the solving of ecological and health problems. Technologies that effectively clean polluted waters or reduce particulate emissions from machines or factories are, or will be, in high demand in the marketplace. Similarly, drugs that cure common diseases not only save the lives and end the pain of hundreds of thousands of people, but they can make millions of dollars for the producers. According to this perspective, problems become economic opportunities on which capitalism thrives.

Many examples of just such successes can be used to support this optimistic view. Green industries, or those that concentrate on being nonpolluting, are expanding throughout industrialized nations. Processes that are polluting but not essential to ensure the integrity of products, such as the bleaching of paper, are eliminated at the expense of superficial appearance. Companies are then able to advertise their products to an increasingly ecologically aware public that values antipollution efforts over luxury.

Other industries have arisen in the quest for cleaner techniques for existing facilities. Most factories in the United States and other Western nations now employ extensive technology to clean up the emissions in smoke and water which used to escape into the wider environs. Disposal of this waste is now a profitable industry in itself. Photographs of American cities taken early in the twentieth century contrast markedly with contemporary pictures. Dark soot from the smokestacks of neighborhood factories once covered buildings; today, this urban pollution has been significantly reduced. Many urban rivers, including the Hudson River which flows by Manhattan Island, have been similarly cleaned to the point that fish species that had disappeared are returning. The free market has played its part in cleaning up the environment.

While such examples clearly support the high-technology perspective, it is also true that other factors have contributed to these successes. Government regulations, not private market forces, have been important in forcing much of this industrial cleanup in the United States. Also, the flight of factories from the urban North to less expensive areas in the South and other countries eased the pollution at the cost of local unemployment.

In the realm of health care, the power of technological innovation is apparent. New treatments for diseases appear daily in the news, and the idea that eventually modern medicine will be able to cure all ailments is common. Organ transplants, vaccines for childhood diseases, fetal surgery, and genetic testing, which would have seemed impossible a generation ago, are now almost routine. This means that some fatal diseases have been cured, dangerous children's diseases have become rare, and fewer children are born with fatal conditions.

On a global scale, the most extraordinary success has been the eradication of smallpox through large-scale vaccination. Smallpox, a highly contagious, deadly disease, once killed millions yearly around the world. In 1967 the World Health Organization directed a worldwide vaccination attack on the disease. Individuals in the most urban and the most remote areas of the globe were injected with the smallpox vaccine. Countries barred their doors to travelers who could not prove they had been vaccinated. Within a decade most countries could declare themselves smallpox free, and in 1979, after two years with no report of the disease, the vaccinations ended. Since then the only smallpox virus remaining has been kept in laboratories as a guarantee against its return. All samples were scheduled to be destroyed before the year 2000, but as the case in this chapter will show, that did not happen.

The apparent destruction of smallpox, and a correspondent control of poliomyelitis (more commonly known as polio), supports the vision of a world in which sophisticated technology can overcome deadly diseases. Less optimistic scientists point to the fact that the vectors of these diseases resist mutation and need human hosts for survival, and these characteristics made them easier to conquer these most contagious diseases (Karlen 1995, 154). Some proponents of the high-technology perspective might regret the fact that it was the United Nations, rather than private business, which led the attack against smallpox. They can point to more extensive contribution of private enterprise in the polio campaign, however, to show that such programs need not be the exclusive domain of states or international organizations.

The most significant agenda for attacking the problems of world agriculture from a high-technology perspective has been called the **green revolution**. Promoted by the Rockefeller Foundation and championed by Nobel Prize–winning agronomist Norman E. Bourlaug, the core concept of the green revolution involves the transfer of high-technology farming techniques to the developing world. By increasing the production of crops in the less-developed areas of the world, world hunger might be dramatically reduced or eradicated, and developing states could use exports to improve their positions in the world market. In the 1960s and 1970s, concentration was placed on new grain hybrids that had been created for high production. This entailed the wholesale replacement of local varieties with imported, genetically engineered crops. To prepare the soils for these new plants, the intensive use of water, chemical fertilizers, and pesticides was required. The immediate increase in wheat and maize output in a number of countries dramatically highlighted the claims of success, and many predicted the end of world hunger (Bodley 1996, 138).

The promise of this beginning soon gave way to grave doubts about the universal applicability of the green revolution. Both ecological and cultural factors worked against the long-term success of the operation in many areas. Local people did not like the crops that were imported and rejected them in favor of local crops. The new crops had no immunity to the diseases in these environments. Even where there were no inherent local barriers to success, in many areas the intensive use of delicate soils led to erosion and loss of water supplies.

Most criticism of the green revolution focuses on the intensive use of fertilizers, herbicides, and pesticides. The dangers that such chemicals bring to an uncontrolled environment were made clear. The runoff from fields to water supplies threatened the health of local residents and negatively affected the plants and animals that were necessary elements of the local ecosystem. Some of the chemicals used early in the green revolution are now widely banned. Others critics cite the economic problems associated with a dependency on petroleum-based resources. With the increases in the price of oil since the 1970s, only the wealthy can afford the crucial resources needed to continue this form of agriculture. Many individuals, and even states, incurred heavy debt in an attempt to maintain high crop production.

Other economic concerns soon became apparent. The green revolution fostered a dependency on the industrialized nations that generated the techniques and produced the necessary tools and chemicals, as well as a growing dependency of peasants on the rich. Not only did wealthy countrymen purchase peasant farms when peasants could no longer afford the fertilizers and pesticides, but the peasants, themselves, could no longer work in the agricultural field. Because the new farming techniques were not labor intensive, fewer people with sophisticated machines could manage farms which had previously employed many workers. The displaced farmers were forced into low-paying wage labor or destitution in the cities. According to Richard Franke, in a review of a program which spent over $100 million in Indonesia, "For the poor, the Green Revolution in Java offers only the choice between servitude and homelessness" (1974, 87). At best, the green revolution caused an increase in the number of large farms owned by elite families, who produce food that is too expensive for the unemployed peasants to buy. At the worst, the green revolution has destroyed formerly fertile lands and clean waters and has decreased overall food production in the area.

From the high-technology perspective, the green revolution remains a work in progress. The technological failures of the past were to be expected as with any new complex technology. Improved technology can overcome this. New disease-resistant high-yield seeds and more careful use of new pesticides and fertilizers will solve most of the previous problems of technology. The social and political difficulties that have deterred the success of the program can be overcome by the efficient work of dedicated governments. The rise of an agribusiness elite is not an inherent concern since this educated elite can lead the transformation from peasant farming to modern farming.

SHARED-TECHNOLOGY PERSPECTIVE

While proponents of shared-technology perspectives also consider technology to be a major tool in the fight against human hunger and planetary pollution, they also believe that such technology works only in an open and cooperative social association of world groups. Ecological problems are global and must be solved globally. Social factors, in this view, are not unfortunate distractions; rather, they are central to any successful project and often the reason behind the failure of others. The key words in this perspective are cooperation and sustainability. First, projects should be created with the input and agreement of all parties affected. The goal must be the equitable distribution of resources and technology throughout the world. All states, ethnic groups, classes, and genders have played roles in creating ecological problems, and they should all be agents in creating solutions. As an end, all people should benefit from modern technology. Second, new industrial projects must be sustainable. **Sustainability** means that the solutions are designed for long-term success. It should be demonstrated that there are planned solutions to the problems the project will inevitably cause. This is notably different from the high-technology perspective, where each step is taken one at a time, and any problems caused by the first solution will encourage research to solve them. Effective incentives, in this view, are assumed to be private, individual, and financial. For shared-technology projects, the solutions to foreseeable problems should be devised before the first step is taken and be designed for the general good.

The major philosophical requirement for the global success of such a perspective is a universal agreement on the importance of ecological stability as a central human priority. Hope for such a consensus depends largely on education. It is assumed that, given all the facts, only one conclusion could be reached by an intelligent person: without a healthy environment, the human race is in peril.

Within the last two decades, a number of international events have spurred the creation of a state-based international ecological movement, joining hundreds of existing ecological nongovernmental organizations (NGOs). In 1983 the United Nations established the World Commission on Environment and Development to investigate the state of the world's environment and to propose solutions. Named after the prime minister of Norway, the **Brundtland Commission** issued its report in 1987. Called "Our Common Future," the document affirms the validity of concerns about the fragility of the world's environment and stresses the importance of broad actions that will address the issues of the poor rather than those of the rich. Fully embedded in this document is the concept of **sustainable development**. Successful development is defined here as improving not only the lives of contemporary people but also those of generations to come. While the concept of development as a purely economic issue (as seen in state statistics) is directly challenged, the document affirms technological development as a means to attack poverty.

The World Commission on Environment and Development formulated policies, in 1989 and 1992, to address the challenges of the report. At the Rio Earth Summit in 1992, heads of state from over 100 of the 178 states represented attended, but the summit was largely ignored by the United States, a critical state in development. The conference ratified Agenda 21, a blueprint for sustainable development, as a plan for the twenty-first century. It explicitly mandates the inclusion of all people in development programs and emphasizes the need for full participation of the poor, women, youth, and indigenous people. The agreement is broad and difficult to enforce. The ideals of the document, however, form a moral core that has international support.

Concerns over the protections proposed in the documents from the Rio Earth Summit arose almost immediately. The rights of indigenous people are recognized, for example, but their rights to the resources of their lands and their knowledge of the uses of these resources are defined as **intellectual property rights**, and these rights may be exercised by states rather than ethnic groups. While some businesses contract with indigenous people to use their inventions and knowledge and to promote their products to the public as "ethnic" and "green," most businesses do not. The Body Shop, a lotions and cosmetics chain, has contracted with the people of the Santa Ana Pueblo of the U.S. Southwest to use their domesticated blue corn. Many other businesses have used blue corn or have hybridized a blue-white corn and advertised it using Native American symbols and terms with no compensation to the indigenous people who developed the crop. When the principle is applied to medicinal plants, the potential income can be calculated in the millions of dollars.

The environmental agreements of the Rio summit are being modified and elaborated on each year. The rights of indigenous people, which could clarify the problem of rights, is under consideration by the United Nations. There are also ongoing annual, or biannual, meetings which continue to call for a number of environmental regulations, such as the 1994 appeal for an end to the use of leaded gasoline.

Critique from the High-Technology Perspective

While there appears to be growing support for the shared-technology perspective in the international arena, critics from the high-technology perspective still abound. Some suggest that the shared-technology perspective is simply too idealistic and, perhaps, a luxury that only the rich can afford. The countries of the world have never fully agreed to any goal of this breadth, and it might be foolish to assume that they would now. There are many other interests in the way, including states and corporations. In a sense, shared-technology advocates are trying to solve problems that do not exist. They believe these problems will occur, but there is no solid evidence that would mandate expensive programs. Business, however, will invest money in the research and infrastructure necessary to develop worthwhile solutions to real problems, which will, in the long run, earn good profits. As problems arise, business will address them.

The economic needs of developing countries mandate increased energy utilization, and they are unlikely to welcome any barriers to their use of new technologies. Likewise, the expense of ecological cleanups appears to be beyond the means of such countries. Finally, it is in just these states that the world is most likely to find relatively undisturbed ecosystems. The preservation of these areas falls disproportionately on the poorer nations. These countries have repeatedly argued that the industrialized nations, which have become wealthy from the exploitation of both their own natural environments and environments in the developing world, now demand that developing nations do not benefit from even their own resources. In partial response to this, most international agreements include clauses that place the economic responsibility for ecological expenses worldwide largely in the hands of the industrialized nations. Advocates of high technology would argue that, if these plans were implemented, the costs of doing business in these countries would increase. Employment for local people would disappear if industries were forced to relocate because of economic pressures. Rather than help people, this would harm them.

APPROPRIATE-TECHNOLOGY PERSPECTIVE

Advocates of the appropriate-technology perspective point to neocolonialism as a barrier to the successful ecological future of the planet. **Appropriate technology** is the mechanism that works best in a specific case. It may not be the most complex technology available. Advocates believe that only those projects and techniques that fit both the culture and physical setting of the people involved will work and serve the ecological purpose in the long run. This is considered to be true in industrial and nonindustrial states alike. Projects should be locally devised and locally supported to be successful. Transplantation of projects from one place to another can be done only with the utmost care and with the full cooperation of the residents of the new site.

The idea of a global agreement or worldview on ecology challenges the diversity of cultural belief systems. Demands are made in UN documents for equitable treatment of men and women, and indigenous and migrant populations. Others assert the value of animals and plants as living organisms. All focus on the good of the planet as more important than local disputes. Many world cultures and religions inherently disagree with these basic assertions. Some cultures argue for the inherent superiority of men and the inferiority of nonhuman life as the plan of human creation. Women may be seen as protected by men, and animals and plants as created for human use. For many, to see things otherwise is heretical. For international governmental organizations (IGOs) and NGOs to demand action based on such heretical views, they would charge, would be colonial paternalism at its worst. The faith in education, in a way, supports this charge. Education means teaching people new ways of thinking and approaching problems, but if it is based on a Western technological paradigm, then it is likely to be viewed by those of different perspectives as a neocolonial form of education.

The focus of the appropriate-technology perspective tends to be on small, low-energy designs; it rejects the wide use of high technology as a solution to environmental problems. In this sense, it differs radically from both of the other perspectives. Popular awareness of the appropriate-technology perspective dates to the 1973 publication of *Small Is Beautiful: Economics as if People Mattered,* by economist E. F. Schumacher. In this book, Schumacher argues that the goals of agriculture should be to perfect methods that are "biologically sound" and "produce health, beauty, and permanence." The goals of industry should be small-scale, nonviolent technology "with a human face" (21). Peace and prosperity would thus go hand in hand. The progress of technology and industry is limited by the realities of the environment. The religions and goals of the people must also define the desirability of modern technology. According to Schumacher, new techniques that bring wealth in the Western economic sense may impoverish the culture and environment of other nations.

Proponents of appropriate technology will point to the majority of development cases around the world where industrial technology has imperiled the environment and the standard of living of local people. The results of some aspects of the green revolution highlight such problems. Smaller cases prove the point with equal clarity. In one well-documented case of inappropriate technology involving snowmobiles, Pertti Pelto (1973) describes the impact of this new form of transportation among the Sami of northeastern Finland. On the surface, the snowmobile appeared to be perfectly suited for modernizing transportation in the Arctic north. With it drivers could travel quickly over long distances that formerly had to be transversed using sleds and domesticated animals, and Sami herders could herd their reindeer with greater ease. To own and operate a snowmobile, however, a Sami driver or herder had to have cash for purchase and upkeep. Also, lack of technical skill often meant that broken machines were discarded rather than repaired. Pollution problems mounted in this fragile environment as a result of the gasoline and discarded machine parts. Inequality in this formerly cooperative culture grew between those who could initially support the new technology, thereby collecting larger herds, and the poorer Sami, who were driven into wage employment. Even the reindeer suffered. The new machines frightened the animals and interrupted their breeding cycle. After less than a decade with the new technology, Sami culture had changed, and the people faced more problems than ever before. The nearly pristine northern ecosystem was compromised as well. The snowmobile, an apparently superior technology, was actually less appropriate for this situation than the simpler reindeer sled that had preceded it.

The appropriate technology for a given situation may be a familiar traditional tool or it may be a new technology created out of easily accessible local resources. An example of the latter might be seen in the case of the Peruvian cooperatives discussed in Chapter 4. The cooperative political structure and the farming techniques that were developed fit the environmental and cultural needs of the village people.

India provides many other examples. The continued use of oxen-drawn plows for most work in village communities, which could economically afford individual tractors, demonstrates their understanding of suitable techniques. They rent tractors when such power is needed. Other, poorer Indian villagers have been successful with an innovative dung-burning stove. Wood for fuel has been depleted in many areas of India, so dung from the ever-present roaming cows is dried and used as fuel. Rather than encouraging oil or propane stoves, which would be too expensive and polluting for most families, an appropriate new technology has been developed by researchers. This new stove, inexpensively made of locally obtainable clay, burns the widely available cow dung. It is an improvement over the old, open-fire techniques because it makes the fire more fuel efficient. These seemingly small advances in technology prove to be far from insignificant to the people who use them. Plows drawn by oxen and efficient dung-burning stoves allow people to live happier, more comfortable lives. In other words, they fit Schumacher's goal of technology with a human face.

Critiques from the High-Technology and Shared-Technology Perspectives

While it is difficult for anyone to criticize the ideals of appropriate technology, advocates of both high-technology and shared-technology perspectives doubt the practical effectiveness of it in the face of the worldwide ecological crisis. Instead of solving problems for millions at a time, the solutions of appropriate technology involve only small local populations using rudimentary technology. Each solution must be reinvented for each community and each culture. Each community, furthermore, must commit itself to ecological ideals for the regional cleanups to work. This is clearly not an efficient approach in economic terms.

Matrix 7.1
ECOLOGY PERSPECTIVES

	High Technology	Shared Technology	Appropriate Technology
Goals	Private enterprise (to protect interests and the environment)	Equal distribution of technology	Egalitarian treatment and local control
Key Concepts	Progress	Sustainability and cooperation	Appropriate technology
Strategies	Market system	International joint uses	Individual solutions
Locus of Power	Private enterprise	Governments	Communities
Technology	Complex	Complex	Simplest for task
Sees Current System as	Good, but with too many constraints	Controlled by powerful states and businesses	Dominated by colonial forces

Proponents of the shared-technology perspective criticize the appropriate-technology approach for its lack of interest in the world community. From the shared-technology perspective, varied individual solutions work against the notion of concerted world co-operation. Although local solutions can solve local problems, local solutions cannot solve the problems of the worldwide commons.

Proponents of the high-technology perspective note the lack of incentive for intensive research and development in the appropriate-technology approach. Because there is little money to be made in local technologies, the best research facilities will turn their interests to other, more profitable projects. Since this view, like the shared-technology perspective, places its faith in the efficacy of modern industrial technology to save the environment, it concludes that appropriate technology cannot solve the important problems.

CASE STUDY   New Epidemics

During the 1990s, a new entry into the genre of horror fiction emerged in best-selling novels and films. Replacing monsters made huge by radioactivity, the new horror feature was the out-of-control epidemic. In the plot, a newly mutated or laboratory-synthesized virus escapes into the general population and rapidly kills millions around the world. Like Godzilla, the radioactive giant lizard that ate Japan, killer viruses of this ilk are not plausible, but like the monster, they reflect real environmental threats. Atomic energy is dangerous, as has been seen in the reactor disaster at Chernobyl and medical waste disposal. New epidemics are real and can be deadly, but their spread is more complex than popular fears suggest.

Early in the twentieth century, Americans and citizens of other technologically advanced societies celebrated the end, or at least the beginning of the end, of epidemics of infectious diseases. Antibiotic drugs being developed were hailed as the panacea that would ultimately cure these often-deadly diseases. The attitude grew that modern science had prevailed against the most negative elements of the environment. Early in the twenty-first century, however, Americans and others are again becoming fearful of infectious diseases and the potential epidemics that could follow. Diseases including AIDS, SARS, mad cow disease, West Nile virus, Lyme disease, and monkey pox, which most Americans had never heard of until recent years, appear in newspaper headlines and create economic, political, and health problems in the United States and throughout the globe. These new diseases, called **emerging infectious diseases** in medical literature, are new and very disturbing. Other serious diseases have largely disappeared in the industrialized world but have continued their deadly rampages in rural and developing settings. Diseases including tuberculosis, cholera, and malaria, which are treatable when discovered in wealthy nations with high-technology health care, are not treated, or are poorly treated, in the rest of the world. Consequently, they have continued throughout the twentieth century and into the twenty-first to kill millions of people. Additionally, the danger of their mutation into forms that cannot be controlled by medication, even in wealthy areas, is quite real and has most recently been seen in new drug-resistant strains of tuberculosis and malaria. Finally, fears over terrorism have brought other diseases including, most notably, anthrax and smallpox, to the public awareness. The global environment has changed in many ways in the last century, and new diseases have thrived in new environmental settings. A hard-learned lesson was that the smallest living parts of the natural environment, especially the viruses and bacteria, are worthy opponents of the most sophisticated technology.

Perils of a Global Ecosystem

The most devastating modern new epidemic arguably has been **acquired immunodeficiency syndrome (AIDS)**. Since 1981, when the disease was first recognized, millions have become infected and died. During this period, the HIV virus (human immunodeficiency virus) was isolated and drug therapies were formulated that can control, if not cure, the disease. Scientific research on AIDS is international. Four institutions—the World Health Organization (WHO), the United States Centers for Disease Control and Prevention (CDC), the United States National Institutes of Health, and the French Pasteur Institute—have led the research (Grmek 1990, 13). Laboratories around the world are involved in the search for a cure and a preventive vaccine for the disease. While no cure is at hand, encouraging advances have been made in drug treatments that have lengthened the lives of sufferers. These medicines are expensive and, so far, limited in use. Today the life expectancies of HIV-positive people in the developed world and those of their fellow sufferers in the developing world could not be more different.

In the early years of the AIDS epidemic, the disease was misunderstood on a variety of levels. Scientists had difficulty discovering the cause and nature of the disease. The nature of contagion was argued, and fear was widespread. The public believed that casual contact with those with the disease could spread it. Victims of the disease were shunned in businesses, schools, and housing. First identified as a disease of homosexual men, who had a high rate of AIDS, the discrimination gay men already suffered in American society was intensified. Some religious leaders even declared that the disease was a heavenly punishment for behavior they found sinful. Even after it was discovered that the means for spreading the disease was through intimate contact with bodily fluids and that the disease would not be caught by casual interaction, the stigma remained. Only after children, media celebrities, and sports heroes made their own AIDS status public did the attitude toward the victims begin to change.

With the discovery of HIV, the nature of the disease appeared more ordinary: a virus that was spread through contact with blood and other bodily fluids, most often through shared needle use or heterosexual or homosexual relations. Now personal protection was possible and the fear lessened. Soon new drug treatments were developed that permit longer, healthier lives for HIV-positive individuals and AIDS victims. While the cure and vaccines to prevent the disease are still in the future, the futures of those exposed to the disease today are brighter than those ten years ago—that is, if the victims live in the developed world.

The picture in the developing world is horrific. According to the CDC Global AIDS Program (GAP), a vast majority of the new cases of AIDS are now in developing countries. The worst hit area by far is sub-Saharan Africa where it has become the number one killer, taking the place previously held by malaria. Three million people were infected and 2.2 million died of the disease in this region in 2003, accounting for more than 75 percent of the world's deaths from AIDS (UNAIDS Fact Sheet). Adding to the misery is the fact that few can afford to buy the modern drugs that have improved the lives of wealthier victims. The WHO defined this epidemic as a "global health emergency" in 2003 because only 50,000 people in Africa were receiving the antiretroviral treatments (Mitchell 2004). The ambitious goal of WHO and UNAIDS in their "3 by 5" initiative is to get these needed medications to 3 million people by 2005. While the goal may not be met on time, they emphasize that this is a long-term commitment since the drugs need to be used for the rest of AIDS patients' lives.

The foremost result of this epidemic, which is quickly moving beyond Africa to Asia and Russia, is human misery for the victims and their families. Beyond this, however, there are structural problems that affect even more people. Life expectancies have decreased. The breakup of families is devastating. The number of orphans without family support has gone beyond the capability of social service agencies in many countries. Many of the victims are young adults who should be at the height of their contributions to the economy. Challenges on the workforces in developing countries have become extreme. Political scientists Catherine Boone and Jake Batsell have described the devastation to farms in Zimbabwe, where crops on small farms declined precipitously in 1999. Maize declined by 61 percent; cotton, vegetables, and sunflowers by almost 50 percent; and cattle raising by almost 33 percent (2001). They also point out that ten times more people died of AIDS in Africa than died in war in 1998.

The World Bank recategorized AIDS from a health issue to a development issue in many of its papers.

HIV/AIDS, despite improvement in health care, is unlikely to decrease as a world problem in the coming years. Increased access to expensive health care and better education to increase prevention rates should help improve the situation. The loss of life already felt cannot be undone. A generation of development potential is lost in Africa and perhaps other regions of the world. Private funding and funding in foreign aid have increased in the last few years. The threat of this epidemic to all states, regardless of health care, is being recognized. The world cannot afford losses of this magnitude.

In February 2003, a new disease reported in China was soon known around the world as **severe acute respiratory syndrome (SARS)**. Symptoms of this disease, caused by a corona virus, resemble those of many respiratory ailments, but SARS patients often developed high fevers and pneumonia. The disease spread quickly by person-to-person contact, and by the time it disappeared in the late summer of that year, cases had appeared in more than twenty countries: 8,422 people had become sick, and 916 had died (CDC Fact Sheet, August 2003). The effects of SARS reached far beyond its place of origin, causing economic woes half a world away.

Apparently, the first SARS cases were discovered in southern China and Hong Kong, but they were not reported immediately (Morse 2003, 43). Consequently, the epidemic was well under way and no longer contained in that area when international public health agencies took action. Soon after WHO alerted doctors around the world to look for and report possible cases, the virus was identified and tests were developed to identify the disease in patients. By the end of the summer, the last cases of SARS were identified and the epidemic was controlled for that phase. While many doctors expected the disease to return, the protocols for identifying it and limiting it were well established.

China appeared to be the origin of the epidemic, and the initial suspicion centered on the exotic wildlife markets found in southern China. If this proves to be true, it will be one of the increasingly common cases of diseases jumping from unusual animals to humans. In Hong Kong, the high residential density of the city may have helped the spread of the disease. In September 2003, WHO reported that inadequate plumbing systems in apartment buildings could have contributed to SARS transmission.

Once it began, and before it was well reported, people traveled out of China and took the disease with them. One of the areas most dramatically affected by SARS was Toronto, Canada. Air travel, of course, makes the distance between China and Canada of little importance. Over forty people had died in Toronto from the disease by the end of the summer.

The CDC put out travel advisories to Hong Kong, China, and Toronto during the epidemic. Such advisories warn the public against traveling to these areas for other than essential purposes. The Women's World Cup in soccer was moved from China to the United States as a result of the SARS epidemic. One overall effect, of course, was the devastation of the tourist industry in these regions. Perception of danger proved much more important than the actual danger that existed. According to an article in the *New York Times* (August 8, 2003), Air Canada, which has Asian as well as Canadian flights, lost more than 400 million Canadian dollars in the second quarter of 2003 due to SARS. Likewise, another *Times* article (August 30, 2003) noted that Hong Kong's second quarter economic output was 3.7 percent lower than the first.

In a very short period of time, this new disease appeared, spread throughout the world, and disrupted countries and individuals alike. Quickly the public health organizations around the world took up the challenge and limited the epidemic. Only in a global context with contemporary technology could such a scenario have unfolded.

Humans and Animals in the New Ecosystem

Not all diseases pass from people to people; some pass from animals to humans. Several such diseases have begun to spread beyond their usual boundaries in recent years. West Nile virus, mad cow disease, and monkey pox have suddenly become concerns throughout the developed world. Other new diseases, including AIDS and ebola, according to the CDC (August 3, 2002), may have also begun with animal-to-human transmission. Today, not only do people move freely from one part of the globe to another, but so do animals. Living animals, pets and breeding stock, and dead animals, for food, are transported regularly as part of the international market. Other animals, especially insects, stow away on planes and boats and enter new ecosystems in this way. As noted in Chapter 6, once they enter a new environment, there is no limit to the effects they can have on the existing ecosystem.

West Nile virus is a good example of how quickly such a disease can spread. The disease causes infections and fevers in the people who contract it. In most people the disease passes unrecognized since the symptoms often mimic a simple cold. In some, however, especially the elderly, the symptoms may become deadly. The disease was first recognized in 1937 in Africa and western Asia. Mosquitoes that feed on infected birds carry the disease. The mosquitoes pass the disease on to humans and other animals through bites. West Nile virus first appeared in the United States in the summer of 1999. Centered in New York City, it was the first occurrence of the disease in the Western Hemisphere, and seven people died and fifty-three were known to be infected (Chyba 2001, 94). The disease spread quickly from birds, especially crows, to mosquitoes and back. According to the U.S. Geological Survey (CDC, 2004), in 2001, the disease was identified in ten states with nine deaths that year; in 2002, there were more than 4,000 cases in forty-four states and 284 deaths. In just two years, the disease went from being unknown in the United States to being a coast-to-coast health concern. While the death rate is relatively low from this disease, the swift spread of West Nile virus has to be taken as a warning since the next such disease to spread this rapidly might not be so benign.

A more unusual transmission may have other lessons. The CDC facts sheet on monkey pox (CDC 2003) describes it as a rare viral disease which is found more commonly in Africa and was first described in 1958 as occurring in laboratory animals. It has now been found in wild rodents, rabbits, and squirrels in infected areas. The first human cases were noted in 1970. The symptoms are similar to those of smallpox but not as severe. The death rate of people in Africa who contract the disease has ranged from 1 to 10 percent. In June 2003 the first outbreak occurred in the United States. More than thirty people who had contact with pet prairie dogs came down with an unfamiliar illness. The disease was traced to a shipment of exotic pets, including a Gambian giant rat, from Ghana. Scientists concluded that the prairie dogs contracted the disease from the Ghanaian animals and soon spread it to their owners. The humans survived, but another public health issue was brought to the American public. With globalization, trade in exotic animals is increasing at an enormous rate, and only limited protections are in place. An article published in *Health and Medicine Week* asserted that trade in these animals had expanded by 62 percent in the last decade (2003, 278).

Bioterrorism: Poisoning the Ecosystem

A third concern of public health professionals in the twenty-first century is bioterrorism. Since the sarin gas attack in 1995 in the Tokyo subway, which killed twelve people and injured over 5,000 more, the reality of the threat has been heightened. At that time, the Aum Shinrikyo religious group not only released the deadly nerve gas, but also released *Bacillus anthracis* (the cause of anthrax) in four different areas in the city (Chyba 2001, 93). Anthrax came to the United States as a bioterrorism concern in 2001. Between October 4 and November 20, 2001, there were twenty-two cases and five deaths from seemingly purposefully placed *Bacillus anthracis*. Letters containing the contagious agent were sent to media and government agencies. Postal facilities, and their employees, were more directly affected. With no swift identification of the perpetrators of this attack, the vulnerability of the general public in developed countries became very clear. The economic impact of the Japanese and U.S. cases were enormous, causing even broader disruption.

The most pressing, and in many ways most extraordinary, terrorist-connected public health threat may be **smallpox**. What makes the threat extraordinary is that smallpox had been eradicated by 1980. Smallpox is not a new disease. It was known in antiquity and found throughout the modern world. Highly contagious, it typically killed about one-third of its victims. No effective cure was ever discovered. The victory over smallpox was the development of an effective vaccine and an international effort to get the vaccine to everyone. The success of the effort is apparent in WHO figures: in the 1950s, there were 50 million cases a year; in 1967, there were from 10 to 15 million cases; in 1977, there was 1 case. That last case, in Somalia, was the last naturally occurring case of smallpox in the world. While an additional case occurred the next year in the United Kingdom, that was contracted in a laboratory setting. There have been no known cases since then. In 1980 the disease was declared eradicated. This was perhaps the most successful international effort ever made for the health of humanity. Samples of the virus were stored in two laboratories—at the Centers for Disease Control and Prevention in the United States and at the State Centre of Virology and Biotechnology in Russia—so that further vaccine could be produced if the disease ever appeared again. Plans for the destruction of these samples were made, but a variety of concerns stopped the destruction from taking place.

While most people had accepted the eradication of this dread disease, fears of its use as a bioterrorism agent grew after the September 11 attacks on the United States. Since it is highly contagious, extremely dangerous, and easily transported, it appears to be a likely weapon for bioterrorism. Some people also express concern about the safety of the Russian supply. The dilemma is what to do about the situation. One obvious solution is to reintroduce the vaccination program. Arguing against this solution is the limited supply remaining and the side effects that can be produced by the vaccines. The WHO recommended against vaccination where there was "no or little risk of exposure." In the United States, a government program mandated the vaccination of health care workers and other emergency workers who would be called upon in case of a smallpox bioterrorism attack. Many workers refused to take part in the program, and by late 2003 fewer than 40,000 health care workers had been vaccinated. Still, this many people took part in the program despite the fact that the disease has not existed for a generation.

PERSPECTIVES ON THE NEW EPIDEMICS

Advocates of all these perspectives have strong views on the best way to solve the health problems of the world. These new diseases can cause human misery beyond comprehension. People, well beyond the personal grief of the victims and their families, feel the pressure of health care costs, lower economic productivity, and fear for their own well-being. Until recently citizens of developed states could celebrate the triumph of medical invention over disease and could reasonably hope for cures for those diseases that still imperiled them. People in developing countries also saw an improvement in health using basic cures from developed countries. While their general health lagged behind the people in the developed countries, the promise of better medicine was real even there. These new epidemics, then, appear as a shock, as an anachronism. The health of the world is supposed to be improving, not failing.

A view from the High-Technology Perspective

The emergence of new epidemics is a setback, but it is exactly the type of problem that can be solved by the use of high technology and private enterprise. The breadth of the problems means that there is a great deal of money to be made and that big business will invest heavily in the research needed to produce new, effective medications. Additionally, these problems negatively affect big business by limiting markets and downgrading the workforce. In both business and human terms, these problems need to be solved quickly.

The pharmaceutical industry has been highly successful in transforming the discoveries of medical researchers into medication that has cured or, at least treated, the symptoms of countless diseases. The medical industry in the United States is among the most profitable and fastest growing. Profits have made investment into basic research good business. Good business practice dictates that a company focus on research that can be expected to turn a good profit. Cures for diseases that affect large numbers of people logically should be more profitable than those that affect small numbers. Most of these new epidemics are in this potentially profitable category. The efforts of governments and IGOs should be focused on diseases that affect fewer people.

The industry faces a number of problems that limit its efficacy, and all people would benefit if these problems were lessened or eliminated. Among the problems are pressures on pricing, lack of protection from lawsuits, lack of support for purchasing in developing countries, and rigid regulations on new drugs.

First, price protections have taken the products out of a free market arena in which businesses prosper. Individual governments in developed states, including Canada, have put price limits on important drugs. Consequently, the prices of drugs in the United States, which does not have such limits, are considerably higher than those in Canada. Many U.S. citizens on the northern border travel to Canada to buy their medications, further eroding the profits of the pharmaceutical companies. Similarly, medical care has been socialized in many countries, including those in Europe. There the government is central in the choice and use of drugs. The European Union, which has long allowed price controls on drugs, became concerned about the effect on drug companies in Europe in the fall of 2003, and it has moved toward recommending the elimination or easing of these controls. Even in the United States, where the free market prevails on drug prices, relatively short patents on new drugs allow generic drugs (those of the same chemical composition without the patent name) from other companies to compete with those of the company that paid for the research and development. The returns from significant investment in such medications are thus diminished.

Second, in a litigious age, the danger of significant lawsuits related to harm from drug use is extremely high, even when all the rules for production have been met. In the 1960s, in one of the most famous of these cases, the drug thalidomide was developed and used for morning sickness in forty-six countries. When it was discovered that this drug caused birth defects in about 10,000 infants born to mothers who used it, hundreds of millions of dollars of lawsuits followed. By the end of the twentieth century, individuals who had had severe reactions to a particular drug often sued the company that produced the drug for multiple millions of dollars. Attempts to limit excessive jury payouts largely have been ineffective. New drugs, even after extensive testing, can have rare side effects on a small number of individuals—effects that could not be foreseen. Such suits discourage the development of new drugs.

Third, the huge expenses incurred during research and development are increasing. The price of drugs has to reflect those costs. Consequently, new drugs for new diseases will be expensive. It is unreasonable for companies to carry the costs of invention without compensation. In the developing countries, unfortunately, people and governments do not have the resources to pay the fair prices of the drugs. As has been seen, the new epidemics have been most severe and most widespread in these countries. Who will pay for the drugs? It is unreasonable to ask the businesses to carry the costs. If they cut the costs to the poor countries, they will have to raise the prices to richer people in the developed countries, to prevent losses and ensure a reasonable profit. Unfortunately, IGOs and governments are pressuring them to do just this. Some help has come in large donations by foundations, most notably the American Gates Foundation, which has pledged over $600 million to fight AIDS around the world. Likewise, some governments are pledging aid to do the same. President George W. Bush of the United States promised $15 billion in 2003 toward this cause.

Finally, government regulations controlling research and development of drugs and their approval for sale have become draconian. While no one wants an unsafe drug marketed, many safe drugs have waited years before they could be offered to victims of diseases. Countless people have died while an effective cure has been tied up in bureaucratic red tape. It is in the companies' interests to be sure that the drugs are safe for general use in order to avoid lawsuits and expensive recalls. The existing rules, however, put an undue burden on promising drugs that could be used immediately. Further, the costs of unnecessary testing and delay are borne by the drug companies, which pass this on in even higher prices. An efficient, but thorough, testing regime that is regulated by the industry that understands it would solve many problems.

A View from the Shared-Technology Perspective

The threat of the new epidemics is worldwide and should be solved by the world. The poor countries, which suffer the most, do not have the resources to solve the problems, and the rich countries, which have the resources, have an interest in limiting and destroying these diseases. As with the eradication of naturally occurring smallpox, the world must come together under the umbrella of IGOs like WHO and jointly fight this scourge which threatens us all. It is not a time for profit and industry standards; it is time to unite against killers.

A victory over worldwide epidemics is essential to the well-being of people throughout the world, and programs for the eradication of these diseases must be debated in the world arena. The sovereignty of any country must be respected, but those governments with policies which allow the spread of these diseases must, along with the governments of other nations, cooperate through the NGOs and IGOs to ensure the health of the planet. Wealth and technology from rich states must be made available to the poor states to help them in their health efforts. All must recognize that the Earth is one ecosystem.

IGOs, especially WHO and UNAIDS, with governmental agencies, like the CDC, must take the lead. First, they have the expertise and the experience in dealing with international health threats. Individual governmental aid to these agencies can be combined to fund the fight against these extraordinary modern threats. Second, the huge costs involved in fighting diseases like AIDS, and any return of smallpox, are more than even the richest country can afford. Third, the immense costs incurred from the loss of trade, tourism, and other important elements of their economies put them in weaker positions to carry such expenses. Finally, no private businesses could make a profit when so many disease victims are poor.

IGOs also have a different authority than any individual government to negotiate with individual countries. Both moral authority and preexisting channels of communication are already vested in these organizations. While they do not have the power to force any country to do anything, they can negotiate with any member country in a way other countries cannot. They do not treat any contagious disease as a problem of one state. They recognize that such a disease in any state is a potential threat to all others. Only a coordinated effort can limit the contagion.

IGOs are, and must be, involved in counteracting the recent threat of biological terrorism. The UN Charter and the Universal Declaration of Human Rights define all terrorism and the use of biological weapons against any people as basic violations of international law. Consequently, the use of such tactics anywhere is the concern of all states. The return of smallpox, for example, as weapon against any state or people would incur the condemnation of all UN states. It is a war crime, and once unleashed, the disease could threaten all the people of the world.

Since the world is a single ecosystem in this globalized world, biological threats to the people of the world must be fought at the international level.

A View from the Appropriate-Technology Perspective

There is no doubt that epidemics can become global problems, but it must be recognized that most contagious diseases spread from person to person, and each victim must be cured individually. The place to stop an epidemic is in local communities. Preventative medicine is the only successful strategy for the eradication of contagious diseases. Vaccination, preventative behavior, and appropriate health care must occur locally in a program that takes into account the economic situations and cultural traditions of the people involved. If every community addressed the issues of disease in a manner appropriate to its own social and physical environment, diseases would be stopped there and would not become world problems.

The best solution for a health problem is that it never occurs at all. The easiest end to a contagious disease is to stop the transmission of contagion. Rather than a matter for huge international organizations or businesses, this is a matter for patients and their doctors. While drugs developed using high technology are sometimes necessary, they are effective only if they are used. Focus on sanitation, education, and specific cultural traditions is essential for successful programs.

People cannot contract contagious diseases in isolation. In the case of AIDS, only immediate contact with the body fluids of an individual with the disease can spread it. The virus is spread, then, mostly through sex and by sharing blood by sharing hypodermic needles or transfusions. The disease should easily be limited; however, traditions of sex and gender have, in some areas, helped spread it. In some African cultures, where women have a duty to have sexual intercourse with their husbands, and husbands are allowed to have multiple wives and use paid sex workers, the wives have little means to protect themselves. These women then pass HIV to their unborn children. Even with education about the causes of the disease, women cannot demand that their husbands use condoms. Control over the spread of the disease is dependent on the men whose cultural ideals of masculinity are threatened by the health rules. Education is vital, but so is an understanding of local sexuality. Blood sharing can be limited by testing medical blood supplies and eliminating the sharing of needles. In the West, needle sharing is largely limited to those who use illegal drugs together. In other parts of the world, the expense of new needles can mean that people store hypodermic needles for repeated use for legal drugs for family and friends. The problems of poverty are frequently poorly understood by those who do not live with them. Additionally, cultural traditions, including female genital surgery discussed in Chapter 2, male circumcisions, and puberty tattooing, can spread the virus through the reuse of tools and careless contact with blood. None of these are global issues. The health of the drug user on the streets of Seattle, the circumcised young man in a village in Sudan, and the young female sex worker in urban Thailand are best protected at the local level.

Other diseases are likewise better controlled with an understanding of local practices. Diseases spread by animal contact need to be addressed by limiting that contact, perhaps by training in sanitation techniques and the nature of disease. Appropriate technology may be a low-technology means to create barriers to contact between animal and human. It may also mean fighting the poverty that creates seemingly unavoidably unsanitary living. Even the environmental disasters stemming from terrorism, which is discussed in the chapters that follow, may best be dealt with at a local level. Many argue that the elimination of the conditions that lead people to this extreme action is the key to stopping it. Local conditions of despair often make a ready audience for teachings of hatred, and these teachings lead to more environmental destruction.

The successes of disease control in the twentieth century involving high technology were centered in the developed world, where the local traditions fit the technological cures. The new epidemics now taking form in the developing world must be defeated there in ways that make sense locally. While some technologies, such as vaccinations against diseases, seem broadly applicable, proponents of appropriate technology do not claim to have specific solutions that fit all situations. Individuals and local groups must be listened to and encouraged to take control over their own lives and land. There can be no one simple solution to any one disease. There must be many solutions to each problem. Different people in similar physical settings may not accept the same methods of exploiting their environments. On the other hand, people of similar cultures may need different technologies to deal with their environmental problems. The inventiveness of people in each community will solve not only its own environmental problems but ultimately and jointly those of the globe.

TERMS AND CONCEPTS

Acquired immunodeficiency syndrome
  (AIDS) *140*
Appropriate technology *137*
Brundtland Commission *135*
Emerging infectious diseases *140*
Green revolution *133*
Intellectual property rights *136*

Severe acute respiratory syndrome
  (SARS) *142*
Smallpox *144*
Sustainability *135*
Sustainable development *135*
West Nile virus *143*

DISCUSSION QUESTIONS

1. How have the lives of people in the beginning of the twenty-first century changed because of the spread of new diseases?
2. Americans have long valued capitalism, and much of the prosperity of the West can be traced to free enterprise. How do the goals of business conflict with those of global human and environmental health? How can these latter goals be good for business?
3. Disease prevention has cultural and economic implications as well as environmental. Discuss one such disease by looking at all these components.
4. How are the issues in the Brazil case and those relating to New Epidemics case related?
5. This has been called a throw-away society. Many things are thrown away instead of fixed. What does the concept of sustainability mean in such a society? Should it be more important?

RESEARCH PROJECTS

1. Review newspaper articles chronicling the discovery, spread, and impact of SARS in 2003. What assumptions were made in these articles? Did they prove true?
2. Conduct some library and online research on the types of environmental issues currently being addressed by the United Nations. What types of problems are getting the most attention? Choose one or two of these issues and analyze their global impact.

3. Choose two stories from today's newspaper that deal with environmental issues. Using the perspectives from this chapter, analyze the assumptions apparent in the articles. Are both written from the same perspective?
4. Choose one ecological problem from a specific place in the world. Analyze the problem from the point of view of a local resident, from the point of view of a regional political leader, and from the point of view of an environmental scientist in an IGO.
5. Review the UN commissions on environmental issues since the Brundtland report. What successes do they claim? Which environmental problems are not addressed at these meetings? Which perspectives are clearly reflected in their public statements?

INTERNET RESOURCES

World Health Organization's webpage: www.who.int It contains updates on all major diseases.

U.S. Agency for International Development: www.usaid.gov It contains information about environmental issues and sustainable development.

Pan American Health Organization's webpage: www.paho.org This covers health and environmental concerns important in the Americas.

CDC website: www.cdc.gov The Centers for Disease Control and Prevention maintains an overview of health issues around the world as well as in the United States.

International Institute for Sustainable Development: www.iisd.ca This Canadian NGO's homepage provides archives of information about sustainable development projects and links to other sites of interest.

CHAPTER **8**

Peace and War

A t any given time, somewhere in the world, violence is used by individuals, organized groups, and states as a means to achieve political ends. Whether the situation involves the taking of hostages, other terrorist incidents, mass killings, torture, or war, humans have proven adept at inflicting suffering in the name of a cause. The 1995 Oklahoma City bombing and the passenger airplanes used as missiles on September 11, 2001, illustrate well the vulnerability of any society to politically inspired violence. Because they capture headlines, war and other violent acts seem an almost normal occurrence. In fact, they are not. Rarely do groups or states fight to achieve their objectives. Conflicts, from minor disputes to major clashes of interest, are dealt with peacefully virtually all the time, whether they occur within countries or internationally. This chapter discusses several concepts that explain why groups or states sometimes react violently to unresolved conflicts while most of the time they do not.

The concepts discussed also define degrees of both peace and war, which reflect the different relationships among the communities and countries in conflict. The word **war** refers to a range of violent actions—from all-out full-scale clashes of armies to smaller-scale incidents of terrorism. **Peace** can describe situations ranging from an uneasy and tense absence of war to a permanent peace wherein the participants consider the use of force unimaginable. Peace and war are not opposites; they merge with each other when force is threatened but not used. In such a situation, peace may be said to exist but only tenuously.

Earlier chapters have provided a general context for explaining why conflicts exist at the beginning of the twenty-first century. Increasingly severe economic problems, exacerbated by destruction of the natural environment, can cause a society to split along its existing cultural and class fault lines, or states to act on long-smoldering grievances against other states. Political ideologies play their role as well by allowing the antagonists to perceive the causes of conflict as linked to higher principles, such as religious beliefs, ethnic or state nationalisms, stability and order in defense of an existing political system, or general ideals like freedom from oppression.

Much of this chapter focuses on the circumstances in which communities or countries decide not to debate their opponents but to defeat them. Although abstract explanations represent real human suffering, the following account of the Segetalo family in Bosnia brings to life the terrible toll violence extracts from its victims. The family's situation was reported by Chuck Sudetic in the *New York Times* on September 30, 1993.

> Dzevahira and Asim Segetalo are among the 35,000 people hanging on in eastern Mostar. This Bosnian city became a battleground like all the rest. With nowhere

else to go, the Segetalos and their daughter Sabina, aged seven, endure snipers and shelling. Their eleven year old son had been killed in 1992. Since Asim's house is east of the Neretva River, he had avoided being rounded up and herded into a concentration camp when Mostar's western section fell a few months earlier in 1993.

Asim had worked as a metalworker before the war. Now he, Dzevahira, and Sabina remain in their house as much as possible. Survival has become their occupation because life's basics cannot be taken for granted. Water is supplied from a tank trucked in by soldiers from the United Nations. If allowed to by the enemy's forces, they also bring food after it parachutes down from a United States cargo plane. There has been no electricity for months and cooking relies on whatever pieces of wood can be found. Most of eastern Mostar has been reduced to rubble by bombardment. The smell of sewage hovers in the air mixing with smoke from stovepipes sticking out of sandbagged basement windows. Life alternates between boring and frightening. Yet however bleak the city, it is better than the outskirts where 20,000 or so refugees try to stay alive in caves or bombed out buildings. Everyone fears the coming winter.

Asim has the dubious honor of owning a house used by hundreds of people each day as a cut off from what had been a main shopping street. By going through the house, they avoid being hit by a sniper. One man who tried the street was wounded the day the Segetalo family was hosting a journalist. About 600 people in eastern Mostar had died in the last four months from snipers and shelling. Dzevahira and Asim understand the need for people to constantly walk through their home, but the path goes through the kitchen. The family finds it disconcerting particularly when eating dinner. Some of the passersby even ask for food. Asim worries about his house, in the family for all of its 130 years, because it has taken two direct hits and several very near misses. Dzevahira complains about the never ending flow of people but has become adept at cutting hair. "I cut about 20 heads of hair each day, men and women," she reports. Most of the time Dzevahira works for free, but some of her clientele give her cigarettes and soap. She expresses the beginnings of a post-war plan in wanting to open a beauty salon after the war, if she lives through it.

Her daughter shows off some possessions. One is a turtle she found in the garden. Another is the metal casing of an exploded shell. "It's a 105 millimeter," Sabina explains. (Copyright © 1993 *The New York Times Co.* Reprinted with permission.)

This family was caught in circumstances beyond its control. Wars have deeply important but incompletely considered effects on individuals because explanations of the causes and results of wars focus on large-scale long-term trends and decisions made by political leaders. Most often society's elites determine major events. International relations specialists often begin an analysis of why political leaders choose peace or war by considering the nature of the **international system,** defined as the organizations and processes that people and states use to interact across state borders.

ANARCHIC NATURE OF THE INTERNATIONAL SYSTEM

It often seems that people assume wars are more or less spontaneous. The phrase "war has broken out" implies a nondirective causation. Upon closer scrutiny, however, each use of violence "erupted" because decisions to do so were made by specific people for explicable reasons. Understanding why people decide to use war to get their way requires knowing how the international system works. International relations theorists identify the two most prominent, interrelated characteristics as state sovereignty and international anarchy. These two concepts apply to the behavior of states; however, when groups within states reject the authority of the government, they take on the attributes of sovereignty, at least as they see it. Some groups even declare independence from their former state, perhaps because, as explained in Chapter 1, states remain the most powerful units in the international system, and groups want one of their own.

Sovereignty

As an international legal principle, as well as a practical political one, **sovereignty** means that states accept no political authority as superseding their own. This presumption, enshrined by centuries of hoary tradition, is considered by states to be their chief characteristic in relating to each other. According to the principle, no international institution exists with the right to determine what laws and policies apply to the people within the borders of any state. Sovereignty has the effect, then, of designating governments as the sole representative of the population of a state. At least since 1945, violations of sovereignty have been denounced as aggression; for example, when states have used war to take over the territory of another state or to change the governments or policies of other states. To be effective, sovereignty must be mutually respected by all states.

Some people think that because international organizations have proliferated in number and influence since World War II, state sovereignty has been substantially eroded. As this chapter's following section will illustrate, a solid case can be made for this point of view. Yet the opposing opinion can also help explain world events; namely, that state sovereignty retains its validity. States have the vote when international governmental organizations pass resolutions, and, even then, the resolutions do not apply within a state's borders until its government enacts implementing legislation. Thus states remain central in carrying out any internationally validated policy. Even "binding" resolutions are subject to interpretation and enforcement by each member government. Transnational corporations and other nonstate actors are gaining in number and importance, but governments still set the rules for interactions across state borders. Governments also have military forces, unlike corporations and other organizations.

More than 190 sovereign states make up the current international system; 191 of them are members of the United Nations. In recognizing no political authority as superior to their own, they behave very differently from organizations within a domestic political system in one major way. Governments can threaten or use force in relating to each other, whereas businesses, unions, colleges, issue groups, and ethnic organizations cannot legitimately threaten violence, at least not in stable societies.

International Anarchy

Anarchy is perhaps more difficult to understand than sovereignty because it seems contrary to the practical experience of most people. Sovereignty conjures up thoughts of loyalty to the institutions of government, if not also to the government's present officials. Such patriotism is a common phenomenon. In thinking about anarchy, however, people who live in a stable state have a hard time imagining how force can seem a reasonable alternative in the absence of a highly structured social environment.

International relations theorists use the term **international anarchy** in explaining why force can be considered within the bounds of acceptable behavior in cases of extreme international conflict but unacceptable in domestic political contexts. Defined as an absence of governance, of political rule, anarchy applies to the international system of sovereign states. Each state acts as judge in its own cause because it recognizes no higher political authority. It can make a case for and act on whatever policies and tactics it chooses, including war. Compared with what appears to be the certainty of centralized domestic institutions—courts, police, legislatures—internationally the Security Council cannot enforce its resolutions. UN member states must implement UN decisions.

Yet in spite of the absence of an assured appeal to authority, states handle most of their disputes peacefully and even settle some now and then. Thus anarchy as applied to the international system definitely does *not* mean an absence of order. Whole networks of rules and relationships condition and even limit the leaders of states in their choice of political as well as economic actions. In the final analysis, though, anarchy allows states the freedom to use violence if their leaders think they can get away with it. That they choose not to most of the time reflects their calculation of the consequences, such as retaliation by other states often sanctioned by international institutions.

The existence of known standards of behavior refutes the commonsense connotation of anarchy as chaos, confusion, lawlessness, and disorder. To the contrary, states conform to recognizable patterns of behavior. Diplomatic immunity provides one case in point. For centuries, governments have mutually ensured the physical safety of foreign ambassadors and other representatives. This is why most of the world's leaders were so shocked at the complicity of the revolutionary Iranian government in the 1979 seizure of the U.S. embassy in Tehran and subsequently holding its officials hostage for over a year.

The concept of anarchy can apply within the borders of states where domestic order has disintegrated. Groups take on a semblance of sovereignty by renouncing the authority of the government, as in Lebanon in the 1970s and Bosnia in the 1990s. Thus, groups feel free to use violence just as states do when they fight. Such actions by groups greatly add to the complexity of international events. When domestic political systems destabilize, it virtually invites other states to intervene. An interventionist state can legitimize its seeming violation of the sovereignty of another state by labeling the leadership of one of the domestic groups a potential government that has requested help.

Power

Whatever the policy choices of states, or groups within states, power determines their relationships with other states or groups. **Power** is the ability of persons, groups, organizations, and states to cause others to do what they want. Thus power exists in relationships that enable those with greater power to achieve their desired results by affecting the behavior of others. Power is exercised most effectively when compliance is voluntary and the presence of power in a relationship is not obvious. This occurs when those in leadership positions are aware of the needs and thoughts of others in the system and design strategies that make sense to them. Power is built up and exercised in three ways—through persuasion (political power), economic inducements (economic power), and, rarely, physical force (military power).

This definition counters the commonsense assumption that equates power with control and coercion. Such an overemphasis on power's negative connotation obscures the real way most decisions are made and leadership is exercised. Some analysts, recognizing the voluntary nature of much compliance, try to distinguish between control and influence. Then they get into the problem of determining whether people are doing something somebody else wants them to because they agree or because they have no choice. Trying to draw such a fine line may be impossible in many real situations and often is not worth the effort. To summarize, as defined by many social scientists, power applies to most human relationships and includes both influence and control, recognizing that they are often intermingled.

Whereas in domestic politics the role of physical force is minimal, international decision makers are aware of their state's level of power and that of their counterparts in other states. States are termed small, regional, or great powers and, since World War II, the word superpower has been added to the international relations vocabulary.

Small powers, such as the Slovak Republic, can make decisions affecting their own affairs, but they have little influence elsewhere. **Regional powers**—India, for example—can have a direct effect on their neighbors and thus in their region of the world. **Great powers** can extend their reach out of their region and wield some worldwide clout. Germany and Japan's global economic influence and France's use of its military in central Africa serve as examples. A **superpower's** political, economic, and military effectiveness can be exercised around the world and sustained for some time. A narrower definition of superpower that is sometimes used includes only those states with extensive nuclear missile capability. Under this definition, Russia may still qualify. Yet such weapons are irrelevant in almost every daily interaction with other states.

INTERCONNECTED NATURE OF THE INTERNATIONAL SYSTEM

International relations theorists divide over their analysis of the current international system. Many understand it as essentially anarchic with sovereign states still the dominant decision makers in spite of huge increases in the number of other important entities, such as transnational corporations and nongovernmental organizations (NGOs). Another mainstream assessment among international relations analysts regards the international system as having undergone much more substantial change. They note that states are often sidelined as nongovernmental interactions of major importance take place. When governments do make policy and take action, it often supports the realities created by private groups interacting with counterparts in other countries, such as corporations, aid organizations, or academic researchers. Both the anarchic and interconnected conceptualizations of the international system recognize the phenomenon of globalization, but they differ as to whether or not it has made major changes in the codes and customs that govern international interactions. They also disagree as to the impact globalization has had on peace and war, usually referred to as "security issues." Those understanding the international system as interconnected see as obvious the need for stability and cooperative interaction. Those with anarchic assumptions assume states must first focus on their own levels of power and negotiate when it will enhance their position.

This section explains some of the reasons why many people who study international trends think that globalization indeed *has* changed how the system functions by making it measurably more interconnected. Four trends constituting globalization were highlighted in Chapter 1. A growing number of people think that these trends, taken together, have so greatly transformed life on the planet that now we live in a global world not an international one (with "international" connoting the past state-centered world).

As the first trend, exponential increases in international economic transactions have characterized the twentieth century, especially after World War II. In 1913 world trade amounted to about $20 billion; by the early 1990s, about $3.7 trillion in goods were exchanged per year. The post–World War II era especially brought about a trade boom: in the two decades between 1948 and 1968, world trade increased from $53 to $350 billion, or 660 percent, and the pace in more recent years has not slackened (Rourke 1993, 442). In the 1990s trade generated about 15 percent of the world's total production of goods and services. For the United States and Japan, it amounted to about 20 percent of gross domestic product (GDP), whereas for members of the European Union, it averaged about 50 percent (Balaam and Veseth 1996, 113).

Some would argue that economies have become so interconnected that, for many industries, it is outmoded to think of goods as produced in a single country. A decision made in one U.S. town illustrates the point. Its local government decided to "Buy American" and chose a John Deere earthmover priced about $15,000 higher than one sold by Komatsu, a Japanese company. Unfortunately for the town's nationalistic objective, the John Deere machine was made in Japan, except for the motor; the Komatsu was actually made in Illinois (Brown and Hogedorn 1994, 162).

A second trend, integration of international/global economic decision making, connotes that the international economic system consists of IGOs—the World Bank, the International Monetary Fund, and the World Trade Organization—as well as private corporations, state agencies that set commercial policies and administer aid programs, and NGOs such as private development aid organizations and labor unions. The issue of developing world government debt provides an example of how public and private international economic entities work together. When a government is in danger of defaulting on its debt payments, transnational commercial banks, such as J. P. Morgan and Citibank, devise and coordinate strategies with the International Monetary Fund and often with the U.S. Treasury Department. In global credit markets in general, debt security rating agencies, such as Moody's Investors Service and Standard & Poor's, fill the regulatory role (Baylis and Smith 1999, 24).

Strengthened Political International Governmental Organizations, a third trend, focuses on the role of the United Nations since it operates at the center of a large network of "universal," meaning worldwide, IGOs. Over 120 UN-related organizations, commissions, and programs cover a wide variety of international issues, including human rights, threats to the natural environment, and global development. They work not only with relevant state agencies but also with private individuals who have relevant expertise. As an example, the International Whaling Commission, an IGO, sponsors workshops where scientists present their findings. These papers and accompanying consultations provide the organization with data on the world's remaining whales.

Many people consider the issue of peace and war as central to the UN's mission. As the one universal IGO expressly charged with handling threats to the peace, the Security Council attempts to carry out the UN Charter's vision of creating a comprehensive system of international security to deter war. Its mechanism, **collective security**, refers to Security Council–authorized military action against an aggressor state without that state's consent. Examples often cited include the Korean War and the first Gulf War. Such forcible **intervention**, however, denies state sovereignty, another UN principle. The Charter itself makes explicit state sovereignty's norm of noninterference in other states' domestic problems. According to the Charter's wording, "Nothing contained in the present Charter shall authorize the United Nations to intervene in matters which are essentially within the domestic jurisdiction of any state or shall require the Members to submit such matters to settlement under the present Charter but this principle shall not prejudice the application of enforcement measures under Chapter VII" (Chapter 1, Article 2, section 7). The last phrase means that a state's sovereignty can be abridged only when the Security Council has authorized it because that state has violated another state's sovereignty by committing an act of aggression or threatening the peace.

The UN Charter thus embodies dual principles. State sovereignty, with its territorial integrity and noninterference implications, appears to contradict provisions for intervention by collective action. The Security Council reconciles these two principles when it determines that an aggressor state has violated the Charter and thus collective intervention can trump its sovereignty.

Changing historical circumstances have expanded the Security Council's role. The Charter does not mention peacekeeping, yet in some cases managing threats to the peace has called for deploying troops from member states in a police role, sometimes including the delivery of humanitarian food and medical aid. In addition, UN-authorized personnel have actually administered the government until local people could take it over: examples include the Congo in 1960–1964 and East Timor, now Timor-Leste, from 2002. These interpretations of the Security Council mandate have come to be called **humanitarian intervention.**

As a fourth globalization trend, increases in international non-governmental contacts and communication characterize the late twentieth and early twenty-first centuries. People move internationally in their careers in IGOs, NGOs, and government agencies, or as immigrants and refugees hoping for a better life. Also, international tourism has exploded. Estimates put the number of world tourists in 1990 at 457.3 million people. By 2000 the number had grown to 698.8 people, a 53 percent increase and reflecting an average annual growth rate of 4.9 percent (calculated from World Tourism Organization data).

More efficient person-to-person communications have exponentially increased international contacts. Fiber-optic cable networks and satellite communications allow not only vocal interactions but teleconferencing as well. The explosive growth in e-mail usage seems the more striking because computer Internet technology has developed so recently. An estimated 604 million people used the Internet in 2002 (CIA Factbook 2003). Immediate international communications mean that networks of international activists concerned about land mines, human rights abuses, deforestation, species extinction, and a myriad of other issues can become much more effective in gathering information and focusing public pressure.

MODEL OF PEACE AND WAR

Analyses of international events made by the leaders of states have high-stakes consequences, particularly when they concern peace and war. Figure 8.1 offers a simplified model of international foreign policy making as it relates to security issues. The following pages discuss the three general choices states make to achieve their objectives: war, balance of power, and international rule of law. The explanation refers to states because they are the main international actors, but it can also apply to groups when they assume sovereignty and act like states.

The figure depicts relationships among several concepts used by international relations theorists to explain peace and war. The figure's three prongs represent how states

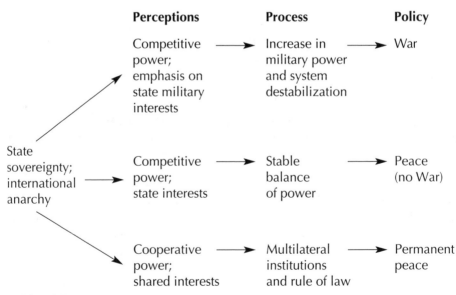

FIGURE 8.1
Three International System Contexts

in three different international political contexts respond to conflict. The first refers to the use of force. The second policy choice also assumes a context of hostility, but this time it leads to competition without violence. The third alternative assumes that a sense of commonality or even community has developed; therefore, cooperative actions manage conflicts without violence.

War Strategies

A state or group that decides to use force has several choices to make in waging war. The choices, which reflect the state or group's level of military power, are listed as five categories: show of force, terrorism, guerrilla war, conventional war, and nuclear war.

A **show of force** refers to the movement of a state's military forces into a conflict situation as an implied threat. Such an action is designed to cause the adversary to back down. Bluff is the intention rather than the initiation of actual fighting. A show of force has a chance to succeed only when the state making the threat has considerably more power in the situation than its adversary. An example of a show of force occurred in 1903 when U.S. President Theodore Roosevelt sent a warship to prevent Colombian forces from entering Panama. A former province of Colombia, Panama had declared its independence. The United States wanted to build a canal in Panama, and the Colombian government had not accepted the U.S. terms. An independent Panama, however, signed the treaty dictated by the United States. In this case, the United States used its political, economic, and military power to create a new state by violating Colombia's sovereignty.

Unlike a show of force, **terrorism** is a tactic of the weak. It uses specific acts of violence perpetrated by small numbers of people for the purpose of destabilizing an existing political system, or at least revealing it as oppressive, inept, and unworthy of support. Groups within states generally use terrorism when they have little power but want to make a big impression. Because they are few in number, terrorists employ clandestine, hit-and-run tactics, often against civilians. Targets are chosen to make the terrorists appear strong and to publicize their grievances. They hide by blending into the general population. Although terrorist bombings, assassinations, robberies, and other attacks can be labeled as criminal acts rather than acts of war, the terrorists consider themselves to be engaged in war. What muddies these seemingly clear waters, however, is the fact that sometimes governments use clandestine operations against another state. Such government-sponsored terrorism uses the same tactics as group or individual terrorists.

Fighters of **guerrilla wars** often use small arms and hit-and-run tactics like terrorists, but they are organized in larger, more coherent groups, and they can attack defended targets. They assault military outposts and ambush army patrols. Guerrilla wars, like terrorism, occur in domestic conflict situations, ironically called civil wars. The term guerrilla war, first used during the Spanish Civil War in 1936, combines the Spanish word for war, *guerro*, and *illa*, which is a Spanish suffix meaning little. Like terrorists, guerrilla fighters blend into the local population as their main defense. In some cases, though, they gain enough size and strength to establish strongholds within a specific territory. When they attract enough support, a full-scale civil war can ensue, with the guerrillas setting up their own government functions. In these cases, the size of the military operations and use of heavy military equipment can make the level of violence in a guerrilla war akin to that of a conventional war.

The word *war* to most people means **conventional war**, with formally organized military forces of states, complete with uniforms, differentiated functions, command and control hierarchies, training, and sense of historical mission. Governments with sufficiently large economies invest in trained, fully equipped, permanent military forces. Since industrialization has made possible mechanized armies and high-technology weapons, the scale of killing greatly increased in the twentieth century.

The most destructive conventional war of all time, World War II, ended with a weapon so powerful that it has been given a category all its own. **Nuclear war**, unlike the previous categories of force, is defined by the kind of weapon rather than the manner in which it is used. Nuclear, including atomic, weapons are produced from the release of molecular energy. They were developed by states with large-scale scientific and military establishments and, therefore, the requisite advanced technology and military capability. Currently seven states have officially acknowledged production and possession of nuclear weapons: the United States, Russia, China, the United Kingdom, France, India, and Pakistan. Israel also is commonly understood to have nuclear weapons. Many people fear proliferation because the states with nuclear weapons may sell the technology and components to previously nonnuclear states.

The fact that the type of weapon is the distinguishing characteristic of nuclear war has raised a hotly debated issue with important policy implications. Both military strategists and international relations theorists disagree over whether nuclear weapons can be treated as just another, although more devastatingly powerful, weapon system or whether the difference is so great as to require completely new strategic thinking. A further issue has been raised over whether such weapons can be used in warfare like any other weapon or whether they act only as a deterrent to keep other states from using them. U.S. policy makers accepted the former position when they dropped atom bombs on two Japanese cities in 1945, ending World War II. During the Cold War, however, U.S. policy makers seemed to shift to the latter policy—the use of nuclear weapons was unthinkable except in retaliation for a direct nuclear attack.

Perhaps the U.S. policy change occurred because the destructive capability of energy-based weapons greatly increased. A one-megaton warhead is over eighty times greater than the bomb used on Hiroshima, Japan, and some ten-, twenty-, and thirty-megaton warheads were produced by the Soviet Union and the United States during the Cold War. In addition, the United States experienced severe adverse political fallout from being the only country to ever use an energy-based weapon in war. Commentators point out as well that U.S. policy may have been influenced by the fact that when the atomic bomb was dropped, there was no threat that Japan could reply in kind. In contrast, the Soviet Union not only had what was called "the Bomb" but also delivery systems able to get it to the United States.

This section has summarized the various fighting strategies used by states and groups when engaged in armed combat. Many who read it will assume that peace is preferable to war by definition; however, wars have been used to change things for the better, as judged by the winners. Israelis, for example, would make the case that fighting was necessary in 1947 and 1948 to establish their country's existence. The U.S. Revolutionary War may be cited as another example. Opponents of the opinion that sometimes force is needed point out that violence sets the context for the use of countering violence. World War II and the Holocaust directly produced the perceived need by Jewish people to create Israel as soon as possible. Perhaps the independence of the United States could have been achieved in the long run without war, as it was in Canada. Arguments over history can go on and on, but the point remains that people will choose violent means to achieve what they perceive to be a vital objective if they feel justified, think success is possible, and can see no other way to gain it.

In the early years of the twenty-first century, one war strategy has come to dominate headlines in the United States. The question could well be asked whether terrorism is an international inevitability in the twenty-first century. As the war strategy of the weakest groups wanting to influence international events, terrorism before 9/11 earned less attention from U.S. top officials than other military issues. Security priorities changed, however, when hijackers used commercial airliners as missiles to attack the Pentagon and the New York World Trade Center. The United States then came to share with France, the United Kingdom, Germany, and other leading world powers the experience of international terrorist incidents on its home soil.

As acts of inhuman horror, suicide bombers and commercial airlines smashing into buildings may mark the twenty-first century much as gas chambers and atomic weapons characterized the twentieth. However, a distinction exists. Major world powers committed the twentieth-century acts which continue to appall people decades later; in the new century, the weak can carry out the tactics most people consider ruthless, revolting, and inhuman.

Having experienced such incidents themselves, Americans may find it difficult to analyze the 9/11 attacks as an example of a commonly used tactic of international violence. A deeply felt identity with the victims of a terrorist attack often builds understandable mental barriers to a careful consideration of the causes and consequences of terrorism. Yet emotionally charged reactions do not necessarily produce effective responses, even by the world's predominant military power. As others before them, such as the British, Israelis, Turks, Egyptians, Indians, and Philippinos, Americans must move through their emotions to accomplish effective analysis and action. Of all countries, the United States must provide leadership in meeting the new century's major military challenge.

Terrorism's causes do not fester in the obvious, that is, in pathological blind hatred or mental maladjustment. If psychosis created the problem, finding and eliminating the perpetrators could solve it. Unfortunately, such a direct cause and effect exists only as a popular misperception often parroted by those who play at analysis. In reality, terrorists have frighteningly lucid objectives based on their thinking about what is wrong with the world. Their assumptions make sense to many more people than themselves, sometimes numbering in the millions. This constituency may not condone the horrific tactics used but may agree with the terrorists that the enemy is "oppressive," "dominating," and "evil."

Understanding this larger context—that terrorist groups may have a broad sympathetic constituency—explains the dangerous depth and longevity of terrorism. Military retaliation by the perceived oppressor can perpetuate terrorism when it produces more individuals who join those using violence. Therefore, opponents of terrorism must undermine the appeal of its ideas. Simply using violence against violence will not work. It takes a multifaceted approach. Violent countermeasures have a role, if they prove effective. Yet fighting terrorism must include policies that erode its tacit mass support. This requires an accurate analysis of how the terrorists explain their actions to themselves and to those who share their perspective.

In figuring out how terrorists think, it helps to compare seemingly unrelated acts of terrorism and see if any common patterns emerge. At first, little overlap seems possible because of major differences in the actions, the ideas used to justify them, and the perpetrators' identities. Yet looking for more general similarities can reveal useful comparisons. The following analysis is adapted from remarks made by James L. Taulbee subsequent to 9/11 as summarized in "The One That Gets Past You: Trends in Terrorism," published in the *Academic Exchange*. Prior to the 9/11 attacks, news analysts considered the bombing of the federal building in Oklahoma City, Oklahoma, as the single most heinous act of terrorism ever committed on American soil. Could any general category of causation link the two incidents?

Terrorists, among them Timothy McVeigh and the 9/11 plane hijackers, regard themselves as part of larger groups of people who share their beliefs. Although considerably outside their groups' mainstream, terrorists self-identify as among the most devoted to their ideals. They have dedicated themselves to taking action while others, more squeamish and less heroic, shrink from engaging in necessary violence. Both radical Islam and the American militia movement harbor a visceral hatred of the U.S. government sanctioned by religion and justifying "collateral damage," or, as the hijackers would explain about attacking civilians, "there no innocents."

Terrorists live lives saturated with inflammatory speech and thought. They formulate elaborate explanations for why the rules of civilized behavior do not apply to them. They regard the enemy as thoroughly corrupt and absolutely repressive, with no hope of redemption. They think their sacrifice, as well as that of their victims, will hasten the time when their hope for a better world will be realized, when destruction will come to the existing order and a purer society will take its place. Their "heroic" act will be just one incident in a long war.

Terrorists dwell in a destructive never-never land of their own devising. As members of subcultures existing at the fringe of a larger constituency, they indulge in blinding hatred, and their self-vindicating violence freely festers. When speaking to people in the larger constituency, however, terrorists often use more generally accepted rhetoric. Homegrown U.S. terrorists, for example, speak of limited government and individual rights. They say America has to make wholesale changes to be true to its own ideals. The 9/11 plane hijackers spoke of living according to the Koran's teachings, of freeing the world from the West's materialistic temptations and the corruption proliferated by U.S. power.

The most dangerous of radical beliefs are those derived from plausible explanations for world problems. In the present global context of vast and growing disparities of wealth and power, current governmental leaders seem to be without a clear plan to achieve positive incremental change. Hopelessness and despair can make radicals appear to be right, to some people anyway.

Always a weapon of the weak and alienated, terrorism in the contemporary world can take advantage of modern technologies. Globalization has made more efficient the systems of international transportation, communication, and financial transaction. Terrorists can use these structures as well as anyone else. These structures enhance the physical reach of terrorists as well as their capacity to distort ideals shared by millions. If no serious attempt is made to address the actual grievances of disaffected groups, terrorism will continue to be a significant threat in the foreseeable future.

Balance-of-Power Strategies

When governments or groups in conflict choose a balance-of-power strategy, the result is not war but peace, although the peace may be temporary. In a **balance-of-power** system, states or groups choose not to use force because they consider the potential cost too high. They may lose the war or experience so much destruction that their populations judge the deaths, suffering, and material sacrifices not worth the foreign policy objective. In a balance of power, decision makers adopt the deterrence of an attack as their aim. To be successful, they rely on military power, but it does not necessarily have to be equal to that of potential enemies. Even small powers can pose a real threat to larger ones if they can fight a long-term guerrilla war and thereby split opinion in the attacking country. The Vietnam War is an obvious example.

In a balance-of-power situation, by definition, force is threatened but not used. Military power retains its importance but becomes one of several strategies instead of the only tool for achieving foreign policy objectives. It remains important to remind other states that a potentially hostile alternative exists to the peaceful strategies currently being employed. Peaceful strategies are derived from the other two types of power: economic power and political power.

States can draw on several economic strategies, some providing positive incentives, others negative ones. All favor the powerful. Aid and the granting of favorable trade treatment can establish the basis for future positive relations. For example, granting most-favored-nation trade status to China, which will reduce tariffs on many of its products, was an ongoing debate in the United States before China joined the World Trade Organization (WTO). Many Americans took exception to China's treatment of its political dissidents and preferred punishment to business as usual. Others realized that not granting China the same access to U.S. markets enjoyed by most other countries would only hurt importers and U.S. consumers, while angering China's leaders and doing nothing to help those jailed for their criticisms of the government.

Governments employing negative economic strategies can cut off aid and reduce trade by setting a quota, or eliminate trade by carrying out an embargo. States employ **economic sanctions** individually, or collectively in the form of votes cast by the UN Security Council. Sanctions are punishment for actions deemed to be in violation of international norms. In Iraq, for instance, economic sanctions were applied after its 1990 invasion of Kuwait and continued for years, given Iraq's harsh treatment of its rebellious ethnic groups. Sanctions are also designed to encourage states to change their policies. Cutting off trade and financial flows, admittedly long-run strategies, have a chance of success only when carried out by virtually all the target country's trading partners. The strategy worked over time in the case of South Africa; however, Cuba provides an example of how economic sanctions can fail.

After Cuba's 1979 revolution and subsequent seizure of foreign-owned property, the Organization of American States voted to impose economic sanctions against Cuba. In addition, the United States eliminated its Cuban sugar quota, a trade policy that had assured a high level of Cuban sugar imports. This action virtually eliminated the U.S. market for Cuban sugar, the country's one major cash crop. In response, the Soviet Union became Cuba's main trading partner. The economic embargo has had no visible effect on Cuban political policies to this day. On the other hand, evidence exists that years of economic sanctions had an influence on South Africa's ruling white minority in its decision to hand over the government to elected representatives of the black majority. These examples show that most states in the international community, and all great powers, must cooperate for economic sanctions to be effective.

States also can use political power to influence other states. Announcing policy positions and providing information are strategies designed to have a desired impact whether communicated formally, through diplomatic channels, or informally, using public media. Like those based on economic or military power, sometimes political strategies work while at other times they do not. Take, for example, propaganda. Defined as an attempt to influence through emotional appeals, **propaganda** can be either true or false, but its negative connotations prevail in the public mind. Its strategies include public statements by government officials, articles planted in the written media, informational fliers, and films, among others. Their purpose is to affect the opinions of other government leaders or the general population in the same or other countries.

The problem with propaganda as a political strategy is the danger that targeted groups might react differently than policy makers intended. Iraq provides a case in point. During the months of waiting to see what would happen after his invasion of Kuwait, Saddam Hussein evidently wanted to send a message portraying himself as a reasonable, decent human being. He invited worldwide television coverage of his meeting with the Europeans his government was holding in Iraq. Unfortunately for the benevolent image he wanted to project, the world saw malevolence as the Iraqi president awkwardly attempted to put his arm around a young British boy whose face reflected confusion and fear. As with economic strategies, the powerful have a disproportionate chance of success; however, the clever use of public media can allow a weaker state to make its case to the world. President Fidel Castro of Cuba, for example, seems adept in meeting with prominent figures from other countries, allowing tourism to prosper and encouraging educational contacts.

Diplomacy, another political strategy that is often overlooked but can prove potent at times, includes all the communications between two or more governments or IGOs. As the most commonly understood form of diplomacy, **negotiation** takes place when officials talk to each other directly or through an intermediary. Indirect communications have come to be considered diplomacy as well. Called signaling or **tacit negotiations**, this process involves officials saying or doing something with the intent of sending a message to another government without telling it directly. Stating a shift in position can signal a willingness to break an impasse and negotiate a peaceful resolution to a dispute. Devising an offer to accompany a threat enhances the chances of reaching an agreement. The Cuban missile crisis in 1962 provides a much studied example. Reconnaissance photographs taken by a U.S. spy plane showed that the Soviet Union was deploying missiles with nuclear warheads in Cuba. The United States demanded their removal and signaled how seriously it considered the crisis by mobilizing its forces and blockading Cuba. The Soviet Union faced a hard choice: back down or risk a war with the United States. The confrontation was resolved peacefully when the United States promised not to invade Cuba in exchange for the Soviet Union's removal of the missiles and their warheads.

Politics refers to the process of bargaining and negotiating involved in making international as well as domestic decisions. It is the opposite of using force, but all involved in the process have an awareness of their varying levels of power. They assess the effect the potential agreement and its enforcement will have on their political, economic, and/or military power. In general, states choose between the options of negotiating or using force. Unfortunately, politics has a bad name for many people in the United States. It seems like common sense to Americans that governmental power corrupts inevitably, and therefore the decision-making process of cutting deals somehow works against the interests of the "average person." People with this narrow view fail to realize that politics and power are exercised in many public and private relationships involving businesses, universities, and community organizations. Politics describes not only what happens in making government decisions; power and politics are also inherent in all hierarchical organizations. In the international system, peace requires politics as the alternative to the use of military force.

In choosing policies and tactics, government leaders do not only consider their relative level of international power. They must also take into account the interests of their country and the perceptions of their people, as well of those of other states. Therefore, the concepts of interest and perception are crucial in analyzing international events.

Persons, groups, organizations, and states are said to have **interests** when they are able to use relationships or resources for their own benefit. As a practical matter internationally, the term interest relates to one or more of the three elements of power. States adopt positions and take actions that enhance their political, economic, and military capabilities. The problem arises in applying the concept to a specific situation. Most of the time, people disagree over exactly when their country's interest is at stake and when it is not.

In many international conflicts, no obvious, clear-cut interpretation of their country's interest is accepted by most of its people. The reason lies in the ambiguous nature of power itself. A state's reputation for power and its willingness to use it are just as important as any appraisal of exactly what capabilities the state may have. Such capabilities include the number, location, and battle-tested experience of troops; weapons and their sophistication; the level of economic resources that can be committed; and the political support of the population. These objective factors are only a part of the calculation made by a government's leaders in deciding what action they can take. The probable use of these elements of power figures just as much into another state's reasoning. In other words, power is not just a condition, like the sum of currency and troops for example. To influence decision making, states must be perceived as willing to apply the factors of power to a given situation. Here interpretations, assumptions, and perceptions become important.

To illustrate, during a crisis somewhere in the world, a knock-down drag-out argument breaks out in the United States over whether its interests in the situation are strong enough to warrant taking action. Sending troops to Bosnia is a good example. All involved in the verbal joust solemnly claim that their position reflects the true U.S. interest. Supporters of sending U.S. soldiers to monitor compliance with the peace agreement argued that the United States had an interest in the Balkans because if instability were to spread, Greece and Turkey could become directly involved. Since both countries are U.S. allies as members of NATO, the United States would be dragged into an even more volatile situation than if this country had dealt with the problem in the first place. Opponents to committing American troops vehemently countered by asserting that the United States had no real economic or strategic interest in Bosnia. The problem was in Europe, and the Europeans should have handled it.

Interest relates to the elements of power but, in applying it to a set of international events, policy makers filter it through their own **perceptions**. These attitudes and points of view are selective by definition and are determined by cultural-historical, nationalistic, ideological, or religious preconceptions. The resulting values and beliefs cause **perceptual selectivity**; that is, some information gets through to conscious thought, while other facts may be ignored or misinterpreted.

Humans often act on expectations. Such actions prove effective when they fit the circumstances, partly defined by the expectations of others. When they do not, failure often results. To illustrate, although U.S. leaders were convinced that the 1958 domestic violence in Lebanon was inspired by communism, it was subsequently revealed that their assumption was without any evidence or support. The landing by U.S. Marines helped shore up a minority government friendly to the United States but, within eight years, the country had dissolved into an ugly civil war. In a similar example of how perceptions can obscure reality, Kuwaiti and U.S. officials in 1990 did not think Iraq would invade Kuwait. They interpreted Iraq's threatening troop movements as a bluff. Unfortunately, they were wrong, and it took the 1991 Gulf War led by U.S. troops to force Iraq out of Kuwait.

Interests and perceptions directly relate to the intergovernmental politics needed to keep a balance of power operating. Some state relationships are volatile; others are more stable. The difference depends on the existence of a minimum of states with revisionist foreign policies and a maximum of status quo states. States are labeled **revisionist states** when they aim to change their existing level of military power by accumulating more troops and weapons. Sometimes they do this because they have decided a war may be needed to get what they want (such as a piece of a neighboring state's territory) or to stop a perceived enemy from becoming a major influence in a third country. Other times, revisionist actors aim for a preponderance of power to use fear and bluff in forcing adversaries to back down. In contrast, **status quo states** are satisfied with their existing level of power; nevertheless, they may feel threatened by a revisionist state's power buildup. Such a reaction is prudent in an anarchic situation. If a revisionist state continues its aggressive policy, other states will add to their arsenals, producing in turn higher levels of fear, tension, and overall instability. A degenerating cycle sets in as destabilizing relationships result in less predictable behavior and more unknowns, thus increasing distrust, fear, and misperception. The greater the destabilization, the greater the military buildup.

The Middle East is a regional power system long noted for its great instability. In the decades since World War II, at least ten wars, innumerable terrorist incidents, periodic domestic demonstrations and rebellions, and several high-profile assassinations have taken place in the Middle East. Much of this violence can be explained by the fact that the region is filled with revisionists, including Syria, Israel, Iraq, Iran, Libya, and, arguably, Lebanon. All do not accept their present boundaries for various reasons, and several have substantial numbers of people who retain revolutionary ideologies with expansionist overtones. Palestinians may be the ultimate revisionists because they are demanding part of the land they regard as their historical heritage so they can have a state, and this is the same territory many Israelis perceive as theirs. This leaves few status quo states in the Middle East: Egypt, Jordan, the oil-rich gulf sheikdoms such as Qatar and Saudi Arabia, and Turkey.

In contrast, northeast Asia has been a relatively stable region since the Korean War ended with a cease-fire in 1953. Violent incidents have occurred, but they have not led to war at least partly because every state in the region has a status quo foreign policy. All wanted to expand their economies and keep the sea-lanes open. China restrained the one potentially destabilizing state, North Korea.

Maintaining an effective balance of power requires understandable policies that are clearly communicated to both friend and foe. Some ambiguity may prove useful as a tactic in a specific situation, but general intentions must be seen as peaceful. Particularly with adversaries, decision making must be flexible with a willingness to negotiate. Unknowns heighten anxiety and create a context fostering suspicions that military power exists not for defense but for offense. In a viable balance of power, states can remain adversarial but do not fight each other. Some international relations analysts consider such a situation, however tenuous, as the best hope for peace. Others, however, think a stable balance of power can evolve into a more permanent kind of peace, as it has in Western Europe. As the third set of policy choices shown in Figure 8.1, a rule of law is both an indicator and implementor of permanent peace.

International-Rule-of-Law Strategies

An **international rule of law** evolves when states follow commonly accepted rules of behavior and orderly processes for peacefully working out conflicting interests. There are two ways in which behavioral standards become established. First, they develop traditionally as norms because they are commonly practiced over time, such as human rights standards. Resolutions of the UN General Assembly are taken as evidence of such customary law if they are passed over and over again by virtually all the world's states. This kind of consensus formed around resolutions condemning colonialism.

Second, rules are formulated by states negotiating and ratifying treaties. Security Council resolutions fall into this category because their authority is derived from the UN Charter, which is, in effect, a treaty. Thus peaceful patterns of state interaction are legitimized formally and by common practice. The standards of behavior become reinforced by peaceful, problem-solving interactions.

The number of international organizations has continued to grow in the decades after World War II. States and groups have become woven together through these institutions because they are deemed necessary for dealing with the whole range of human interactions. IGOs have become important in diplomacy for all states—small, regional, and great powers. The United Nations, World Bank, and other IGOs, such as the African Union, provide representation for small powers which are at a disadvantage when interacting with larger ones bilaterally, one on one. They gain at least some leverage within a multilateral context because they assert common positions and vote with other less powerful states. Such blocs can have an effect on the development of international institutions.

To take the point one step further, the regularity and confidence evident in some interstate relations even amounts to a sense of community, complete with commonly accepted rules. People in countries that are members of the European Union (EU), for example, cannot imagine a war among themselves. This situation presents a striking contrast with their history during the first half of the twentieth century. Decades of effective cooperation after World War II have eliminated force as a means of settling disputes among Western Europeans in the foreseeable future.

The development of this permanent peace came after two all-out world wars within thirty years. World Wars I and II, in turn, produced history's greatest volume of slaughter and material devastation. World War II occurred when Nazism took nationalism to its illogical extreme. The Nazi brand of fascism eventually denied even the right of existence to its imagined enemies. Europe's Jewish minorities, as well as millions of other people, were killed, not as a means of winning a war, but because of a perverted principle. World War II's unimaginable destruction, plus the horrifying barbarity of the Holocaust, compelled Europeans to create new international institutions potentially able to affect state behavior. The institutions of the European Union have eroded the sovereignty of their members, and thus anarchy no longer provides the context for how member governments relate to each other. Yet for centuries the concept of anarchy did apply in Europe.

The **European Union** provides an example of a set of international institutions that actually causes its member states to do what they otherwise would not. For example, its administrative institution, the European Commission, sued in the European Court of Justice seeking to compel Greece to end its policy of denying landlocked Macedonia use of a Greek port. This lawsuit was a significant factor in Greece's decision to drop its trade embargo of Macedonia. There are many other examples of EU member states enforcing rules with which they disagree and rejecting their own policies inconsistent with agreed-upon rules. In other words, EU members accept constraints on their own behavior imposed by international institutions. EU member states have yielded sovereignty even to the extent that individuals from other states as well as their own can sue them in the European Court of Human Rights.

Even analysts who assume anarchy to be the nature of the international system note that IGOs have modified state behavior to some extent. The European Union certainly has eroded the sovereignty of its members. International relations specialists debate the degree of sovereignty handed over to EU institutions, but the organization's evident success cannot be ignored. As evidence, the EU accepted ten new members in 2002, joining the existing fifteen. While the process of community creation is far less developed in every other IGO, the EU models how to end war and establish permanent peace.

Within universal IGOs, however, the state sovereignty principle is not only alive but well—all the more reason actively to support the expanding and enforcing of international law, say its advocates, through strengthened UN institutions. Institutional development has only begun with the World Court and the Security Council. As the barest beginnings of an international legal framework, neither can enforce its decisions. Yet their actions can confer the legitimacy needed to attract support from the international community, often useful to even the most powerful states.

The **World Court**, headquartered in The Hague, Netherlands, has jurisdiction only in cases where both states are parties. Individuals have no standing to sue. Established in 1946, the World Court consists of fifteen judges from different countries elected to nine-year terms by both the UN General Assembly and the Security Council. Private citizens, groups, or businesses cannot bring a grievance against their own or another state in the World Court. Some states have refused to obey World Court rulings. In 1984, for example, Nicaragua sued the United States for placing mines in that country's main harbor. After losing the case, the United States announced that it did not have to comply with the court's decision. An example of success occurred in the 1992 settlement of a border dispute between El Salvador and Honduras when both countries accepted the World Court's ruling.

World policing is carried out by states. The UN Security Council can impose economic sanctions on a specific state and authorize election observers or peacekeeping missions. The first such mission was sent to Cyprus in 1956; by 1996, peacekeeping forces were still in Cyprus as well as in Lebanon, Cambodia, Haiti, and Bosnia. All material and personnel for peacekeeping missions are paid for and provided by specific states. Actual wars have been fought under United Nations authorization. The Korean War in 1950 and the Gulf War in 1991 implemented UN Security Council resolutions. Both were conducted under U.S. command as the coalition's organizer, most powerful state, and contributor of the most troops. In fighting the two wars, the international community had responded to the purest form of international aggression, that is, territorial invasion with the goal of taking over the victim and eliminating its sovereignty.

This last point illustrates the fact that, since it was introduced, international law has been in the interest of the great powers. The first two issues in the seventeenth century were the need to protect commercial shipping from seizure during peace, and the treatment of noncombatants and prisoners during war. Both were in the interest of countries with the most trade and wars, but they also benefited smaller powers. Establishing rules sets principles of behavior that any state can use in making a diplomatic case. Because it legitimizes a universal consensus, international law can establish a moral imperative as well as accomplish the more mundane task of regulating common-place interactions across borders. In spite of well-publicized violations of international standards in extreme cases, mostly involving human rights, the vast majority of inter-national rules govern ordinary transactions and are followed most of the time. States honor passports, issue visas, deliver mail, and enforce contracts. The world's daily interactions are regulated by international law, and compliance is the norm.

Even concerning their political and security interests, states would have to invent the United Nations and its specialized agencies and formulate international rules if they did not exist. They offer states, particularly the great powers, the cover of legiti-macy not granted by bilateral negotiations. Rules governing state interaction and authorized by international institutions give structure to cooperation and reflect a gen-eral consensus. Such institutions also provide for participation by all interested parties. Thus international law and organizations parallel domestic rule of law because power-ful people in a society pass the laws which they too should obey.

The issue of peace and war illustrates the evolution of international rules of behavior because it involves high-risk policy making by definition. International law concerning war and peace has long been focused and filtered by the concept **just war**. Debated for centuries by philosophers, theologians, political leaders, and writers, a consensus has developed that a war is "just" when the combatant fights in self-defense and accepts limits on its actions, such as preventing the slaughter of civilians and pris-oners of war. The problem of interpretation exists because virtually every group or state using violence claims self-defense in blaming its enemy for causing the conflict. Also, when the tactics of war result in "collateral damage" (the U.S. military term for civilian deaths in the Vietnam War), states shrug and say such unfortunate events are a by-product of war.

In the latter half of the twentieth century, **human rights** became a much broader issue concerned with the treatment by governments of their own citizens. After World War II, the first War Crimes Tribunal tried and punished Nazi leaders for committing "crimes against humanity" in their planned, systematic annihilation of ten million Jews, Gypsies, and others designated as "undesirable." A 1948 international agreement codified international law by specifying **genocide**—acts committed with the intent of destroying in whole or in part an ethnic group—as a crime against humanity. Most of the world's states and, with the ratification by the United States in 1992, all the major powers have signed and ratified the Convention on the Prevention and Punishment for the Crime of Genocide.

Another statement on human rights was adopted by the UN General Assembly in 1948. Called the **Universal Declaration of Human Rights**, the document specifies fundamental freedoms including religious and political rights, a ban on torture, and the right to economic well-being. The broad range further expands human rights norms by covering abusive actions of governments and groups in peace as well as war. Schol-ars disagree as to whether the Universal Declaration of Human Rights should be con-sidered international law. Most think the General Assembly does not have the authority to legislate international law. Since 1948, eight additional human rights treaties have been negotiated and signed (for example, the Convention against Torture and Other Cruel, Inhuman, or Degrading Treatment or Punishment), but they have not been ratified by enough signatory states to go into effect. A case can be made that human rights are basic principles of law, and thus violations could be punished; however, in every case but genocide this represents a controversial position. As with other major issues facing the world at the beginning of the twenty-first century, NGOs monitor compliance by gathering information and pointing out problems. Amnesty International and Human Rights Watch are the two most prominent international human rights NGOs.

A grand debate among international relations specialists is occurring over how far international law and institutions have advanced in their development. The arguments for and against are compelling, as Chapter 9 will illustrate. There is a general acknowledgment of the importance of IGOs and of the European Union's supranational authority in specific areas of state interaction. Yet the argument attempts to assess the extent to which these factors substantially affect the policies and actions of governments: Has the international system undergone such a transformation as to make the concepts of anarchy and state sovereignty outdated and irrelevant? Suffice it to say that international institutions continue to have a role in framing state responses to threats to the peace.

CASE STUDY   Gulf Wars I and II

The two short wars between the United States and Iraq in 1991 and 2003 link the last decade of the twentieth century and the early years of the twenty-first century. They highlight the international role of the United States as one of the most important issues bridging the two centuries. Will the dominant military state with the world's largest economy behave as though it were first among equals and use its great clout to manage and reduce conflicts multilaterally, by working cooperatively with other states? Or will the United States use its power primarily to serve its unilateral interests and take into account the positions of others only as they serve its own?

The August 1990 invasion by Iraq of its neighbor Kuwait triggered the first Gulf War (called the Persian Gulf by Iran and the Arabian Gulf by Saudi Arabia). In January and February of 1991, the United States, under the administration of president George H. W. Bush, responded with over 500,000 land, sea, and air forces supported by military contingents from several states in an international coalition. The forty-two–day war included air bombardment followed by ground combat that sent remaining Iraqi forces fleeing from Kuwait. A clearly worded Security Council resolution had authorized the collective security action.

The U.S. president in the second Gulf War, George W. Bush, the son of President George H. W. Bush, made the case that Iraq's President Saddam Hussein had to be removed from power and that Iraq had weapons of mass destruction (WMD) which posed a major threat in one of the world's most strategic regions. (WMD includes nuclear, biological, and chemical weapons.) In March 2003, over 140,000 U.S. and approximately 20,000 British troops defeated scattered Iraqi resistance and occupied the country. Saddam Hussein and his supporters went into hiding. Because of opposition in the UN Security Council, no resolution specifically mandated the use of military force.

Macro Factors Causing the Wars

The Gulf wars had common underlying causes that explain why the United States and Iraq fought two wars in twelve years. Analyzing these causes reveals the opposing interests and perceptions of the United States and Iraq, their differing levels of power, and contrasting interpretations of international law. For the purposes of this discussion, the underlying causes fall into six categories: (1) Iraq's borders and ethnicities, (2) increasing U.S. intervention in the Persian Gulf, (3) intra-Arab regional politics, (4) Saddam Hussein's government, (5) international law, and (6) U.S.–Iraqi power imbalance.

Iraq's border and ethnic issues result from the state system established under colonial rule during and after World War I. The British and French carved out several new Middle Eastern countries from territories formerly ruled by the defeated Ottoman Empire. The British laid claim to Iraq as its protectorate. Yet, even when indirectly governed by the United Kingdom, no Iraqi government ever recognized another British protectorate, Kuwait, as a separate, sovereign state because Iraq claimed Kuwait as its nineteenth province. For centuries the area now known as Kuwait was part of the province of Basra. When the British drew the boundaries of the new country of Iraq, they included Basra City and some of its surrounding area. Kuwait remained a separate country which the British recognized as independent and under its protection in 1914.

Iraq's European-drawn borders built in another major long-term problem. Three main cultural groups found themselves in the same state. The minority Sunnis, who have ruled the country, and the majority Shiites are distinguishable by their differing interpretations of Islam; the Kurds have a separate culture and language. Being made up of three ancient and strong national identities while being ruled by only one of them stunted the growth of a common Iraqi nationalism.

Since its creation, Iraq has had little internal agreement on a state's basics: its borders and what group should legitimately rule. Thus Iraq has evidenced authoritarian regimes comprising military elements that have taken power by force. The country also has had revisionist foreign policies in claiming territories in neighboring countries and stridently opposing Israel.

Increasing U.S. intervention in the Persian Gulf became a second factor leading to war. Oil caused the first foray by U.S. interests in the region in the 1930s. American oil companies negotiated concessions with Saudi Arabia which took effect in 1933 (Polk 1981, 276–77). Decades and billions of dollars in investments later, economic interests became overtly strategic when, in 1979, the U.S. Navy began a constant patrol of the Persian Gulf. President Jimmy Carter initiated the Cold War naval show of force in response to the Soviet Union's invasion of Afghanistan. Since then, U.S. policy has viewed the presence of its navy as a stabilizer in the regional balance of power. In effect, the United States protected the oil-rich but militarily weak Arab sheikdoms. Their small populations make them vulnerable to the two larger and more powerful states on the Gulf's northern coast, Iraq and Iran. Before the first Gulf War, the United States had established naval bases in several countries; after the war, the number expanded and included army as well as naval installations. Every Gulf state except Iraq and Iran had a U.S. military presence before the second Gulf War. Many of the bases were used by the United States in launching sporadic military actions against Iraq in the years between the two Gulf wars. The U.S. public, as well as its political elite, generally accepted their country's deepening involvement in the Gulf.

Regional politics constitute a third underlying factor explaining the Gulf wars. Contradiction characterizes Iraq's place in the Arab world. As the historic home of the Abbasid Empire, Iraq was part of the Arab world's heartland and an integral element in the Arab people's common identity. Saddam Hussein's Iraq often attempted cooperation with other Arab states in lobbying for their acquiescence as it developed weapons it said challenged Israel's regional military superiority. Yet, as one of the larger Arab states, Iraq also competed in intra-Arab rivalries and in the region's balance of power.

As a revisionist state, Iraq wanted to rearrange its borders with its neighbors, Kuwait and Iran. Redrawing boundaries also meant gaining control of more oil reserves since they lie under present international borders. Adding Kuwait's approximately 9 percent of the world's known oil reserves (fourth in the world) to Iraq's about 11 percent (second in the world) would enable the Iraqi government to control about 20 percent, thereby rivaling the state with the largest reserves, Saudi Arabia, with its about 25 percent. (Percentages were calculated from data compiled by the Energy Information Administration, U.S. Department of Energy.)

Saddam Hussein's government itself can be cited as a fourth causal factor for war. In 1979 Saddam Hussein took power with elements in the military providing his support base as well as the Baath party, the country's only party. The principles of the Baath party, which means "renaissance" in Arabic, include socialist government policies, pan-Arab nationalism, and opposition to neo-imperialism. These principles provide an ideological appeal to Arabs outside Iraq. Saddam Hussein's internal policies included building Iraq's economic infrastructure and brutally suppressing dissent. Externally, Iraq attacked Iran in 1980. Taken together, Saddam Hussein's actions have provided ample evidence of an enthusiasm for violence both internally and externally.

Analysts who know Saddam Hussein's personal background and rise to power point out that he used personal and official violence to project an image of strength, the kind that equates mercy with weakness. Force provided at least part of his legitimacy and fear a means for his rule. He said that building military strength would enable Iraq to adjust its borders and carry out pan-Arab aims by countering Israel's military dominance. With such a political posture, Saddam Hussein could never back down from a fight.

The two Gulf wars highlight the role of international law in modern conflicts, and it is cited here as a fifth factor. Both Iraq and the United States have used international legal principles to support their positions. Iraq evoked the sovereignty and nonintervention principles in both wars. In the first war, Iraq claimed Kuwait was not a sovereign state but part of Iraq. Since sovereignty resided with Iraq, its dealing with Kuwait was an internal issue not subject to outside interference. In the second war, Iraq claimed that a U.S. invasion not expressly authorized by the Security Council constituted a violation of its sovereignty and an act of aggression.

In contrast, leading up to the first war, the United States argued that Iraq had clearly committed an act of aggression by crossing an international border and invading Kuwait with the goal of ending Kuwait's sovereignty. In the second, the United States asserted that for years Iraq had not complied with Security Council resolutions when it failed to cooperate with UN inspectors searching for evidence of WMD. Indeed, Iraq was still under economic sanctions imposed by the Security Council for noncompliance. Iraq had also previously engaged in acts of aggression against its neighbors, not only Kuwait but Iran, in 1980. In addition, the Saddam Hussein regime had violated human rights and international law when it used chemical weapons on Iranians and Kurds. Finally, the United States claimed that Iraq was supporting international terrorism. (Most of the international community disputed this last U.S. assertion.) Clearly, said the United States, Iraq constituted a threat to the peace.

The sixth factor takes into account the U.S.–Iraqi power imbalance. When one state is perceived as weaker than its enemy and as having no support from a powerful third state, the likelihood increases that conflict can lead to war. The implosion of the Soviet Union in 1991 deprived Iraq of the powerful international supporter that it had counted on in the past as a counterweight to the United States. U.S. worldwide political, economic, and military power left few with the perception that Iraq as a regional power could win a war with the United States.

Micro Analysis

Beneath their macro-level similarities, analyzing specifics about the two Gulf wars reveals contrasts rather than comparisons. Differences surface concerning the two wars' explicit causes and objectives, international legitimacy, and choice of war strategies.

As to specific causes and objectives, the fact that the two wars were fought in two different places offers a clue as to a major difference between them. In the case of the first, U.S. forces, with some coalition support, chased Iraq's troops out of Kuwait; in the second, the United States invaded Iraq aided by the United Kingdom.

The first war began when Saddam Hussein's troops overran Kuwait after making a case that it had unfairly demanded immediate repayment of the billions it had loaned Iraq to fight its war with Iran. In addition, according to the Iraqi government, Kuwait was pumping too much oil out of the shared field on their border. Of course, Saddam Hussein also stated the historic case that Kuwait was actually Iraq's nineteenth province.

In the aftermath of the first war, President George H. W. Bush ordered U.S. troops not to pursue the defeated Iraqi forces as they fled north to Baghdad. The United States had achieved the UN-mandated objective of freeing Kuwait. Also, the U.S. president expected that the rout of Iraqi forces, plus rebellions by the Kurds and the Shiites, would result in the Iraqis themselves ending Saddam Hussein's rule. This assumption proved mistaken because Saddam's loyal forces proved more than capable of crushing any rebellions with indiscriminate violence, resulting in the deaths of hundreds of thousands. U.S. troops remained on the sidelines during the slaughter of Shiites in Iraq's south.

A change in U.S. policy directly caused the second war. The second Bush administration announced "regime change" in Iraq as its objective. This Saddam-must-go policy meant war. As an addendum to his primary policy of regime change, President George W. Bush announced that Iraq must obey UN resolutions to eliminate its WMDs and it must allow UN inspectors back into the country to document compliance. When Iraq acquiesced to the demand, it left the U.S. government needing to make the case that Iraq did not cooperate as fully as it should have. Using this logic to supplement its primary position that Saddam Hussein's Iraq posed a threat to regional and world peace, the United States invaded Iraq in March 2003.

The two Gulf wars differ in a second major way. The first was legitimized by the UN Security Council; the second lacked any such legal clarity. The first war resulted from an overt attack across an international border recognized as such by the international community. This aggression by Iraq violated Chapter VII of the UN Charter, and the Security Council took the firmest action it can in authorizing armed force. In November 1990 it passed resolution 678, which mandated member states "to use all necessary means" in compelling Iraq's withdrawal from Kuwait. Virtually all the rest of the world supported the U.S. military in its collective security action. Some, including several Arab states, supplied troops, and some, like Japan, helped by paying almost all of the needed $60 billion.

In the months preceding the second war, the UN Security Council became the locus for intense public debates. In November 2002 the Security Council unanimously passed resolution 1441, which demanded "full implementation of existing resolutions on Iraq's weapons of mass destruction" and insisted inspectors "be given unhindered access to any suspected weapons sites." The resolution also warned of "serious consequences" in the event of noncompliance (United Nations Information Centre). Under intense international pressure, Iraq allowed UN inspectors to search for evidence of WMD. They searched for weeks and found none. The United States and the United Kingdom introduced a resolution authorizing the use of military force against Iraq but withdrew it when France announced it would exercise its veto instead of just abstaining. Russia and China, also permanent Security Council members with a veto, voiced opposition arguing that the UN inspectors should continue their work. Consequently, the U.S. use of force in the second war did not have clear Security Council validation.

The United States relied on the more murky legal justification that twelve years of UN resolutions demanding that Iraq eliminate its WMD had not produced Iraqi compliance and therefore member states must take action. Indeed, some in the U.S. government thought the United States did not need specific UN legitimization since, as a sovereign state, it could respond unilaterally to the perceived Iraqi threat. Actually, the United States acted bilaterally by negotiating support from each of several countries, most notably the United Kingdom. The question remains as to whether the United States, by implying that it was exercising its sovereign right of self-defense, undermined international institutions and legality. Judgment in the international community about U.S. behavior has been affected by the fact that U.S. troops had located no WMD in Iraq months after the war. In this context, those critical of the United States' use of force remain dubious about President Bush's postwar claim that Saddam Hussein had to be removed because of his "programs for the production of WMD" and not necessarily because of the presence of the weapons themselves.

As the third category of difference between the two wars, the first war's military strategies contrast with those used in the second war, at least on the part of Iraq. Given its preeminent military power, the United States fought conventional wars in both cases. Iraq, however, switched strategies. In the first war, Iraq deployed its conventional army in Kuwait and attempted to fight the American military on its own terms, primarily with tanks. U.S. forces routed the Iraqi army in Kuwait after minimal resistance, and the Kuwaitis welcomed U.S. troops as liberators.

In the second war, Iraq used guerrilla-style tactics instead of fighting major battles. Now and then they slowed the American juggernaut, but in less than a month all of Iraq fell to U.S. and British forces. President Bush announced the end of "major combat" on May 1, 2003. Opposition to U.S. and British occupation continued to be expressed by terrorist tactics: the destruction of infrastructure, bombings of civilian targets, and the killing of U.S. and British soldiers.

Legacy

While both Gulf wars projected unprecedented U.S. power into the region, the second marked a qualitative leap in U.S. involvement. The Bush administration's occupation of Iraq, hard on the heels of the U.S. invasion of Afghanistan and subsequent occupation of its capital, marked a much more intrusive intervention than any contemplated by a previous U.S. government. Instead of being a balancer in the Gulf's balance-of-power equation, the United States became embedded as a direct player in the Gulf and in the larger political arena of Arab politics. Unknown at the time of this writing, the ramifications of direct U.S. rule of an Arab state will emerge over time.

The second Gulf War will leave a second significant legacy. While the United States carried out the will of the international community in the first war, the second threw the constructive U.S. multilateral role into serious question. The first war reinforced established international law and the United States as the world's leader in creating a world of orderly stability. In the second war, however, the United States attacked Iraq after withdrawing the authorizing resolution from Security Council consideration when three of its five permanent members announced their opposition. Many state, IGO, and NGO decision makers and opinion leaders consider U.S. hegemonic activism in Iraq as having undermined progress toward an orderly and peaceful world. U.S. policy makers, however, regard the overthrow of Saddam Hussein as necessary to increase the possibility for stability in the Gulf. Whichever position subsequent events show to be the more viable interpretation, all can agree that the second Gulf War propels to the forefront of the international system agenda the question of whether the United States implements or threatens an international rule of law.

TERMS AND CONCEPTS

Balance of power *163*

Collective security *157*

Conventional war *160*

Diplomacy *164*

Economic sanctions *163*

European Union *168*

Genocide *170*

Great powers *155*

Guerrilla war *159*

Human rights *170*

Humanitarian intervention *157*

Interests *165*

DISCUSSION QUESTIONS

1. Give examples of states that fit into each of the four power classifications: small powers, regional powers, great powers, and superpowers. On what basis did you make your determinations?
2. What is the difference between state politics and international politics?
3. In your opinion, why do groups or states sometimes choose violent means to achieve their objectives? Which of the following three categories best summarizes your answer: characteristics of human nature, certain kinds of states, or the international system itself?
4. Do you think international law affects state behavior? Why or why not?
5. Explain the changes currently affecting the international system. How do you think they enhance or detract from the power of international states?

RESEARCH PROJECTS

1. Read news accounts of the events that led to the first Gulf War (August 1990–February 1991). How do the following concepts explain what took place: interests, levels of power, international law, economic tactics, propaganda, and diplomacy?
2. Conduct some research on a civil war in recent history (for example, in El Salvador in the 1980s). Analyze the case by determining the factors that caused the war as well as those that played a role in the peace process.
3. For one international issue, such as human rights, list the NGOs that deal with the issue. Choose one and describe what it is doing to address or resolve the issue.
4. Choose a world region, such as southern Africa, and find some basic information about the states located within that region. Use what you find to interpret the states' interests in relation to each other.
5. Read news accounts about a foreign policy issue, such as the U.S. occupation of Iraq, noting in particular how members of the U.S. Congress reacted to the issue. What different perceptions do their reactions reflect?

INTERNET RESOURCES

Foreign and Commonwealth Office, UK: http://www.fco.gov.uk/reference/briefs/yugo chronology.html The chronology of events in the former Yugoslavia (from January 1990 to November 1995) found on this site is among the most inclusive and useful.

U.S. Department of State: http://www.milnet.com/milnet/state/1996/year.htm The State Department's reports on terrorism are included on this site.

World New Index: http://www.stack.nl/~haroldkl This is one of the best inclusive link sites to news articles in papers from around the world.

United Nations Peacekeeping: http://www.un.org.depts/dpko/ Here summaries are available of all UN peacekeeping operations past and present.

CHAPTER **9**

Perspectives on Peace and War

> *"Until these war criminals are delivered to justice in The Hague, we will not have the basis in this country for free elections with democratic principles and therefore we will continue to have a country that is divided."*
>
> — MUHAMED SACIRBEY, BOSNIAN FOREIGN MINISTER (QUOTED IN SCIOLINA 1995)

> *"I will not embrace an agreement that trades justice for peace."*
>
> —JUDGE GOLDSTONE, CHIEF PROSECUTOR, INTERNATIONAL WAR CRIMES TRIBUNAL ON THE FORMER YUGOSLAVIA (QUOTED IN "BOSNIAN TALKS SNAG ON FATE OF TWO SERBS," *NEW YORK TIMES*, NOVEMBER 17, 1995)

> *"A sovereign state, recognized by the world community, is under attack from forces encouraged and supplied by another power. This is not a civil war but a war of aggression. . . . A well-armed Muslim–Croatian alliance would confront the Serbs with a quite new and unwelcome challenge. It might even prompt the Serbs to settle."*
>
> —MARGARET THATCHER, FORMER PRIME MINISTER OF THE UNITED KINGDOM (THATCHER 1994)

War has been considered one of the four scourges of humankind for centuries, joining disease, starvation, and death. It seems as though these four horsemen of the apocalypse have galloped around the world nonstop throughout the twentieth century. Their human agents have been active particularly in war, the calamity directly caused by people themselves. Except for extreme nationalists who regard war as necessary in eliminating enemies, people view peace as a desired normalcy. The three perspectives presented in this chapter diagnose why wars occur, and what it will take to diminish or maybe even eliminate them.

When people think about peace and war, they often make either conscious or unconscious assumptions about what institutions deserve their primary loyalty and, therefore, should be the means for interacting internationally. The dominant perspective regards the world as primarily made up of states held together and legitimized by the patriotism of their citizens. Another perspective, which has persisted for centuries and has been reinforced and revitalized by the veritable explosion of international institutions in recent decades, emphasizes the similarities shared by all humans and views states as historical artifacts perhaps now artificial and outdated. A third perspective focuses on what may be termed *nationhood* instead of statehood. As the often neglected but ever present primary source of identity, cultural groups should determine the form their international interaction should take, whether in states, international organizations, or their own newly developing interactive processes.

STATE SOVEREIGNTY

Clearly, the prevailing perspective holds states as the main means of international inter-action. As the most prominent and powerful actors in the international system, states benefit from centuries of legitimacy enshrined in international law and enlivened by patriotic emotion. They have fought wars but have achieved peace as well. At this time, war is far from probable and may be not even possible among the world's most power-ful states. Thus, people with a state-centered perspective consider themselves vindi-cated since a case can be made that states have proven capable of managing conflict in an increasingly complex world.

The state sovereignty perspective is not solely based on the state's functional role as the most effective unit for setting the rules for international economics and politics. People ardently loyal to their country also view it as the embodiment of the best of their own history and group values. They consider their state as more than the sum of its parts—not simply as everybody living within its borders under the authority of a common government. A patriotic feeling of identity has power in its appeal to the sense of loyalty and self-sacrifice in people. With the decline and even demise of other ide-ologies, particularly those of the left, nationalism has become the dominant ideology at the beginning of the twenty-first century. Whereas other ideologies, such as commu-nism, are not specific to a group of people, nationalism offers a time-honored, often uncontested idea of a person's location in the world and place in the flow of history.

People with the state-centered perspective realize that anomalies exist in the inter-national system, including multinational corporations, international governmental organizations (IGOs), and nongovernmental organization (NGOs). Yet states make the rules by which the international system is run and, as armed actors, they are the only enforcers of the rules. International relations theorists call the state perspective *realism* in its recognition that states have the power, and security is their main interest.

Some advocates of the state sovereignty perspective would go further in asserting that states remain the world's central actors not only because they are powerful, but also because their legitimacy derives from patriotism, the emotional loyalty of their population. Therefore they alone can speak for the world's people. Competing loyalties within a state are viewed as a problem. The greatest threat at the present time, ethnic nationalisms at their worst cause wars within states. In fact, this kind of war is flourish-ing even while wars among states are diminishing. Even when it does not lead to attempts to dismember an existing state, ethnic nationalism can undermine a country's ability to act internationally in maintaining a balance of power.

For most people with the state sovereignty perspective, a balance of power remains the way to peace. International governmental institutions can be useful vehi-cles for enhancing the foreign policy interests of states. Thus, they play a constructive role in achieving stability as they facilitate a balance of power. IGOs, however, must not become a means for undermining the power and authority of states. If IGO leaders act independently from the policies of member states, it becomes harder for states to maintain an effective balance of power.

Deterrence and Military Power Paradoxes

To achieve a balance of power, states adopt a deterrence strategy because military force remains an option if economic and political tactics prove ineffective. **Deterrence** means states must pose a credible military threat to enemies and potential enemies. If a state seems weak, it could invite attack. An adversary may calculate that using economic or political strategies will take too long, prove ineffective, or end in an unwanted compromise. In this situation, the temptation exists to use force. To deter such a decision, states must have not just military power alone but also the reputation for a willingness to use it. This leads to a balance-of-power paradox. To be credible, military force has to be regarded as potentially effective. Using it now and then is the surest way to demonstrate military potency. Thus, policy makers sometimes argue that to forestall a large war, a small one may be necessary. Balance of power is defined as an absence of war but, according to its own rules, it can be used to justify military actions.

Policy makers must deal with another paradox in establishing deterrence. They are presented with what international relations theorists call a **security dilemma**. Governments have to decide how much military power is enough to deter potential aggressors. If they increase their force capability too much, it will threaten other states in the region, which, in turn, may build up their own military forces. The result is the same or less security than existed originally. In a context of distrust and conflicting interests, an enemy regards any expansion in military forces as an aggressive act. An arms race may result, which will destabilize the existing balance of power. Instability emphasizes mutual fears and hostile perceptions, which become reinforced by a cycle of actions and reactions. People who forestall such a cycle, called *statesmen*, perform the difficult task of putting military power at the service of political power and achieving foreign policy aims without using force. This task is easier for a great power than for a small one.

The nuclear arms race between the United States and the Soviet Union during the Cold War provides an example of deterrence and, some would say, a security dilemma. Both states built weapons during the 1950s and early 1960s, employing a policy called *mutually assured destruction* (MAD). Each superpower planned to deter an attack by the other nuclear superpower by building more weapons with bigger payloads. Therefore, it could launch a devastating second strike even after it had taken a first strike. Later in the Cold War, both sides adopted another policy. Called *nuclear utilization theory* (NUT), it assumed that a nuclear war could be won if it were limited to smaller nuclear weapons, allowing some of the population to survive. Each superpower then sought to deter the other by producing a wide range of weapons so that they would not have to rely on a massive, all-out retaliatory strike. With first the MAD and then the NUT strategies dictating policy, the nuclear arms race produced more than 40,000 warheads. The question could well be asked whether they produced more or less security for the cold warriors. People with a state sovereignty perspective, however, would point out that this security dilemma question is irrelevant: the fact that no nuclear war occurred means deterrence must have worked.

WORLD ORDER

The world order perspective sees states as the problem, not the answer, to minimizing war and maximizing peace. Unfettered state sovereignty and international anarchy have allowed the most destructive human tendencies to dominate too often. People with a world order perspective hold a wide variety of basic principles, with some contradicting others (which will be explained on the following pages). Yet all the world order advocates emphasize the development of international law and institutions as the means of achieving the conditions for peace. The proliferation of NGOs, in particular, is inherently beneficial since people interact with each other beyond state boundaries without the filter of state power. The world is more and more tied together through growing networks of human interaction, whether they are IGOs or NGOs.

There are at least four variations of the world order perspective: one world, functional interdependence, U.S. leadership, and world government. People advocating any one of these four perspectives agree to strengthening international law and organizations, but they have different reasons for doing so.

One World

The first set of assumptions leading to the world order perspective believes the world is one in its essentials. It recognizes that all the world's people share a common humanity as well as economic needs and dependence on the natural environment. It considers building a sense of community based on social justice as the only path to true, permanent peace. Differences among people, their languages, behavioral characteristics, and identities are not inherent. They have to be taught. As people come to realize that they are held together by increasing global interdependence, more and more will learn that their similarities are more basic and important than their differences. The true realists are those who understand how interwoven human life on the planet has become.

The need to develop a sense of community by learning to cooperate can arise from idealism but also from interest. Interdependence produces conflicts as well as the need for cooperation. Communities do not end tensions among the different interests and perceptions of their members; they provide incentives for managing them. Advocates of this interpretation of world order accept the idea that international organizations will develop processes like the pluralist political systems in Europe and the United States. They also define human rights as belonging to individuals, not to culture groups. Establishing processes for dealing with and solving common problems produces trust. It is in everyone's interest to interact and negotiate disagreements peacefully. In learning how to make decisions together, one-world advocates see themselves as appealing to the best in human nature not by ignoring the worst, but by coping with it.

Functional Interdependence

Those identifying functional interdependence as the most effective way to achieve an orderly world illustrate their approach by pointing to the ongoing integration of European states. Based on a set of ideas articulated in the 1940s and 1950s, **functional interdependence** was envisioned as a way to make war obsolete. The theory offers at least two reasons why economic integration would lead to permanent peace: (1) economies would become so tied together that a state could not produce war-fighting material on its own, and (2) shared economic vested interests would require increasing social and political cooperation because of the need for common policies. The integration process was to proceed incrementally beginning with specific, technical, economic activities. The European Coal and Steel Community was the first step, chosen because its products were so essential to a modern industrial economy. Encouraged by free trade policies, the European Common Market followed the European Coal and Steel Community as the integration process continued in other economic sectors. The density of contacts created by the common market had spillover effects by revealing a need for cooperative social and political policies. To illustrate, member states encouraged the movement of workers by adopting similar social benefits so that workers would move from one country to another as needed and not be influenced by better unemployment compensation programs. The name of the organization was changed to the European Community when a common legislature was instituted. The latest step produced an integrated banking system and currency, called the *euro*. When this decision was made in 1992, the name was changed again to the European Union.

U.S. Leadership

Some analysts, as well as U.S. foreign policy makers, define world order as requiring U.S. hegemony. As the remaining superpower, it falls to the United States to mediate many of the world's conflicts and, failing this, to fulfill a police function. Yet this assertion of the central role of one state, with its own interests and perceptions, is not what many advocates of the world order perspective generally have in mind. They are uncomfortable with U.S. dominance. Theoretically, the development of cooperative decision making can occur among participants with varying levels of power, maybe even with one having more power than the others; however, rule making and enforcement must be a group effort. Those distrustful of U.S. hegemony saw their fears realized by the U.S. go-it-alone policy in the second Gulf War, which heightened the ongoing debate inside and outside the United States over its appropriate role in the world. Will it choose sovereignty or promote the rule of law by accepting the fact that it too must be held accountable?

World Government

Sometimes the world order concept is taken to mean world government. It seems to be the logical antidote to state sovereignty and international anarchy, and the nascent institutions already exist in the United Nations. To many with a world order perspective, however, the idea of a world government misses the point. Multilateral decision making in response to mutually experienced, global problems can and does take many forms. Answers are needed now and cannot depend on instituting a world government. Besides, if such an institution behaves like current governments, it may not be an improvement over the current multi-institutional, international complexity.

As demonstrated by this discussion, the world order perspective includes a wide variety of viewpoints since, unlike the state sovereignty and ethnic autonomy perspectives, it does not have one kind of institution as its focus. One of the most important differences among one-world perspective adherents is their varying attitudes toward the state. Some think that loyalty to country is compatible with their advocacy of international cooperation because states, as well as private groups, businesses, and international organizations, need to work together on global problems. Yet loyalty to a state cannot be blind. Governments make mistakes concerning global issues that can prove destructive to their own people in the long run. In cases of mistaken policies, criticism becomes a public duty. This reasoning implies that true patriots take an enlightened, long-term view of their state's interests and see them as intertwined with those of other countries.

Those with a one-world interpretation of world order consider nationalism, whether state or ethnic, a major problem. It can become a central cause of war. Permanent peace is possible, at least in the long run, but only if nationalist identities diminish and stop inhibiting cooperation among peoples of varying countries and ethnicities. At their worst states, or groups acting like states, insist on absolute loyalty and justify killing people for nationalistic reasons. Increasingly outmoded, indeed irrelevant in this global age, states developed long ago in a different age. The institution of the state spread at the expense of other political forms of organization and, like empires in their time, must now face decline and demise.

Critique from the State Sovereignty Perspective

Those with the state sovereignty perspective prefer to call the world order perspective idealistic. Actually, this is the kindest of their possible repertoire of responses. Downright dangerous would be another. One-world advocates, to choose an example, want to make the world better, more peaceful, and just, while ignoring the fact that states remain the only real means of taking action. What they should be doing is participating in the policy-making process of their own governments to develop effective solutions to global problems. Ardent state nationalists would go further in criticizing world order thinking. They believe it undermines loyalty to country. This constitutes a threat because, if such disloyalty spreads far enough, states will not be able to fulfill their essential role as protectors of the livelihoods and lives of their citizens.

ETHNIC AUTONOMY

A growing number of commentators, academics, and members of ethnic groups acknowledge that cultural groups provide the primary identity for human beings. The loyalty this engenders can challenge the loyalty required by centralized states. A state's government expects, indeed demands, the ultimate loyalty of every person within its jurisdiction. This can create a major source of tension, particularly when many people do not consider their state legitimate in demanding their loyalty. Coercion and sometimes violence can result.

Those with an ethnic autonomy perspective think that the structure of the international system should allow ethnic representation in addition to states, corporations, voluntary NGOs, and IGOs. Because the ethnic autonomy perspective is relatively recent, its institutionalization is still taking shape. Only the barest beginnings have emerged, indicating how cultural groups will organize *themselves* internationally. International conventions of representatives from many of the world's cultural groups have established cultural rights—not individual rights—as the basis for their representation. Article 27 of the Universal Declaration of Human Rights reads, "Everyone has the right freely to participate in the cultural life of the community." The Universal Declaration on Cultural Diversity, adopted by UNESCO's General Conference in 2001, elaborates **cultural rights** more fully:

> All persons should therefore be able to express themselves and to create and disseminate their work in the language of their choice, and particularly in their mother tongue; all persons should be entitled to quality education and training that fully respect their cultural identity; and all persons should be able to participate in the cultural life of their choice and conduct their own cultural practices, subject to respect for human rights and fundamental freedoms. (United Nations Educational, Scientific, and Cultural Organigation)

The Nunavut case study presented in Chapter 2 provides an example of a state that will allow a cultural group to govern itself. The case study described Canada's granting local autonomy to the Inuit living in part of its Northwest Territories. The experiment granted the Inuit semisovereignty, called **autonomy** by political scientists, and the new territory will be able to make decisions about all government functions except foreign policy and defense, which remain with Canada's government in Ottawa. This Canadian initiative remains unique as a method of addressing an ethnic group's demands for self-rule. Generally, state governments have insisted on subordinating group interests to what they term the "national interest." At their best, states have granted only individual rights which, by implication, require people to subordinate their cultural identities to their individualism. Those with an ethnic autonomy perspective may acknowledge the Canadian attempt to grant Inuit group rights and redress past wrongs; however, other ethnicities who live in Canada have issues requiring attention. People with a pro–ethnic group perspective thus feel an ambivalence toward the Canadian experiment.

Ethnicities more powerful than indigenous peoples are demanding greater participation in governmental decision making within existing states. Others are fighting for states of their own. The breakup of the Soviet Union provides a compelling precedent. Virtually every country in the world is experiencing some form of increased political pressure from its underrepresented groups; examples include French-speaking people in Canada, Scots in the United Kingdom, Tibetans in China, Kashmiri Muslims in India, Latinos in the United States, and Muslims in Norway. More demanding nationalists in some ethnic groups are using violence to achieve their own states, such as Kurds in Turkey, Basques in Spain, Chechins in Russia, Tamils in Sri Lanka, Hutus in Brundi, and Abkhazis in Georgia. Lists could go on and on of examples in both categories of ethnic group assertiveness; that is, those wanting sovereignty and those wanting more power within existing states. The issue of conflicting loyalties between state and ethnic nationalisms will preoccupy world leaders over the long term. Cultural identities do not go away. They remain basic to how individuals learn what it means to be human. For states to remain viable, they will have to establish more effective political processes for accommodating the interests of their less powerful ethnic groups. If they cannot, then various forms of autonomy will be invented, or more parts of the world will fragment into ministates.

Critiques from the State Sovereignty and World Order Perspectives

People with the state sovereignty perspective find worrisome the potential for state fragmentation. They think the creation of more ministates, driven by their own nationalistic animosities toward their neighbors, bodes ill for peace. The world needs more stabilizing influences, not fewer. The future would be frightening if every cultural group tried to establish its own sovereignty or even autonomy. Cultural groups should make use of the political processes within states to achieve their aims. Established state politics allow the leaders of groups to bargain and adjust governmental policies in their interest.

Advocates of the world order perspective differ with each other over whether ethnic groups will act in ways compatible with international law and institutions. Such groups have used international institutions as a means to present their grievances and recommend action. In so doing, they have expanded the number of NGOs and thus created institutional expressions of their interests and perceptions. There is a danger, however, because some ethnic groups choose not to develop peaceful ways to articulate their grievances. As the Bosnia case study that follows illustrates, unless an international rule of law is strengthened, groups can use violent strategies and cause extensive human suffering. World wars may not loom as an immediate threat, yet people in various parts of the world continue to find reasons to fight each other. Wars are smaller in scale but just as lethal to the people involved. Thus war remains a major world problem.

CASE STUDY   The War in Bosnia— Three Peoples in Search of a State

This case study illustrates how applying the peace/war concepts can help explain an appalling example of mass violence that occurred in Europe between 1992 and 1995. In Bosnia, certain ethnic groups recognized no authority higher than their own because they had no loyalty to the "state" formally recognized by other states. Bosnia's experience illustrates state disintegration, called **failed states** by international relations specialists, a situation that has also occurred in Africa and may happen again.

In 1991 two member republics of the state of Yugoslavia, Slovenia and Croatia, declared their independence. A year later, Bosnia-Herzegovina, another Yugoslav republic, announced its sovereignty. Within a few weeks, leaders of the Serb minority within Bosnia declared their own Serb Republic of Bosnia-Herzegovina, and the war in Bosnia began. Fighting lasted until a 1995 agreement was reached in Dayton, Ohio, brokered by the United States. The disintegration of Yugoslavia was accompanied by large-scale brutality reminiscent of World War II. The dead in Bosnia were estimated at about 200,000, and more than a million people, of a prewar population of 4.3 million, were displaced.

The war in Bosnia produced casual cruelty; systematic, ruthless torture, rape, and murder; and the establishment of internment camps. These tactics were designed to create ethnically pure areas either by killing people or by forcing them from the homes where their families in many cases had lived for centuries. With the intentional slaughter of innocents, the war in Bosnia matched other examples of pitiless bestiality in the twentieth century, the most brutal century so far. Called "ethnic cleansing" by the news media, and "genocide" by the United Nations, the violence in Bosnia went on in one form or another until the Dayton Accords established a cease-fire, the separation of warring factions by European and U.S. troops, and various political measures designed to foster peaceful interaction. The question remains, however, whether in the long term the antagonists will accept the status quo or resume fighting if outside forces are withdrawn.

A Tangle of Participants

In the years before the 1990s, Yugoslavia, and particularly Bosnia, had been extolled as an example of how a cooperative, sophisticated multiethnic society could emerge from a history of mutual antagonisms. The 1982 Winter Olympics held in Sarajevo, Bosnia's capital, had showcased the vibrant lifestyle created by the interaction of various cultures. A developing economy encouraged the flourishing of art and architecture, music and entertainment, literature and media from several cultures. Not a thin veneer, the multicultural lifestyle was part of daily life in Bosnia. In the 1980s approximately 30 percent of marriages in urban areas were reported as "mixed" (Malcolm 1996, 222). Only a decade later, the war in Bosnia destroyed what had been a flourishing multiculturalism. Symbols of diverse heritage—churches, mosques, libraries, and other historically important buildings—were demolished by artillery bombardment. Multicultural personal relationships were destroyed by individual acts of fiendish cruelty.

The war in Bosnia raises compelling questions: Why did the war explode so quickly? How did it degenerate into such depths of depravity? Answers are complex, but a useful explanation begins with an assessment of the perceptions and interests of the various participating groups, states, and IGOs. Sorting out the participants takes some effort, given their large numbers and the complex, changing nature of their relations.

Participants included the three major ethnic groups within Bosnia: Muslims, Serbs, and Croats. In addition, several outside governments are vital to explaining the war's causes, particularly the governments of Serbia and Croatia. (Serbia, the main part of what is left of Yugoslavia, kept the formal name of Yugoslavia because it included not only Serbia but also three other smaller sections of the former Yugoslav state.)

Furthermore, news reports of the Bosnian war add to this list of participants several states that played a secondary but important role in the flow of events: the United States, the United Kingdom, France, Germany, and Russia. Finally, IGOs played their parts, specifically the United Nations (UN), the North Atlantic Treaty Organization (NATO), and the European Union (EU). To help simplify this complex assortment of groups, states, and organizations, the following discussion categorizes the various participants into three levels of involvement: (1) groups within Bosnia, (2) states within the Balkan region, and (3) other states and IGOs in the larger international system.

Groups Within Bosnia Bosnia's three main ethnic groups provide the context for the conflict. Before the death and displacement brought on by the war, the breakdown of the groups was generally given as about 44 percent Muslim, 31 percent Serb, and 17 percent Croat. Of the five countries carved out of the former Yugoslavia, only Bosnia had no majority ethnic group. Most towns, and all cities, had mixed populations.

To an outsider, the similarities in the three groups seem obvious, but as the situation in Bosnia disintegrated in the early 1990s, the differences became more important. All three groups spoke a language called Serbo-Croatian before the breakup of Yugoslavia. Now each group considers its language different from that of the others. For centuries, Croats have written using the Latin alphabet of Western Europe, whereas Serbs write in the Cyrillic script used in Russia. Other language differences, such as in vocabulary, have become central as the two groups seek to put more distance between each other historically and culturally. Religion reinforces the linguistic distinctions— Croats generally identify with Catholicism and Serbs with the Eastern Orthodox version of Christianity. Muslims are the descendants of those who converted to Islam when the Balkans were ruled by the Ottoman Turks. The entire region was part of the Ottoman Empire for over three centuries.

Nationalistic perceptions based on linguistic and religious distinctions are reinforced by each group's notion about its place in history. As is often pointed out, Bosnia lies right on the fault line where three great civilizations meet: Western Europe, Eastern Orthodox Europe, and Islamic Asia. As a result, the most ardent nationalists among the Croats and Serbs see themselves as outposts defending the rest of their civilization against its enemies. Symbolized by their defeat in the 1389 Battle of Kosovo, Serbian nationalists portray their role as a bulwark against Islamic barbarism poised to invade the Christian world. They believe themselves to be the true Christians firmly holding out in the epic struggle, as compared with the weaker Catholics. Dominance in the region, therefore, is believed to be the well-earned historical right of the Serbs.

Croat nationalists, in contrast, perceive their role as upholding an enlightened, economically progressive Europe as it stands against the forces of the east, be they Orthodox or Islamic. Muslims regard themselves as synthesizers of the best in Eastern and Western traditions as well as the preservers of their own Islamic distinctiveness. Whereas, before the war, Muslims tended to take pride in Bosnia's multinational and multireligious character, during the war many began instead to extol their Islamic identity, particularly its opposition to oppression.

The differences among Serbs, Croats, and Muslims had existed for centuries. Nevertheless, the three groups lived side by side in peace for most of their shared history.

As with any multicultural society, Yugoslavia's ethnic groups evidenced "both coexistence and conflict, tolerance and prejudice, suspicion and friendship" (Bringa 1995, 6). Since the war, however, only a few accounts have included points illustrating the capacity of the country's people to interact positively. One example cites the fact that, in the 1980s, more than 3 million of Yugoslavia's population of 22 million were either in ethnically mixed marriages or a product of them (Woodward 1995, 36). Although religion distinguished Bosnia's three major ethnic groups, there is evidence that, as late as the 1980s, it was not important to a sizable majority of the republic's people; a 1985 survey put the proportion of religious believers at 17 percent (Malcolm 1996, 222).

Contrary to the impression left by news coverage of the war, reinforced by the comments of many analysts and U.S. political leaders, simmering ethnic hatreds did not spontaneously combust to create a violent conflagration. Nor was the war inevitable. To the contrary, it took years of menacingly nationalistic propaganda for polarized politics to become the norm. As made evident in the next section, specific events caused those with aggressively hateful nationalisms to dominate political decision making within the various Yugoslav republics.

The Balkan States Many analysts think that the breakup of Yugoslavia was foreshadowed by the death of its leader, Marshal Tito, in 1980. Tito, who had ruled the country since World War II, stood for a multiethnic Yugoslavia under the leadership of the Communist party. One-party rule was designed to foster a set of ideals that superseded narrow ethnic nationalism. After the leader's death, those with ambition were freed from the historic and countrywide basis of Tito's appeal. Aspiring leaders in Serbia, Croatia, and Bosnia needed to build their own base, enabling them to unite large numbers of people under their leadership.

In Serbia, Slobodan Milosevic used the Serbian Communist Party as the means for building support by promoting followers. He shifted the party's emphasis from equality and multiculturalism to an extreme form of Serb nationalism. As a result, during the late 1980s and early 1990s, Serb paranoia about the designs of their presumed enemies grew considerably. In response to the presumed Croat and Muslim threat, Milosevic proposed the old nationalistic idea of a "Greater Serbia." This state dominated by Serbs could be Yugoslavia itself or a geographically larger Serbia. After Milosevic became Serbia's party leader in 1987 and president in 1989, he used his party connections to displace the leadership in three of Yugoslavia's other constituent republics, replacing them with people of his own choosing. By 1989 four of the eight parts of the country were under his control. Severe economic problems assisted him in undermining other political leaders. The austerity measures that had been adopted in the mid-1980s to fight inflation and make foreign debt payments worsed an already shrinking economy and aroused a yearning for the strong, decisive, self-assured leadership promised by Milosevic.

In 1990 Milosevic's plans to achieve Serb dominance within Yugoslavia crashed with the disintegration of the Communist Party. This cut off his means for manipulating events in other republics. It also unleashed strident nationalists in each of the republics not controlled by Serbia; namely, Slovenia, Croatia, Bosnia, and Macedonia. With their exaggerated rhetoric, the new nationalistic parties reinforced the fears of the other ethnic groups.

The role of Serbia's President Milosevic in contributing to war highlights the importance of leadership in appealing either to a society's moderates or to its extremists. By using the government-controlled media to foster hypernationalism and placing overwrought nationalists in decision-making positions, Milosevic gained political power over his opponents. The logic of his nationalist ideology included the goal of enlarging Serbia, either through Serb control over Yugoslavia or, failing that, an enlarged and more ethnically homogenous Serbia. Thus, the case can be made that the resulting wars in Croatia and Bosnia did not originate as civil wars produced by a spontaneous outpouring of Serb nationalism with atrocities as an unfortunate by-product. Instead, a deliberate policy of expansion used war and atrocities as the means for achieving a Greater Serbia.

With the Communist Party's collapse, Franjo Tudjman's newly formed political party won the 1990 election in Croatia. With Croatian nationalism as its ideology, Tudjman's party proceeded to pass a law creating an autonomous Croatia. The centuries-old Croatian flag was flown, but, unfortunately, its red-and-white shield evoked memories of the fascist Croatia created by the Nazis during World War II. The military of this 1940s Croatian state had slaughtered, some say, hundreds of thousands of Serbs as well as others before being overthrown by Tito's forces.

Stirred by these memories and their own nationalism, Serbs in Croatia reacted against Tudjman's new government. In an area of Croatia where they constituted a substantial majority, Serbs organized their own militia, held a local referendum, formed their own parliament, and declared autonomy. Their clashes with Croatian police resulted in several deaths. These Serbs then asked local units of the Yugoslav army for help. With an officer corps dominated by Serbs, and implementing Milosevic's policy, the army acted to assist the Serbs in Croatia with arms, equipment, and trained troops.

In 1991 Croatia declared its independence from Yugoslavia. Serb paramilitary forces, supported by the Yugoslav army, fought a war against Croatia. By the time Croat forces became organized, about 30 percent of Croatia was controlled by Serbs. Fighting stalemated early in 1992, but its atrocities and ethnic cleansing had foreshadowed the much longer war soon to be fought in Bosnia.

The violence in Croatia took on a logic of its own. The individual acts of cruelty carried out by the Serb paramilitary units created vested interests. More and more people got caught up in the degenerating, downward spiral of mutual retribution and ever more violence. Hatreds were reinforced and perceptions hardened. The atrocities made real their victims' worst fears. Such actions became justification for similar acts of revenge carried out by Croats and, later in Bosnia, by Muslims. In this context, the exaggerated claims of excessive nationalists seemed correct. The more violence ensued, the more reasonable the claims appeared. The strident nationalists were looked to for leadership, particularly those to whom violence came easily. People surfaced as needed protectors who in peacetime would be considered suspect. Ideologues took over, and for them there were no innocents.

The declaration of independence by Croatia and Slovenia put Bosnia in an untenable position. It was clear that war would result from Bosnian independence. Yet with a government and ruling party predominately Muslim, Bosnia could not remain within the Yugoslavia now controlled by Milosevic's ultranationalist Serbia. There was no hope of redressing grievances through the bargaining and compromise of politics. Caught with no viable option, Bosnia held a referendum on independence in 1992. The ballot read, "Are you in favor of a sovereign and independent Bosnia-Herzegovina, a state of equal citizens and nations of Muslims, Serbs, Croats and others who live in it?" (Malcolm 1996, 231). Since the Bosnian Serbs in areas dominated by their nationalists boycotted the vote, the results were almost unanimous in favor of independence. As in Croatia, Bosnia's new party leader, elected by a majority in 1990, became the country's president. Thus Alija Izetbegovic became the only head of state in a former Yugoslav republic who had not been a leader in the now defunct Communist Party.

The reaction of the Serbian nationalists in Bosnia to the declared independence of a Bosnian state was predictable, given parallel events in Croatia. Their own parliament announced the existence of a Bosnian Serb Republic. A few months later, the Bosnian Croat party, with the same name as that of Tudjman's party in Croatia, declared a Croatian Community of Herceg-Bosnia. The Muslim-majority Bosnian government responded to the Serb and Croat actions by claiming to represent the whole of Bosnia. This situation resulted in over three years of war, with each group claiming different reasons for it. The Serbs, who called the war in Bosnia a civil war, asserted they had to fight for their own survival against Muslim oppression and extremism. The government of Bosnia depicted the struggle as needed for Muslim survival against the region-wide attempt made by Serbia to unite Serbs in the Balkans and achieve regional hegemony. The Croats put forth self-defense as their motive in responding to threats made by the other two groups to take them over and, more than likely, force them out of Bosnia. Given their superior firepower, the Serbs controlled about 70 percent of what had been the Bosnia-Herzegovina republic by 1993.

As for the ordinary people in Bosnia, many villagers resisted becoming part of the war. Unfortunately, some joined in when the fighting finally came in the guise of a military unit of outsiders attacking to drive out local people from a different ethnic group. In general, however, many expressed the sentiment, "We always lived together and got along well; what is happening now has been created by something stronger than us" (Bringa 1995, 4).

Belligerents in the war used several strategies. In committing atrocities, members of the Serb paramilitary units acted like terrorists. As the war wore on, some Croats and Muslims also committed torture, rape, and murder. Their strategy fits the commonly accepted definition of terrorism in several ways. In Bosnia, violence was used to terrorize people into abandoning their homes, thus clearing the area for repopulation by the dominant ethnic group. Other fighting strategies were also used in the war. In areas where they were not capable of conducting a conventional war, the warring factions used guerrilla hit-and-run attacks. As front lines firmed up, however, conventional assaults against enemy positions were attempted.

International Actors States in the European Union, particularly the United Kingdom, France, and Germany as great powers, attempted to decide on a policy to stop the war or at least to mitigate its effects. They were horrified by a scale of violence not seen in Europe since World War II. They also feared it would cause more states in the region to become involved. The United States, Russia, the United Nations, and NATO shared the aim of the Western Europeans, but it took years for all these secondary actors to overcome their differences of interest and perceptions and agree on a plan for peace. In the meantime, although self-defined as well intentioned, some of their actions exacerbated an already disastrous situation.

As the situation in Yugoslavia became chronically unstable in the late 1980s, Germany took the lead among the Europeans in setting a policy. One of its most significant actions was to recognize the independence of Slovenia and Croatia before consulting with other members of the European Union. Some analysts point out that this act forced the issue and extinguished whatever faint hope existed of negotiating a compromise. They also note that Germany traditionally had included the Balkans in its area of influence and was particularly interested in expanding political and economic ties with Slovenia and Croatia. Germany explained its unilateral policy by saying that decisiveness in recognizing the two new states had a chance of forestalling a Serbian use of force. Unfortunately for German policy, the opposite occurred.

Russia also had long had an interest in the Balkans as a supporter of Serbia. Serbia had gained its independence when Russia fought a war against Ottoman Turkey in 1830. Serbia and Russia share a cultural affinity through their common alphabet and Orthodox Christianity. Russia has traditionally perceived itself as the protector of the Serbs. Like Germany in Croatia, Russia sought to build friendly political relations and economic interests in Serbia. Strong nationalistic Russian sentiment emphasizing its Slavic heritage explains why some Russians were reported to be fighting for the Serbs during the war in Bosnia.

Support for their potential client states caused Germany and Russia to have a different view of events in Bosnia from the United Kingdom and France. The latter two states had no clear interest until the conflict had degenerated into ethnic cleansing, had become a European embarrassment, and threatened to draw in the Balkans' larger states. The United Kingdom and France coordinated their policy through the European Union and the United Nations. Both contributed thousands of troops to the UN peacekeeping forces.

If Britain and France could be accused of a slow reaction to the problem in volatile Bosnia, the United States realized the need for intervention even later. President George H. W. Bush's administration considered the breakup of Yugoslavia and its violent aftermath a European problem. Policy makers thought little could be done by outsiders if local people were determined to use violence in responding to deeply felt grievances. Anyone caught in the middle would fail no matter how well intentioned. The U.S. approach changed little during the early years of Bill Clinton's presidency. He articulated a U.S. policy of working in concert with European allies; that is, the Europeans were expected to take the lead in setting a common strategy. Clearly, during the early stages of the war, U.S. government leaders had decided that their country had no significant economic or political interests in the Balkans. They later changed this policy assumption.

From 1993 to 1995, the United States squabbled with its allies but took no unilateral action. However, the United States advocated a firmer approach toward the Serbs after they prevented UN peacekeeping troops from delivering food and medical supplies.

The United States also recommended using NATO airpower to take out the Serb artillery that was shelling Bosnia's capital, Sarajevo. The United Kingdom and France opposed military actions because they had lightly armed troops on the ground with the UN forces. Their soldiers were at the questionable mercy of the combatants, particularly the Serbs, who promised retaliation if NATO attacked them. Because, the United States had no soldiers among the UN peacekeepers who were delivering humanitarian aid, it felt free to threaten Serbs with NATO air strikes. Perhaps more than the European states, the United States sympathized with the Muslims as the group that had suffered the most atrocities. This principled position coincided with U.S. interests in maintaining good relations with the oil-producing Arab states which wanted the United States to alleviate the plight of Muslims in Bosnia.

As indicated in the foregoing discussion, IGOs had become involved in the Bosnian war. The institutions of the European Union, the United Nations, and NATO provided the negotiating networks for devising common policies and actions aimed at ending Bosnia's agony. Peace proposals, peacekeeping troops delivering food and medicines, and possible use of NATO air strikes all contributed to the mix of options and actions. One particular decision made by the UN Security Council has taken on long-term significance. In 1993 it established an International War Crimes Tribunal for investigating, indicting, and prosecuting individuals who had violated human rights in the former Yugoslavia. By 1997, according to a *Washington Post* article, a total of seventy-eight suspects had been indicted, most of whom were Serbs. Nine were in custody, not including the two highest-ranking Bosnian Serbs, Radovan Karadizic, the former president of the Bosnian Serb Republic, and Ratko Mladic, the republic's former army commander (Drozdiak 1997, A14).

The Dayton Accord

Since the United States stood back during the first years of the war in Bosnia, the first attempt to negotiate a settlement was sponsored by the United Nations and the European Union. At this time in history, whenever possible, the world's great powers work through an IGO, in most cases the United Nations. Thus international institutions and standards of behavior legitimized their policies. Yet even the most powerful states in the international community cannot directly control the events in and the policies of sovereign states, or local groups that act as though they possess sovereignty. The first peace plan failed in 1993 after its rejection by the Bosnian Serbs. A second peace agreement was proposed in 1994 by the five great powers formalized as a "Contact Group"—the United Kingdom, France, Russia, Germany, and the United States. The Serbs also refused to accept this peace plan because it did not cede to them all the territory they had taken during the war.

By rejecting the peace agreements, the Bosnian Serbs parted company with their main outside supporter, President Milosevic of Serbia, who had recommended acceptance of both agreements. He recognized that, in spite of the fact that the Serbs would have to reduce the Bosnian territory they controlled from about 70 percent to about 50 percent, the international community would legitimize their claim. Milosevic was not without his own interest in ending the war because of the economic sanctions imposed on his country by the UN Security Council for aiding Bosnian Serbs. The sanctions had produced a severe recession in Serbia and would not be lifted until an agreement was successfully negotiated.

The situation changed quickly in the summer of 1995 when the Serb forces were sent in pell-mell retreat from western Bosnia by Croatian and Bosniak armies. (The Muslim-dominated Bosnian government had begun calling their people Bosniaks.) During this time, the United States asserted itself by becoming the leading outside mediator. This change in U.S. policy came in reaction to two key events. The first was the February 1995 shelling of a crowded market in Sarajevo resulting in sixty-eight deaths, a record number for one such incident up to that date. Although no determination was ever made as to whether the mortar round came from a Serbian or Bosniak-government-controlled area, the carnage captured news headlines worldwide and was blamed on the Serbs.

The second shocking event occurred in July 1995 when Serbs overran Srebrenica and Zepa, two of the six "safe areas" in Bosnia protected by UN peacekeeping troops and sheltering thousands of Muslim refugees. In Srebrenica alone, over 60,000 people, barely living on drops from U.S. cargo planes and intermittent truck columns, were surrounded by Serb forces. When the Serb attack came, the few hundred Dutch peace-keepers could do nothing, not only because of their small numbers and light arms, but also because they had orders to fire only if directly fired upon. They were ordered not to respond to attacks on the Muslims under their "protection." After consolidating their control, the Serbs separated women and young children from the male population, as they had time and again in the early phases of the war. Many of the men were never seen again. Dutch soldiers reported that hundreds of bodies littered the routes trucks had taken to carry away the men and older boys. It was estimated that between 5,000 and 7,000 males were killed in cold blood.

With U.S. urging, NATO responded with two weeks of air strikes against Serb ammunition and weapons supplies. This action, plus a successful assault launched by Croatian and Bosniak forces, left the Serbs in disarray. Milosevic gained the upper hand, and he took on the authority to negotiate on behalf of the Serbs in Bosnia. The other parties to the peace talks also fell into line. Croatia's President Tudjman had been quoted off and on as wanting permanent control of western Bosnia. In the areas populated by Croats and taken over by his army, telephones were being connected to the exchange in Croatia's capital and cars began to appear with Croatian license plates. Yet Tudjman's new military strength was built and supported by German and U.S. aid, and his government needed international loans, so he was subject to great power pressure to negotiate. President Izetbetgovic of Bosnia, even more dependent on out-side assistance, had supported the previous two agreements. Thus the stage was set for the three presidents of Bosnia, Serbia (Yugoslavia), and Croatia to accept the U.S. invitation to meet at Wheeler Air Force base in Dayton, Ohio, and negotiate a peace agreement.

The resulting Dayton Accord ended the fighting and established a framework designed to achieve long-term peaceful interaction among the combatants. The agreement's key provisions included territorial adjustments, with Serbs accepting about 51 percent of Bosnia as their Republika Serbska, leaving the rest to be administered by the

Bosniak-Croat Federation, a paper union since 1994. An international peacekeeping force of 60,000 under NATO's command, not the UN's, would separate the armies of the three factions; it included 20,000 U.S. troops. The framework for a unified Bosnia took the form of a constitution creating a common legislature, a court, a central bank, and a multimember presidency. Each of the three factions would retain its own legislatures, presidents, local officials, and armies. The provision on alleged war criminals indicted by the War Crimes Tribunal stipulated that they could not hold elected office. The three presidents pledged cooperation in holding those indicted accountable, but the agreement had no explicit provision for arresting them.

None of the three presidents considered the Dayton Accord in his interest. All had to give up something they held dear. Bosniaks received the form of a unified Bosnia but not its substance. Serbs gave up important territory but got to keep one key corridor, ensuring a connection between the western and eastern sections of their republic. Croats retained their own forces and government but had to remain in federation with the Bosniaks.

The Dayton Accord includes a provision to arm and train Bosniak forces. This implies that establishing a balance of power among the factions within Bosnia is necessary to achieve peace in the short run. If the Bosniak army becomes a credible threat, the forces of the Republika Serbska, as well as of Croatia, may be deterred from attacking when the international forces withdraw. Those supporting the Dayton Accord explain that a strong Bosniak army is consistent with the overall objective of forging a framework for peaceful interaction.

Opponents of the arm-and-train provision point out the inherent contradiction between wanting to encourage the gradual building of trust among the factions while strengthening the war-making capability of one of them. Some Bosniak leaders have stated their view that the Republic of Serbska is an illegitimate reward for aggression and must be reunited with the rest of the country. The Bosniak government might be tempted to win back its perceived lost territory by fighting if it thinks the Bosniak army has enough military power to win a war. In that eventuality, strengthening Bosniak forces as a means of achieving peace would backfire.

In response to the type and scale of violence, outside intervention was required to apply international standards through the Dayton Accord and the War Crimes Tribunal. Most observers consider the tribunal central to the reconciliation process in Bosnia, which is why it is included as a provision in the Dayton Accord. Most of those indicted are Serb, including the former Bosnian Serb president and the army commander during the war. Their continued strong following among Bosnian Serbs has protected them from arrest and prosecution, which remains an ongoing source of tension with Bosniaks. Yet implementation of the Dayton Accord depends on Serb as well as Bosniak and Croat cooperation. Therefore, minimal action has been taken to arrest indicted Serbs. The agreement's inherent contractions cannot be avoided but are often cited as a stumbling block to achieving a meaningful, long-term peace. This situation illustrates the paradox of the international system: since there is no international authority, sovereign governments are not only the subjects of international law but also its enforcers.

The world's great powers had to intervene directly in Bosnia for conflict management via the Dayton Accord to take place. Then they initiated a UN-authorized assortment of institution building and reconstruction programs administered by the Organization for Security and Cooperation in Europe (OSCE) to establish the political processes designed to bring about permanent peace among the three groups. Yet eight years later, a military protection force continues to police what still may be a tenuous peace.

This fact highlights the need for a constructive show of force as an element in implementing international agreements. Force also played a role in arriving at the Dayton agreement in the first place. Not until NATO planes attacked Serb positions and weapons supply centers, followed by Croatian and Bosniak military successes, did Bosnia's Serbs accept an agreement. This shows that in cases of violent conflict, UN-legitimized force provides a necessary support for the imposition of international standards of behavior. Aggressors must be convinced that they cannot win. Such a realization creates the conditions for successful negotiations. The great powers applied this formula again when tensions produced violence in another unit of the former Yugoslavia.

Kosovo Crisis 1998–1999   Tensions between the province's two main groups, Serbs and Albanians, had built up since Milosevic had maneuvered the revocation of the province's autonomy in 1989. Albanians, who made up about 90 percent of Kosovo's over 2 million people, speak a non-Slavic language but share a long history as Muslims. Albanian peaceful resistance to direct, heavy-handed Serb rule had continued with the avowed goal of an independent Kosovo, but in 1997 a small group of obscure origins, the Albanian Liberation Army, began to conduct violent operations. The Serb government's excessive reaction included burning houses and crops, killing livestock, and massacring whole families. The downward spiral of attacks against police followed by brutal government reactions culminated in the summer of 1998 in an out-and-out ethnic cleansing. Government forces destroyed more than 300 Albanian villages and forced the exodus of an estimated 250,000 to 300,000 Albanians (Malcolm 1999, preface).

The international community both threatened and negotiated with Milosevic, but all their bluster and "agreements" produced only a brief interlude over the winter, while the Serbian leader massed thousands of troops on Kosovo's borders. The notorious Serb gangster and militia leader Arkan, who ranked among the most vicious violators of human rights in Bosnia, mobilized his followers for the pending operation in Kosovo. Clearly Milosevic was planning a campaign of destruction and expulsion more thorough than that of the previous summer. Evidence of systematic preparation for the removal of Albanians includes the "seizing of official documents and land-ownership registers" in order to facilitate turning over cleared land to new Serb owners (Malcolm 1999, preface).

The discovery of a site where forty-five Albanians, including children, had been massacred galvanized the great powers into action. They summoned representatives of the Serbian government and Albanian leadership to a conference at Rambouillet near Paris in February 1999 in order to end the crisis with an agreement. The plan called for the restoration of Kosovo's autonomy, far less than the independence the Albanians wanted, but far more than Milosevic would accept. He rejected the plan after two weeks of hesitant talks. By then more than 26,000 Serbian troops had moved inside Kosovo, augmenting the 15,000 poised outside the province. Albanian Liberation Army combatants, Milosevic's excuse for the action he clearly planned to take, probably numbered in the hundreds. NATO began the threatened campaign of air strikes in March and it continued through April. Meanwhile the Serb forces launched their cleansing Operation Horseshoe, the name itself indicating its objective of forcing Albanians from at least northern Kosovo. Over the weeks, the estimated number of displaced people numbered about 850,000.

The NATO bombing of Serbia escalated through April, and finally Milosevic changed policy. He removed his troops from Kosovo, and hundreds of thousands of Albanians returned to their homes under the protection of a UN peacekeeping force that included 7,000 U.S. troops. Within weeks, three IGOs began administering and rebuilding Kosovo: the United Nations, the OSCE, and the European Union.

Analysis

The Bosnia case study provides lessons about peace and war that continue into the twenty-first century. One involves the potential for instability in multiethnic states if leaders choose to exacerbate tensions. Most knowledgeable analysts of events in Bosnia and Kosovo do not accept the "ancient ethnic hatreds" explanation for why the violence happened. The primary fault lies with Milosevic and his cronies and their use of pseudo-history and fantasies to create fear, conjure hatred, and condone cruelty. Other extreme nationalists and thugs certainly contributed to the volatile mix of reckless propaganda and self-perpetuating violence. Since the Kosovo crisis, three events have served to calm the Balkans. President Tudjman died in December 1999. Arkan, perhaps the most vicious of the Serbian paramilitary leaders who operated in Bosnia and Kosovo, was killed in January 2000. Finally, a popular uprising on the streets of Belgrade overthrew the Milosevic government in June 2000. He was arrested by the new government in April 2001 and sent to the War Crimes Tribunal in June 2001.

The violent conflicts in Bosnia and Kosovo also illustrate the conditions often needed for successful intervention by outside mediators. The Security Council's permanent states and most European Union members must concur on a common policy, particularly when it involves the use of military force. Such an agreement is greatly facilitated within the framework of international institutions and rule of law. The point of outsiders threatening or using force is to convince the warring factions that they cannot win. This recognition must occur before they will participate in negotiations that produce an agreement.

International relations analysts disagree as to the impact on the international system of more states dividing into sovereign ministates. Some predict that more wars would likely result. Others disagree, pointing out that the new states would need peaceful and cooperative interaction to ensure their economic viability. Still others contend that the example of Bosnia may have frightened groups in other countries from agitating for their own sovereignty. All commentators agree, however, that the further disintegration

Matrix 9.1
PEACE AND WAR PERSPECTIVES

	State Sovereignty	World Order	Ethnic Autonomy
Goals	Peace, often temporary	Peace, force not an option	Peace Ethnic justice
Key Concepts	International anarchy	International rule of law	Ethnic rights
Strategies	Balance of power	Strengthen international institutions	Decentralize power
Major Problems of Existing System	Ethnic threats to state stability; Aggressor states	State actions based on narrow interest and perceptions	Domination by state governments
Sees Current International Political System As:	Too limiting of state power, at least potentially	Too state centered	Too state centered
Role of Force	Deterrence	Collective security	Dangerous in most situations, given the power of governments

of states into more ethnically pure ones would have a major effect in their world regions. Analyses based on alternative perspectives helps us assess the reasons for war and peace in Bosnia.

PEACE AND WAR PERSPECTIVES APPLIED TO THE WAR IN BOSNIA

Matrix 9.1 summarizes the main points made in this chapter. The war in Bosnia has enough complexity to require analysis using the widest range of concepts, including those explaining war, balance-of-power, and international-rule-of-law strategies. It also has the scale of human suffering and inhuman brutality to capture headlines and, perhaps, frighten people in other countries. Events in the former Yugoslavia may either forestall or foreshadow the breakup of other states. Bosnia's horrors show what can happen if propaganda acts like kerosene poured on inflammatory nationalist passions. Leaders of both ethnic groups and governments must act wisely, with flexible politics.

Yet the different perspectives people possess on peace and war issues cause them to propose opposing recommendations on what specific actions and policies will produce peace.

This chapter's three perspectives provide different reasons for the war in Bosnia and recommend alternative actions to forestall other conflicts from turning violent. They disagree over which institutions are the problem and which are the answer. In claiming that state sovereignty is the answer, the first perspective accepts the prevailing view of the world as primarily a collection of states that hold the key to solving the problems facing humankind, including the use of violence. The second and third perspectives view states as contributing to the problem of war. They demand major institutional changes in how the world's people are currently organized. The world order perspective points out the growth in number and authority of international organizations as sources for standards of international behavior. The ethnic autonomy perspective views cultural identities as the focus of primary loyalty for many of the world's people. Political institutions must, therefore, reflect ethnic group interest.

A View from the State Sovereignty Perspective

The breakup of Yugoslavia proved the key factor in causing the war in Bosnia. Historically, states developed as a means of reducing the kind of chaos Bosnians experienced. Respecting and working within existing states may not solve every interethnic wrong, but it is an improvement on the violence unleashed in Bosnia.

Patriotism by definition subordinates ethnic nationalisms to larger interests and perceptions. Instead of reinforcing narrowly based responses to problems, loyalty to country requires developing the negotiating skills of bargaining and compromise. When this process broke down in the former Yugoslavia, stability eroded and uncompromising, extreme nationalists were unleashed to accomplish their ruthless task. As one of the first to fan the nationalistic flames, Milosevic sought to use them in expanding his own and Serb power. In spite of professing his desire to hold Yugoslavia together, by encouraging and legitimizing nationalist sentiments he knowingly replaced Yugoslav patriotism with Serb nationalism.

The logic of the state sovereignty perspective could also fault German haste to recognize the independence of Slovenia and Croatia. This virtually forced the same decision on Bosnia. In so doing, it negated the already feeble efforts to negotiate autonomy for member republics within Yugoslavia. While the rest of the great powers were hesitating in a search for a negotiated response, Germany acted unilaterally. Its action highlights the importance of the fourth characteristic of a state as defined in Chapter 1—namely, recognition of other states.

Having said this, however, once the world's great powers had recognized the sovereignty of the new states, they should have intervened in their defense against Serbian aggression, at least by providing them with economic and military aid. Bosnia would then have had some chance of standing up to the Serb onslaught. Croatia eventually was strengthened and played a role in thwarting expansionist Serb ambitions. Yet

Bosnia was not. Lady Thatcher's quote in the beginning of this chapter reflects this interpretation of the state sovereignty perspective. The great powers must assume their role and responsibility as defenders of stability and opponents of aggression.

Advocates of a state sovereignty perspective have difficulty with the Dayton Accord even though they realize it may well have represented the only achievable agreement at the time. They doubt that it will work in the long run because its provisions reinforce Bosnia's deficiencies in all four of the basic factors defining a state; that is, its territory, government, patriotism, and recognition by other states. Bosnia's claim to the territory it had when a member republic in the former Yugoslavia remains only on paper. By tacitly accepting partition, the Dayton Accord ratifies the lack of loyalty to Bosnia by the Serbs and Croats living within its old borders. The fact that each of the three ethnic groups has its own governing institutions makes the central government of Bosnia a hollow shell. Finally, some states in the international arena, mainly Russia and Greece, at least tacitly recognize the validity of the Serb Republic within Bosnia.

State sovereignty analysts could take a pragmatic approach and accept the inevitability of partition as the only workable political solution in the foreseeable future. They might advocate assistance to the Bosniaks so they can defend themselves and, in the long run, perhaps either form their own state or negotiate out of strength with at least some Croats in beginning to piece together a new Bosnian state.

A View from the World Order Perspective

The depths of depravity reached during the war in Bosnia provide yet one more historical example of sovereign state ineptitude when confronting ruthless aggressors. By putting their own narrow self-interest first, they cannot take effective, early action. Only international institutions, capable of both setting and enforcing world standards of behavior, will provide a viable, permanent solution.

Whether state-centered or ethnic, virulent exclusionary nationalism can have similar effects. Such ideologies are enemies to orderly, peaceful interaction, the kind needed for cooperative problem solving. Since pressing issues cross international borders, and certainly transcend ethnic differences, building a sense of community is not only a nice idea but a practical necessity. Healthy, constructive interaction is needed not only for economic growth and development, but also to liberate the possibilities for ennobling creativity. World order advocates understand that to make the international community more than just a figure of speech, a commonly agreed to, legitimized rule of law must be established as a prerequisite.

Few benefit from violence and brutality. In the case of the war in Bosnia, ordinary people in all three groups underwent ethnic cleansing. In the summer of 1995, when Croat and Bosniak forces invaded formerly Serb-held parts of Bosnia, it was estimated that about 150,000 Serbs were forced out of their homes. This augments the 200,000 or so people who were killed after the breakup of Yugoslavia, and the more than one million made homeless in Bosnia alone. These figures take on even greater significance in light of the fact that before the war Bosnia had a population of about 4.3 million. In some wars, the winners are hard to find.

World order analysts find plenty of blame to go around in explaining the causes of the war in Bosnia. They would point out there was little to make hyperbolic nationalists think their actions would be opposed. This not only encouraged them but also strengthened their internal position while undermining the moderates. Yet the fact that intervention by the international community via the United Nations and the European Union came late and lame misses the point. Since IGOs can only do what their leading member states will support, they cannot be considered independent actors. The world's great powers remain the problem. Clearly, international organizations need more authority if they are expected to take timely and effective action. The extreme suffering caused by the war in Bosnia lends credibility to those advocating implementation of the UN Charter's Article 47. This article authorizes establishing a Military Staff Committee. If the Security Council took this action and provided the committee with a permanent peace-keeping force, the potential would exist for early reactions to human rights violations.

If the Bosnian calamity will have any positive lasting legacy, it will be through the precedent of the War Crimes Tribunal. The international community will at least in a moral sense redress the carnage if it successfully prosecutes those indicted for crimes against humanity. If, however, the indicted go unpunished, the international rule of law will receive a very real setback, one that in the short term may prove irreparable. Enough countries have ratified the international covenant on genocide for it to go into force, and it provides the tribunal's unassailable legal basis. If even clearly stated, commonly accepted, and enforceable legal standards are not upheld by a prosecutor's office and court set up by the Security Council, then those wanting to flout universal norms of conduct will take heart. In Bosnia, if justice via the law proves ephemeral, those wronged may well think that war is their only option. All groups in Bosnia have reasons for revenge. Thus, without justice providing at least a ray of hope for reconciliation, those advocating retribution will be strengthened.

A View from the Ethnic Autonomy Perspective

Milosevic's actions imposing Serb domination on other ethnicities in Yugoslavia provides the key to understanding how the war in Bosnia happened. Respect for other cultural groups is essential in today's technologically linked yet culturally diverse world. As ethnic conflicts develop, communication must be open and power must be shared. Sometimes this means designing new, autonomous political structures.

Hatred is not inevitable or natural. It must be taught and nourished. Tolerance and mutual respect can become accepted norms, and recognizing the contributions made by cultures to the larger society enhances everyone's life. When the clash of interests and perceptions proves to be too deeply rooted to be solved by existing political processes, various creative relationships can be invented. The war in Bosnia offers a stark illustration of what can happen when ethnic autonomy is not calmly and respectfully negotiated. Mutual destruction and long-term bitterness will preclude working together for years at least.

Developed gradually over time, peaceful interaction and even trust can become a way of life. Substantial evidence for this process can be found in Bosnia before the war. According to an anthropological study carried out in the late 1980s, Croats and Muslims lived side by side in peace and some had established friendships (Bringa 1995, 26). The 1982 Olympic Games provided a forum for many Bosnians to celebrate their various cultural heritages with the whole world looking on. A small but noteworthy number of Bosnia's population, 5.5 percent, had identified themselves as Yugoslav before the war (Bringa 1995, 26) and, by the late 1980s, 30 percent of Bosnia's marriages in cities and towns occurred between people of different ethnicities (Malcolm 1996, 222).

Those with an ethnic autonomy perspective point out that the international state system provided the context, rationale, and means for Bosnia's ethnic groups to fight a genocidal war. Leaders appealed to negative nationalism by inflaming resentments and fears. Serbia's Milosevic initiated the process by using his control of the major media to broadcast misleadingly selective information, even downright falsehoods, about how Croats, Muslims, Slovenes, and others were treating Serbs. The more nationalistic among these groups responded in kind, and voices pleading tolerance and compromise were drowned out. Each group came to believe that being ruled by people of a different ethnicity was dangerous and that only its own sovereignty made sense. Serbia's army aided Serb paramilitary units responsible for ethnic cleansing. Other states provided military aid to Croatia and Bosnia, whose forces engaged in their own violent population removal plans. The concept of the state and its sovereignty lies at the core of the mess.

This chapter's three perspectives differ over the causes of the war in Bosnia and recommend alternative actions to forestall other conflicts from turning violent. State sovereignty advocates blame excessive ethnic nationalism and the resulting breakup of the Yugoslav state for the war. This process unleashed strident nationalists and legitimized massive deaths and destruction. State sovereignty analysis believe that strengthening states is the long-term remedy for such wars. Many states have proven their ability to provide institutions through which ethnicities can constructively work out their differences. Political stability is a necessary condition for peaceful interaction.

World order and ethnic autonomy perspectives both recognize the need for stability but think that states are the problem, not the answer. In the case of the war in Bosnia, the lure of statehood, with its centralized governmental power, heightened real and imagined fears and allowed demagogues to seize control. Proponents of world order and state autonomy propose major institutional changes in how the world's peoples are organized, yet differ significantly over what institutions should be enhanced in order to diminish the power of states. The world order perspective points out the need for strengthening the organizations in the international community and their ability to impose universal standards of behavior on states. In contrast, ethnic autonomy analysts believe that people are demanding more decision-making power over their daily lives. They want local, decentralized institutions in order to have an effect on the global trends that impact them. Because cultures provide people with their primary identities, ethnicities should be the basis for new forms of political representation.

TERMS AND CONCEPTS

Autonomy *185*
Cultural rights *185*
Deterrence *181*

Failed states *186*
Functional interdependence *183*
Security dilemma *181*

DISCUSSION QUESTIONS

1. Which perspective discussed in this chapter do you think best explains the reasons for the war in Bosnia? Which perspective best explains the reasons for the peace in Bosnia?
2. What do the world order and ethnic autonomy perspectives have in common? What do the state sovereignty and ethnic autonomy perspectives have in common? What do all three have in common?
3. Choose a security issue facing the world community today, such as the proliferation of weapons of mass destruction, or a violent conflict in the Sudan, Kashmir, Chechnya, or some other location. How would each of the three perspectives explain its cause? What would each suggest be done about the problem?
4. In your opinion, what are the common assumptions about why wars occur? What do the people you know think about it? Which perspective or perspectives do they reflect the most?
5. What role should the United States play in the international system to achieve peace? Which perspective (or perspectives) does your view reflect?

RESEARCH PROJECTS

1. Read or listen to the analyses of several political leaders regarding an issue of war and peace. What perspectives do their comments reflect?
2. Write a short list of questions about the causes of war from the point of view of each perspective. Pose the questions to five or more people and record their answers. What perspectives do their responses seem to reflect?
3. Research the position of a country's government on a current violent conflict in the world. What perspective does its position reflect?
4. Read about the development of the European Union since its beginning as the European Common Market in the 1950s. What factors account for its success? How do the three perspectives apply?

INTERNET RESOURCES

Amnesty International: http://www.amnesty.org/index.html The homepage of this foremost international human rights NGO includes information about its history and current activities, as well as links to other human rights organizations' sites.

Out There News: http://www.megastories.com/bosnia/index.htm Complete with pictures and maps, this site also offers an interactive policy choices section as well as brief histories of the thee major ethnic groups.

University of Western Australia: http://www.law.ecel.uwa.edu.au/inlaw One of the most useful linkage sites available, it offers a wide variety of sources that contain the texts of treaties and conventions.

Human Rights Watch: http://www.hrw.org This site comprehensively reviews the human rights issues in specific countries and includes information about other global issues.

Glossary

acculturation: A culture is modified by adopting traits from another culture.

acid rain: Sulfur dioxide in smoke chemically reacts with the water in the atmosphere to create sulfuric acid (H_2SO_4). This is maintained in the clouds and falls to earth in rain.

agriculturalism: This subsistence strategy is based on the exploitation of domesticated plants. The social organization of most simple agricultural societies is the tribe.

AIDS (acquired immunodeficiency syndrome): This emerging, contagious disease has become one of the world's major health problems.

alternative perspectives: These sets of interpretive ideas determine how individuals analyze issues.

apartheid: In this recently ended practice in South Africa, the numerical majority in the state, the original inhabitants, were legally defined as inferior and had all aspects of their lives severely circumscribed.

appropriate technology: This technology includes those projects and techniques that fit both the culture and physical setting of people involved.

assimilation: A culture adapts new customs and beliefs which replace the customs and beliefs of a previous culture.

autonomy: Local governments establish and enforce laws covering most governmental functions except foreign policy and defense.

balance of payments: This annual summary of all a state's international economic transactions lists the monetary value of all trade and financial flows, including tourist travel and purchases, business investment and profits, loans, and debt payments.

balance of power: This is an interaction system of states, or groups, which choose not to use force because they consider the potential cost too high.

balanced reciprocity: In this form of exchange, goods of equal value are expected for each gift given.

basic-needs strategy: This approach is designed to enable a preponderant percentage of the population to have life's essentials; that is, adequate shelter, food, clothing, and medical care.

bilateral aid: Official aid from another country's government constitutes bilateral aid.

bilateral diplomacy: In this relationship, two states deal with each other one on one.

bipolar: In this international system, there are two dominant states.

Brundtland Commission: The UN established the World Commission on Environment and Development, which investigated the state of the world's environment and proposed solutions in a 1987 document, "Our Common Future."

capital: The finances and facilities needed to produce wealth are referred to as capital.

capital flight: Capital flight entails sending money out of a country into personal accounts in international banks.

carbon dioxide: CO_2, a colorless, odorless gas, a natural part of the atmosphere, is used by plants as a necessary part of their respiration.

carrying capacity: This term refers to the number of people who can be supported indefinitely in a given environment with a given technology and culture.

cash crops/primary commodities: These products are grown or mined and sold in their unprocessed condition, such as tea leaves, cotton balls, coffee beans, and bauxite ore.

class: This category of a social hierarchy groups people based upon culturally defined differences in wealth, power, or general abilities.

Cold War: This superpower competition engages in threats but not war fought directly between the two antagonists.

collective security: This strategy of IGO members is followed when they act together militarily in responding to an aggressor state.

colonialism: Colonialism is the direct administration of a territory and its people by an outside power.

the commons: These areas are publicly owned and open for general use.

comparative advantage: A good or service is produced at a lower cost than the competition.

conventional war: In this type of war, states battle each other using their formally organized military forces complete with uniforms, differentiated specializations, command and control hierarchies, training, and a sense of historical mission.

cultural pluralism: This perspective prioritizes the autonomous rights of individual cultures, regardless of their power.

cultural relativity: According to this concept, the actions of people within each culture should be understood according to the rules of that culture.

cultural rights: All persons should be able to participate in the cultural life of their choice and conduct their own cultural practices, subject to respect for human rights and fundamental freedoms.

culture: These patterns of behavior and belief are learned by individuals as members of a society. Human culture is the basic adaptation device all people have in common. Specific cultures are those systems of belief and behavioral rules shared by members of a particular society.

culture areas: These analytic categories of geographic regions are based on the similarity of the ethnic groups within them.

deforestation: The rapid destruction of forests, especially tropical forests, which leads to atmospheric and soil degradation is known as deforestation.

demographic transition: This occurs when a society moves from having both high birthrates and high death rates prior to industrialization, through a period of high population growth because of a decline in the death rate, to the low birthrates and low death rates characteristic of economically developed societies. Many developing world states are in the population growth phase of the process without having begun self-sustained industrialization.

dependency: This unequal relationship between the industrialized and developing worlds results from their economic interactions.

desertification: This term denotes an increase in areas of extremely arid land.

deterrence: In this situation, a state presents a credible military threat to a potential enemy.

developing world: States that have primarily agriculture-based economies and low wealth production, as reflected in macroeconomic data, are considered to be in the developing world.

development: This term describes an economy that enables an increasing number of people to produce enough wealth to support an acceptable quality of life.

diplomacy: Diplomacy entails direct negotiations between two or more governments or IGOs.

dual economy: Many developing countries have a small, dominant elite comprising people who live the consumer lifestyle typical of industrial societies and a large majority of the population who live in poverty.

economic growth strategy: This approach is designed to produce enough earnings to invest in machines, the fossil fuels to run them, educated people to fix them, and the constant flow of new technology to update them; in other words, industrialization.

economic sanctions: These actions are designed to encourage states to change their policies by cutting off trade and financial flows.

economies of scale: This economic principle refers to the fact that a product's per-unit cost decreases when a company produces more of it since the plant, personnel, and other overhead costs remain about the same.

ecosystems: The complex interconnections of plants, animals, and the physical and chemical factors that make up environments are known as ecosystems.

emerging infectious diseases: These new contagious diseases, including AIDS, have spread widely in recent years.

ethnic group: This category denotes people who share cultural traits. The term is often used for those constituting minorities in large, heterogeneous nations.

ethnocentrism: Judging the customs of another culture according to the standards of your own is called enthnocentrism.

ethnocide: Ethnocide is the destruction of a culture.

European Union: The EU is the regional IGO furthest along in a process of functional integration. The Maastricht Treaty signed in 1991 initiated an important stage in further integration by setting the goal of establishing a common currency and banking system.

external changes: These new ideas, skills, or inventions enter a society from interaction with another society.

extinctions: The total loss of a specific species or type of plant or animal is known as extinction.

failed states: These states disintegrate as a result of domestic conflict.

financial capital: Monetary investments are needed to produce more wealth, such as bank deposits and interest, earnings from international trade, and currency.

foreign aid: This financial capital is provided by governments of states and IGOs, almost always in the form of loans.

foreign exchange: Earnings from exports are termed foreign exchange.

foreign exchange rate: This term denotes the worth of a state's currency in relation to that of another state.

free trade: This government policy eliminates all restrictions on imports and exports, including tariffs, which are taxes charged by governments on specific categories of goods, and other regulations, such as quotas and inspections.

functional interdependence: This theory holds that integrating the economies of states will make war virtually impossible among them.

gathering and hunting: This subsistence strategy emphasizes the gathering of undomesticated plants and hunting of undomesticated animals. The social organization associated with this is egalitarian bands.

gender: Gender is the cultural definition of the different capabilities and roles of men, women, and sometimes other perceived sexual categories.

General Assembly: In this institution of the United Nations, all member states are represented, each with one vote. The General Assembly serves as a forum for debating and voting on resolutions dealing with world issues.

generalized reciprocity: In this form of economic exchange, people in bands share with one another without the expectation of equal or immediate return.

genocide: Genocide is an attempt to exterminate members of a specific cultural group. It was designated as a crime against humanity in a 1948 international agreement and accepted as international law.

global warming: This denotes a small, but regular and significant, increase in the temperature of the earth.

globalization: Globalization is the process of increasing interconnectedness between societies such that events in one part of the world more and more affect people and societies far away.

government: Government is the one institution in a society that has a legitimate claim to exercise decisive authority over its population.

great powers: These states can directly affect events outside of their world region.

green revolution: This development approach, promoted by the Rockefeller Foundation, focuses on the transfer of high-technology farming techniques, including new seeds and chemical fertilizers, to less developed areas of the world.

greenhouse gases: These atmospheric gases, including CO_2, methane, ozone, and chlorofluorocarbons, decrease the energy lost into space and increase the warmth of the atmosphere.

gross national income: This includes the total monetary value of all goods and services produced by an economy in a given year, including international transactions.

guerrilla war: Organized groups opposing a political system use hit-and-run tactics and then blend into the local population as their main defense.

hard/convertible currencies: These state currencies are used in international markets because corporations and other governments accept them.

high technology: Technological innovations are developed through industry and modern science and represent the cutting edge of complex mechanical and chemical theory.

holism: All traits of a culture influence all others, and, consequently, change in any part of a culture will affect the whole culture.

human capital: This term refers to the educated, healthy, skilled population with able leadership necessary for self-sustaining economic development.

human rights: Just treatment by governments of their own citizens is referred to as human rights.

humanitarian intervention: Threats to the peace are managed by deploying peacekeeping troops and delivering food and medical aid.

ideologies: This set of interrelated ideas is used by people to give meaning to political events and to legitimize political institutions.

immigration: The movement of people from one state to another with the intention of living there permanently is termed immigration.

imperialism: Direct or indirect rule by outsiders over a territory and its local people is known as imperialism.

indigenous peoples, or First Nations: Indigenous people are the original people of an area who have lost political control over their ancestral lands and do not fully recognize the moral authority of the state government to dominate them.

industrialism: This subsistence strategy changes the productive focus of the state system to the manufacturing sector.

industrialization: Industrialization entails the shift from handmade products, using human and animal muscle plus wind and water as energy sources, to machine production, using energy from the burning of fossil fuels—coal, oil, and natural gas.

infrastructure (physical capital): Facilities needed to produce wealth, such as factories, farms, roads, railroads, computers, telephones, banks, and machinery, are called the infrastructure.

intellectual property rights: This concept holds that abstract ideas, knowledge, and creations can be owned just like physical property.

interests: The relationships and resources persons, groups, organizations, and states are able to use for their own benefit and to enhance their own power are called interests.

internal changes: New cultural elements that are invented by people within a society, which is changing, are internal changes.

international anarchy: This is the key characteristic of the international system, according to international relations theory. It means the absence of common political rule.

international governmental organization (IGO): These agencies deal with global or regional interests. Their members are states.

International Monetary Fund (IMF): This international governmental organization provides loans to member states to stabilize their currencies.

international rule of law: States follow commonly accepted rules of behavior and orderly processes for peacefully working out conflicting interests.

international system: The organizations and processes used by people when they interact across state borders.

intervention: States intervene with force and peacekeepers to counter an aggressor state without its consent.

involuntary innovations: In this form of external change, members of a weaker society are forced to adapt traits of a more powerful society.

just war: This military action is taken in self-defense abiding by accepted rules of warfare, such as preventing the slaughter of civilians and prisoners of war.

labor-intensive technologies: Simple tools powered by wind, water, sunshine, and muscles are used in contrast with capital-intensive technologies, which rely on complex machinery needing fossil fuels.

Law of the Sea: This UN-supported treaty of 1984 established general rules for conduct in the oceans. It also codifies the twelve-mile limit of state control over coastal waters and an exclusive economic zone in which the state has rights over natural resources.

legitimacy: This attitude accepts that the existing government is justified, its laws should be obeyed, and its rule conforms to commonly accepted values.

malnutrition: This medical condition is caused by a diet lacking in sufficient calories and balanced nourishment.

market economics: The core concepts of this liberal economic viewpoint include supply and demand, free trade, and laissez-faire government.

most-favored-nation status: This entails agreements between two states which lower their tariffs with each other to match the lowest that each charges any trading partner on a specific category of product.

multilateral aid: This financing comes from an IGO such as the World Bank.

multilateral international interactions: States negotiate and take action within the framework of IGOs.

multipolar: In this international system, several states serve as centers of power.

national identity: This involves a primary affiliation with a group of people who consider themselves unified in a unique culture.

nationalism: An individual's feeling of identity with an ethnic group based on several shared characteristics, such as language, history, and religion, is known as nationalism.

negotiations: Officials talk to each other directly or through a designated intermediary.

neo-imperialism/neocolonialism: These terms are often used as synonyms for dependency— the unequal relationship between the industrial states, the colonizers, and the developing states, their ex-colonies. Dependency theorists draw the conclusion that developing countries have achieved political independence but not economic independence.

New International Economic Order: These United Nations resolutions passed in the 1970s were favorable to the developing world, but they never went into effect.

nongovernmental organization (NGO): These private groups are formed to take action in response to a specified global issue, such as threats to the natural environment or human rights.

nuclear war: This category of war involves the use of weapons produced by the release of molecular energy.

ozone depletion: Thinning of the ozone level in the lower stratosphere, especially in the outermost areas of the world, near the poles, is referred to as ozone depletion.

participatory development: This basic-needs strategy emphasizes the need for local beneficiaries to act as decision makers and use locally available resources and technologies that are compatible with the natural environment.

pastoralism: This subsistence strategy is based upon the use of domesticated animals. The social organization of most pastoralists is the tribe.

paternalism: This term literally means acting as a father. More broadly, it means taking a superior position over others and trying to control their actions.

patriotism: Placing one's primary identity and loyalty in the state is known as patriotism.

peace: Peace reigns when conflicts are handled without the use of violence. This can occur whether interactions take place in an uneasy, tense, potentially violent relationship or in a permanently peaceful relationship in which participants consider the use of force unimaginable.

per capita gross national income: This statistic is derived by dividing a state's gross national product by its total population.

perceptions: Perceptions are attitudes and points of view resulting from a person's particular cultural-historical, philosophical, ideological, or religious preconceptions.

perceptual selectivity: The process of ignoring or misinterpreting information because of prior assumptions is termed perceptual selectivity.

physical capital (infrastructure): Physical capital refers to the facilities needed to produce wealth, such as factories, farms, roads, railroads, telephones, computers, banks, and machinery.

politics: This decision-making process is characterized by negotiation and bargaining.

potable water: Potable water is water that is safe for consumption by humans and other animals.

power: In these relationships, persons, groups, organizations, or states can influence others to do what they want.

primitive states: This social system is based upon centralized political organization. The economic system is elaborated to include complex economic specialization and market exchange built on an agricultural base.

private investment: Financial and physical capital provided by multinational corporations in the states in which they operate is called private investment.

productivity: This economic calculation measures the output of goods and services in relation to the number of work hours used to produce them.

propaganda: Emotional appeals attempting to affect the opinions of others, typically through mass communications media, is termed propaganda.

protectionism: This government policy uses tariffs and other regulations to restrict imports and thus keep out foreign competition.

race, biological: This term is a subspecies designation of animals. The only surviving human race is *Homo sapiens sapiens.*

race, social: This culturally defined classification divides people into categories that are based on perceived physical differences.

racism: Judging groups or individuals based on culturally defined biological differences is termed racism.

refugees: Refugees are people who flee their countries of origin in fear for their lives or cannot return home for political reasons.

regional powers: States whose policies can have a direct effect on their neighbors are regional powers.

revisionist states: These states want more power and generally adopt a policy of increasing their military forces.

rubber tapping: The extraction of rubber from trees is known as rubber tapping. Treated correctly, rubber trees can produce rubber for extraction without harming the tree.

SARS (severe acute respiratory syndrome): This emerging infectious disease became internationally known in 2003 when it caused significant economic damage in Asia and Canada in a short time.

Security Council: The Charter of the United Nations has given this institution the important role of responding to threats to the peace.

security dilemma: This policy problem is faced by states that want to build up their military strength. If their increase in military forces is perceived as a threat by other states that, in response, increase their forces, the result can be the same or less security than existed originally.

sex: These physical categories in animals are based upon differences in reproductive biology.

sexism: Judging groups or individuals based on a culturally defined understanding of the differences between men, women, and any other gender category is called sexism.

shared technology: This concept holds that modern innovations in technology should be used cooperatively throughout the world rather than controlled by private business.

show of force: When a state deploys its military forces as an implied threat, it is a show of force.

small powers: The decisions these states make affect their own people but have very little impact on other states.

smallpox: This highly contagious, widely fatal disease was contained in the 1980s but remains a terrorist threat.

social cohesion: When people in a society attain social cohesion, they share a common identity, value system, and commitment to an established political system and thus have achieved stable economic and political decision-making processes.

sovereignty: States in the international system with sovereignty accept no authority as superseding their own.

specialization: When states specialize they emphasize producing and trading those products in which they have a comparative advantage.

state: This complex political structure includes citizens from a variety of nations (ethnicities). Considered the most powerful institution in the international system, states have four characteristics: territory, government, loyal population, and recognition by other states.

state nationalism: This perspective holds that the primary political identity for any group or individual should be as a citizen of the state of their birth or adoption.

states (with heterogeneous economies): This cultural term describes complex subsistence strategies which developed in early societies.

status (achieved and ascribed): Status is an individual's position in society, from mother to queen to president. An achieved status is one that is earned; for example, a student can achieve status. An ascribed status comes with birth, such as a princess.

status quo states: States satisfied with their existing level of power are status quo states.

subjugation: Subjugation involves people of a stronger culture controlling the lives of people of weaker cultures.

subsidies: These government payments make up the difference between the farmers' cost of raising the agricultural product and the world market price for that commodity.

subsistence: This economic term refers to an agriculture-based lifestyle in which people produce enough to live on and very little more.

superpowers: These states can maintain their direct effect on events in most areas of the world at the same time.

sustainability/sustainable development: This concept holds that development projects must be designed for long-term success.

syncretism: The mixing of cultural ideas from different sources to create a new reality is termed syncretism.

tacit negotiations: Tacit negotiations are achieved by sending a message to another government without telling it directly or using an intermediary. A wide variety of tacit strategies have been used, such as leaks to the press, speeches to another audience, or movements of troops.

technical assistance: These specialists from outside the country are brought in usually to work on a specific development project for a short period of time.

terrorism: This military tactic uses violent incidents perpetrated by small numbers of people for the purpose of calling into question or destabilizing an existing political system.

tolerance: The acceptance of cultural differences without ethnocentric judgment is termed tolerance.

transnational corporations: Private businesses with subsidiaries or operations in more than one country are transnational corporations.

transnational immigrants: These immigrants continue to maintain significant ties and identity with their countries of origin.

United Nations: This worldwide political international governmental organization includes almost all of the world's states as members.

United Nations Environment Program (UNEP): This United Nations agency is assigned the task of monitoring the world's environment.

Universal Declaration of Human Rights: Adopted by the UN General Assembly in 1948, this document lists individual freedoms all humans should be granted, including economic well-being and religious and political rights.

voluntary changes: In this form of external change, members of a society choose to adapt innovations from another area of the world.

war: War is characterized by politically motivated violent acts. These acts can range from full-scale clashes of armies to specific incidents carried out by terrorists.

West Nile Virus: This newly emerging epidemic is spread through animal-to-human contact. It has spread across the United States extremely rapidly.

World Bank: This international governmental organization provides loans to member states for specific development projects.

World Court: This international tribunal has jurisdiction only in cases involving states.

World Health Organization (WHO): This United Nations organization, which was created in 1948, is mandated to promote health throughout the world.

world order: World order entails developing international law and institutions as the means to achieve peace.

World Trade Organization (WTO): The successor to the General Agreement on Tariffs and Trade (GATT), this international governmental organization fosters free trade.

References Cited

————.1953. "A 6-foot 2-inch Queen Arrives for Coronation." *New York Times*, May 19, 20.

————.1995. "Bosnia Talks Snag on Fate of Two Serbs." *New York Times*, November 17, 3.

————.1996. "Croat Is First to Be Convicted by Balkan War Crimes Panel." *New York Times*, June 1, 4.

————. 2003. "Infectious Disease; Exotic Animals May Carry Next Outbreak." *Health and Medicine Week*, August 11, 278.

Alder, Jonathan, Peter Cazamias, and David Monnack. 1995. "Benchmarks: The Ecological and Economic Trends That Are Shaping the Natural Environment and Human." In *The True State of the Planet*, edited by Ronald Bailey, 393–453. New York: The Free Press.

Allotey, Pascale, Lenore Manderson, and Sonia Grover. 2001. "The Politics of Female Genital Surgery in Displaced Communites" In *Critical Public Health*, vol. 11, no. 3, 184–201.

Amstutz, Mark R. 1995. *International Conflict and Cooperation*. Madison, WI: Brown and Benchmark Publishers.

Anderson, Ian, and Rachel Nowak. 1997. "Australia's Giant Lab." *New Scientist*. February 22, 34–37.

Balaam, David, and Michael Veseth. 1996. *Introduction to International Political* Economy. Englewood Cliffs, NJ: Prentice Hall.

Balikci, Asen. 1984. "Netsilik." In *Handbook of North American Indians*, edited by David Damas, Vol. 5, *Arctic*, 415–30. Washington, DC: Smithsonian Institution.

Baylis, John, and Steve Smith, eds. 1999. *The Globalization of World Politics—An Introduction to International Relations*. Oxford, UK: Oxford University Press.

Bodley, John H. 1996. *Anthropology and Contemporary Human Problems*. 3d ed. Mountain View, CA: Mayfield Publishing Company.

Boone, Catherine, and Jake Batsell. 2001. "Politics and AIDS in Africa: Research Agendas in Political Science and International Relations." *Africa Today* (Summer), Vol. 48, no. 2, 3–33.

Bosch, Xavier. 2001. "Female Genital Mutilation in Developed Countries." *Lancet* (October), Vol. 358, 1177–79.

Bringa, Tone. 1995. *Being Muslim the Bosnian Way: Identity and Community in a Central Bosnian Village*. New Jersey: Princeton University Press.

British Medical Association. 2001. "Female Genital Mutilation: Caring for Patients and Child Protection Guidance from the British Medical Association," rev. April (www.bma.org).

Brown, Lester. 1981. *Building a Sustainable Society*. New York: W. W. Norton and Company.

Brown, Wilson, and Jan Hogedorn. 1994. *International Economics: Theory and Context*. Reading, MA: Addison Wesley.

Buckley, Richard. 1992. "Amazonia: An Ecological Crisis." *Understanding Global Issues.*

Carroll, Raymond. 1996. "Water: A Dangerous Endangered Resource?" In *Great Decisions,* 42–51. New York: Foreign Policy Association.

Centers for Disease Control and Prevention. 2002. "Infectious Disease; Wildlife Markets and Disease Transmission: The Problem Is, Pigs Do Fly." *Medical Letter on the CDC and FDA.* Atlanta, August 3, 23.

———. 2003. *SARS Fact Sheet,* August 19.

———. 2003. *Fact Sheet: What You Should Know about Monkeypox* (www.cdc.gov/ncidod/monkeypox/factsheet2.htm).

———. 2004. *CDC West Nile Virus.* Division of Vector-Borne Infectious Diseases. (http://www.cdc.gov/ncidod/dvbid/ westnile/).

Chyba, Christopher F. 2001. "Biological Terrorism and Public Health." *Survival.* Vol. 41, no. 1, 93–106.

CIA. 2003. *CIA Factbook.* (http://www.odci.gov/cia/publications/factbook/rankorder/2153rank.html). Visited September 19, 2003.

Cleaver, Harry. 2003. *The Zapatistas and the Electronic Fabric of Struggle.* (www.eco.utexas.edu/faculty/Cleaver/Zaps.html). Visited October 4, 2003.

Commission for the Creation of the Yanomami Park. 1989. "The Threatened Yanomami." *Cultural Survival Quarterly,* 13, 45–46.

Cushman, John H., Jr. 1996. "Report Says Global Warming Poses Threat to Public Health." *New York Times,* July 8, A2.

Dahl, Jens, Jack Hicks, and Peter Jull, eds. 2000. *Nunavut: Inuit Regain Control of Their Lands and Their Lives.* IWGIA Document No. 102. Copenhagen: International Work Group for Indigenous Affairs (IWGIA).

Damas, David. 1984. "Central Eskimo: Introduction" In *Handbook of North American Indians,* edited by David Damas, Vol. 5, *Arctic,* 391–96. Washington, DC: Smithsonian Institution.

Denslow, Julie Sloan. 1988. "The Tropical Rain-Forest Setting." In *People of the Tropical Rain Forest,* edited by Julie S. Denslow and Christine Padoch, 25–36. Berkeley: University of California Press.

Dickason, Olive P. 1992. *Canada's First Nations.* Norman: University of Oklahoma Press.

Dierks, Klaus. 2002. *Chronology of Namibian History.* Windhoek: Namibia Scientific Society.

Dostert, Pierre Etienne. 1996. *Latin America 1996.* Harpers Ferry, WV:Stryker-Post Publications.

Drozdiak, William. 1997. "German Court Convicts Bosnian Serb of War Crimes," *Washington Post,* September 27, A14.

Earle, Sylvia A. 1995. *Sea Change.* New York: Fawcett Columbine.

Encyclopedia Britannica. 2003. Chicago: Encyclopedia Britannica.

English, Veronica, Gillian Romano-Critchley, Julian Sheather, and Ann Sommerville. 2003. "Ethics Briefings." *Journal of Medical Ethics,* Vol. 29, no. 1, 57–58.

The Europa World Year Book. 2002. 43rd ed. London: Europa Publications.

Facts on File. 1993. "Global Environment: News in Brief." *Facts on File World News Digest,* 153, July 22.

Franke, Richard W. 1974. "Miracle Seeds and Shattered Dreams in Java." *Natural History*, Vol. 83, 10–12ff.

Franke, Richard, and Barbara Chasin. 1994. *Kerala: Radical Reform as Development in an Indian State*. Oakland, California: The Institute for Food and Development Policy.

Goodwin, Paul Jr., ed. 1996. "Chile: Country Report." In *Latin America*. Guilford, CT: Dushkin Publishing Group.

Graburn, N. H., and M. Lee. 1990. "The Arctic Culture Area." In *Native North Americans: An Ethnohistorical Approach*, edited by D. Boxberger. Dubuque, IA: Kendall/Hunt Publishing Company.

Grmek, Mirko D. 1990. *History of AIDS*. Princeton, NJ: Princeton University Press.

Hardin, Garrett. 1968. "The Tragedy of the Commons." *Science*, Vol. 162 1243–48.

Harrison, Paul. 1984. *Inside the Third World*. New York: Penguin Books.

Hileman, Bette. 1995. "Climate Observations Substantiate Global Warming Models." *Chemical and Engineering News* (November), 27.

Human Development Report, 1996, 2001. New York: Oxford University Press.

International Trade Statistics Yearbook. 1994. New York: United Nations.

Karlen, Arno. 1995. *Man and Microbes*. New York: Simon and Schuster.

Klein, Laura, and Lillian A. Ackerman. 1995. *Native American Women and Power*. Norman: University of Oklahoma Press.

Lashley, Felissa R., and Jerry D. Durham, eds. 2002. "Preface." In *Emerging Infectious Diseases: Trends and Issues*. New York: Springer Publishing Company.

Lewellen, Ted C. 2002. *The Anthropology of Globalization: Cultural Anthropology Enters the 21st Century*. Westport, CT: Bergin & Garvey.

Malcolm, Noel. 1996. *Bosnia, a Short History*. New York: New York University Press.

———. 1999. *Kosovo—A Short History*. New York: Harper Perennial.

McElroy, Ann. 1976. "The Negotiation of Sex-Role Identity in Eastern Arctic Culture Change." *Western Canadian Journal of Anthropology*, 6, 184–200.

McElroy, Ann, and Patricia K. Townsend. 1996. *Medical Anthropology in Ecological Perspective*. Boulder, CO: Westview Press.

Minor, Tina. 2002. "Political Participation of Inuit Women in the Government of Nunavut." *Wicazo Sa Review*, Vol. 17, no. 1, 65–90.

Mitchell, Anthony. 2004. *UN Warns Africa to Brace Itself of the AIDS Time Bomb*, October 14 (http://www.cdcnpin.org).

Moran, Emilio F. 1988. "Following the Amazonian Highways." In *People of the Tropical Rain Forest*, edited by Julie S. Denslow and Christine Padoch, 155–62. Berkeley: University of California Press.

Morse, Stephen S. 2003. "Viral Traffic on the Move." *Issues in Science and Technology*, Vol. 19, no. 4, 43.

Myers, Ransom A., and Boris Worm. 2003. "Rapid Worldwide Depletion of Predatory Fish Communities." *Nature*, Vol. 423, no. 6937, 280.

Namibia Statistical Appendix. 1998. Washington DC: International Monetary Fund.

Namibia—The Facts. 1980. London: International Defense and Aid Fund for Southern Africa.

Nanda, Serena. 1990. *Neither Man nor Woman: The Hijras of India*. Belmont, CA: Wadsworth Publishing.

Nunavut Implementation Commission. 1995. *Footprints in New Snow*. Report (March 31).

Odum, Eugene P. 1993. *Ecology and Our Endangered Life-Support Systems*. 2d ed. Sunderland, MA: Sinauer Associates.

Organization of American States. http://www.cidh.oas.org. Visited October 5, 2003.

Paisano, Edna. 1997. *The American Indian, Eskimo, and Aleut Population*. Washington, DC: U.S. Census Bureau.

Pelly, David F. 1993. "Dawn of Nunavut." *Canadian Geographic* Vol. 113, 20–31.

Pelto, Pertti J. 1973. *The Snowmobile Revolution: Technology and Social Change in the Arctic*. Menlo Park, CA: Cummings Publishing Company.

Polk, William R. 1981. *The Arab World*. Cambridge, MA: Harvard University Press.

Prance, Ghillean T. 1990. "Rainforested Regions of Latin America." In *Lessons of the Rainforest*, edited by Suzanne Head and Robert Heinzman, 53–65. San Francisco: Sierra Club Books.

Purich, Donald. 1992. *The Inuit and Their Land: The Story of Nunavut*. Toronto: J. Lorimer.

Reiss, Bob. 1992. *The Road to Extreme*. New York: Summit Books.

Rourke, John. 1993. *International Politics on the World Stage*. Guildford, CT: Dushkin Publishing Group.

Schmink, Marianne. 1988. "Big Business in the Amazon." In *People of the Tropical Rain Forest*, edited by Julie S. Denslow and Christine Padoch, 163–71. Berkeley: University of California Press.

Schumacher, E. F. 1973. *Small Is Beautiful: Economics as if People Mattered*. New York: Harper and Row.

Sciolina, Elaine. 1995. "Enemies in Bosnia Devise Structure for a Government." *New York Times*, September 27, 1.

Sponsel, Leslie. 1994. "The Yanomami Holocaust Continues." In *Who Pays the Price?*, edited by Barbara Rose Johnston, pp. 37–46. Washington, DC: Island Press.

Statistical Year Book 1998. 2001. New York: United Nations.

Stern, Paul C., Oran R. Young, and Daniel Druckman, eds. 1992. *Global Environmental Change*. Washington, DC: National Academy Press.

Stone, Roger D. 1985. *Dreams of Amazonia*. New York: Viking.

Sudetic, Chuck. 1993. "In Moster's Muslin Area, 35,000 Endure in Rubble," *New York Times*, September 30, A7

Tannenbaum, Edward. 1965. *European Civilizations Since the Middle Ages*. New York: John Wiley and Sons.

Taulbee, James L. 2002. "The One That Gets Past You: Trends in Terrorism." *Academic Exchange* (http://www.emory.edu?ACAD_EXCHANGE/December/January). Visited April 12, 2002.

Thatcher, Margaret. 1994. "Stop the Serbs. Now. For Good." *New York Times*, May 4, 23.

Tylor, Edward. 1871. *Primitive Cultures*. London: John Murray.

UNAIDS (The Joint United Nations Programme on HIV/AIDS). 2004. Report on the Global AIDS Epidemic (http://www.unaids.org).

UNAIDS (The Joint United Nations Programme on HIV/AIDS). 2004. USAIDS Fact Sheet (http://www.unaids.org).

United Nations. http://www.un.org/aboutun/charter/chapter7.htm. Visited September 19, 2003.

———.1995. *The World's Women 1995: Trends and Statistics.* New York: United Nations.

United Nations Development Program. http://undp.org/hdr2003/indicator. Visited July 22, 2003.

United Nations Educational, Scientific, and Cultural Organization. http://www.unesco.org. Visited October 5, 2003.

United Nations Information Centre. http:www.un.org/tr/unic_eng/SELECTED%205C%20RES% 20IQ1.htm. Visited September 17, 2003.

United States Geological Survey. 2000–2004. *West Nile Virus Maps* (http://westnilemaps.usgs.gov).

U.S. Department of Energy, Energy Information Administration. http://www.eia.doe.gov. Visited 8/28/03.

———. http://www.eia.doe.gov/emeu/iea/table81.html. Visited September 17, 2003.

Vallee, Frank G., Derek G. Smith, and Joseph D. Cooper. 1984. "Contemporary Canadian Inuit." In *Handbook of North American Indians*, edited by David Damas, Vol. 5, *Arctic*, 662–75. Washington, DC: Smithsonian Institution.

Vandenbeld, John. 1988. *Nature of Australia: A Portrait of the Island Continent.* New York: Facts on File.

Wade, Betsy. 1997. "Warding Off Malaria." *New York Times*, April 20, sec. 4:4–5, 28.

Walker, Alice. 1992. *Possessing the Secret of Joy.* New York: Harcourt, Brace, Javanovich.

Walker, Alice, Pretibha Permer, and Efua Dorkenoo. 1993. *Warrior Marks.* New York: Women Make Movies.

Watson, Robert T., ed. 2001. *Climate Change 2001: Intergovernmental Panel on Climate Change.* Cambridge U Press. (www.ippc.ch).

Wenzel, George. 1995. "Ningiqtuq: Resource Sharing and Generalized Reciprocity in Clyde River, Nunavut." *Arctic Anthropology*, Vol. 32, no. 2, 43.

Williams, Walter. 1986. *The Spirit and the Flesh.* Boston: Beacon Press.

Woodward, Susan. 1995. *Balkan Tragedy: Chaos and Dissolution After the Cold War.* Washington, DC: The Brookings Institution.

World Development Report. 1979, 1994, 1995, 2003. New York: Oxford University Press.

World Bank Group. *WDI Online.* http://devdata.worldbank.org/dataonline/. Visited July 16, 2003.

World Health Organization. 2003. *Inadequate Plumbing Systems Likely Contributed to SARS Transmission.* September 26.

———. 2003. WHO Global Conference on Severe Acute Respiratory Syndrome (SARS). "Where Do We Go from Here?" *Weekly Epidemiological Record*, August 22, 299–303.

———. 2003. *WHO Says Failure to Deliver AIDS Medicine Is a Global Health Emergency.* September 22.

———. 2004. *The 3x5 Initiative* (http://www.who.int/3x5/en/).

World Statistics Pocket Book. 1995. New York: United Nations.

World Tourism Organization. http://www.worldtourism.org/market_research/facts&figures/statistics/ t_ita. Visited September 19, 2003.

Index